POWER
RESUMES

POWER RESUMES

SECOND EDITION

Ron Tepper

John Wiley & Sons, Inc.
New York • Chichester • Brisbane • Toronto • Singapore

This publication is designed to provide accurate and
authoritative information in regard to the subject
matter covered. It is sold with the understanding that
the publisher is not engaged in rendering legal, accounting,
or other professional services. If legal advice or other
expert assistance is required, the services of a competent
professional person should be sought. *From a Declaration
of Principles jointly adopted by a Committee of the
American Bar Association and a Committee of Publishers.*

Library of Congress Cataloging-in-Publication Data

Tepper, Ron, 1937–
    Power résumés / by Ron Tepper. — 2nd ed.
        p.   cm.
    Includes index.
    ISBN 0-471-55185-6. — ISBN 0-471-55186-4 (pbk.)
    1. Résumés (Employment)   I. Title.
    HF5383.T38   1992
    650.14—dc20   91-34366

ACKNOWLEDGMENTS

Although this book would not have been possible without the input of more than a dozen human resource directors, search and outplacement counselors, and hiring managers, a special debt is owed to Mr. Rudolph Dew of Rudolph Dew & Associates, and to Mr. Robert McDonald of Executive Career Services. Their more than 40 years of combined experience in the employment field was of inestimable aid in putting this book together. Equally as valuable was the input, counseling, and original ideas provided by Michael Hamilton, my editor at John Wiley & Sons, Inc.

85467

CONTENTS

INTRODUCTION

I n *Power!*, his classic work of more than 15 years ago, Michael Korda wrote that "All life is a game of power. The object of the game is simple enough: to know what you want and get it."

There is no power game played for bigger stakes than the one the job seeker encounters. As Korda put it, "Why do people wake up to discover the promotion they expected has been given to someone else, the raise has not materialized . . . and they have been 'retired' before they wanted to go . . ."

Power is not *given* to anyone, it must be "assumed, taken, asserted . . . the secret of effectively using power is to pretend one does not have it."

That, too, is the secret of the *power resumes*. On the surface, it may appear to be similar to other resumes. It may be as long and as neatly typed (or printed on a word processor) as any other. However, that is where the similarity ends; beneath the surface there are vast differences.

Power resumes are more than words; they are effective, potent sales letters. In today's competitive job market, the resume has to be more than a chronological employment history; it has to sell. Every power resume has 10 key sales ingredients that other resumes seldom contain.

Power resumes also contain "value-added" benefits for the potential employer. Such benefits show the hiring manager exactly what the applicant can add to the bottom line—without saying it.

The power resume differs dramatically in format and content from the typical resume. It has nuances and information that few job seekers even think about. It lacks narratives, adjectives, and objectives. Instead, it carefully matches the requirements of the job with the qualifications of the individual.

Power resumes can be written by anyone. They do not have to be put together by writers or professional resume firms. The job seeker is perfectly capable of putting his or her own resume together once they understand the 10 ingredients and the power resume approach.

Power resumes are composites of thought and experience from more than a dozen of the finest headhunters, outplacement counselors, psychologists, human resource directors, and hiring executives in the country.

Thirty of the most powerful resumes are utilized in this book to illustrate to job seekers the form, content, and simplicity of the power resume. The second edition of *Power Resumes* now contains 8 more power resumes. In addition, new resumes have been added along with discussions of specific resumes for city, county, state, and federal jobs. Also, a worksheet covering features, accomplishments, and benefits is included.

In addition, the job seeker will also find the components of an effective cover letter. Cover letters are really not letters; they are extensions of the power resume and they must contain certain information if they are to be effective. *Power Resumes* details exactly what that information is and how it should be used.

Power Resumes is the first book that details *the approach* to the power interview. It takes each element in the interview, analyzes it, shows the dialogue that should be used (and how to insure that it is), and then explains in practical terms how the job seeker can control the interview.

Unveiling the "hidden job market" and showing how job seekers can take advantage of it, *Power Resumes* explains the techniques that should be used in order to switch industries as well as the three types of firms that are looking for applicants.

In *Power Resumes,* real advertisements are analyzed to determine what the employers are actually asking for and then shows applicants how to answer.

Power Resumes is a practical, "how-to" text designed for the serious manager/executive who is searching for a new position or even thinking about looking for one. There is no theory in the book, only advice based upon actual experiences—advice that works.

Most important, *Power Resumes* not only shows the job seeker how to open the door for an interview, but how to close it with a "sale."

Power resumes are written and used by men and women equally—anyone seriously seeking a new job. For convenience, I have consistently used the pronoun he, with no intent to imply that the only job seekers are men—it is obviously quite the contrary.

1

TIMES HAVE CHANGED

Gary Townsend was a bright, competent, middle-aged accountant and chief financial officer of a large, northwestern company in a regulated industry that had been dramatically impacted due to a change in consumer tastes. Although the long-term prospects were not hopeless, it was evident that Gary's company would never again grow at the pace it had in the late sixties and early seventies.

The company attempted to counteract slumping profits with layoffs, consolidating departments, trimming labor costs, and bringing in younger employees who the company thought would be more aggressive in the marketplace. In addition, they were paid less than some of the senior management people they were replacing. With wholesale cutbacks, the company's image changed from a paternalistic firm to one that was losing workers almost daily through early retirement and attrition.

Townsend saw it coming and in early 1989, asked for early retirement. "I did not comprehend how fast the changes were coming," he recalls. "My viewpoint was limited by choice. After all, I had been with the company for 15 years. I did not want to admit what was happening."

Matt Belzano of Executive Career Services, an outplacement counseling firm, said Gary was "one of the many victims of the new lean-and-mean mentality that started in 1983 and is sweeping through most U.S. industries. It happened to the steel mills and smokestack industries initially and then spread to other manufacturers."

IMPACT OF DOWNSIZING

Sweeping cutbacks, commonly called downsizing, a term credited to General Motors, are now affecting all sectors of the economy. Gary's company was one of many to feel the cuts.

Townsend, who has taken time to analyze his former company and its industry, cautions other executives who might be in a similar situation about the changes going on in the economy:

> Whether you are employed or unemployed, downsizing, technology, and the tying of local and national to worldwide economies are impacting every company. I thought we were in a protected regulated industry. We were . . . but we failed to recognize the impact of foreign products on our industry. They not only eroded our sales base domestically, but overseas as well.

Townsend's case is not unique. Employment industry analysts estimate that half a million middle-management jobs have been eliminated in the past five years, and there is more to come, especially between the years 1990 and 2000.

Although most think of steel and other manufacturing industries as those hit hardest by the downsizing, there are numerous service industries that have gone through similar reductions. Some of the first employees to feel the thinning squeeze were those in the insurance industry.

"Typically," explains Joseph Izzo, head of JIA Management, a national management and consulting firm, "an insurance application might pass between 10 and 15 people, each a specialist in some area. Companies began to look at the delay in getting applications approved and premiums paid. They trimmed the numbers of people involved and put together teams consisting of four or five workers. Together, these managers controlled more than one function and approval step. The result was better service and faster turnaround."

Service Industries Hit by Downsizing

Downsizing has taken its toll on other service industries. Larry Senn, who heads Senn-Delaney, an international management and consulting firm, points to one large telecommunications company that decided to go from six management levels to four. The change, when completed, eliminated thousands of jobs for middle managers.

"Every organization," says Senn, "is examining similar cutting and layoff alternatives. They are asking, 'do we need these layers?'"

Robert McDonald, an industrial engineer who is a partner in Executive Career Services, says financial and financial service industries are cutting back along with medical services, aerospace, and computer-related fields. At the same time, "there is a shortage of environmental engineers and engineers who can deal with waste disposal. You have to take each industry and examine it to see whether it is going up or down."

"Companies in the oil patch area," says Ben Greco, who runs his own executive search firm, "are prime candidates. Any firm you find in the states of Louisiana, Texas, Oklahoma, or the city of Denver is thinking about cutting back."

"Watch out," says Fred Peters, who runs his own executive search firm and specializes in placing numerous $30,000 to $50,000-a-year engineers, "for defense industry companies. The budget for defense is not growing rapidly. We are seeing cutbacks on contracts. That can only mean downsizing and layoffs in the future."

"Managers," says Izzo, "see downsizing coming. Most close their eyes and say it cannot happen to me—but it does. Look at your company's bottom line. Is it healthy, growing? Look at your contribution to profits. Are you adding value to the product being sold or the service being offered? As a rule, those managers who fall into the sales category or aid in sales are in much better shape than those who do not."

What is more startling is the cutbacks that started with the 1989 to 1990 recession. For the first time, white collar professions were hit harder than the blue collar sector, and in many instances the professional who was laid-off occupied a seemingly safe and secure position. Ted Jacoby is a prime example. He was vice president/ marketing of a major, national real estate company. However, Jacoby, who was thought of as one of the brightest and best administrators in the company was given the word by the president that his services were no longer needed. In some instances, companies fill a senior position, with a younger, less expensive worker.

In Jacoby's case, the company did not replace him at all. Instead, it restructured another vice president's job to include his duties. A year later, the same firm eliminated an entire desktop publishing department and an editor with a $53,000-a-year salary. The rationale was that the company could save considerable funds by going to an outside typesetting facility if it got rid of the editor's salary and fringe benefits.

You can blame downsizing on competition, computers, or even greed, but more likely, the fault rests with an economy that has not only gone through radical changes, but whose domestic vigor relies equally as much on foreign countries as on its own internal pulse. Regardless of who or what you blame it on, there is no question that the American employment market has changed and will never return to its previous state and neither, quite possibly, will the stability of positions in the middle-and upper-management level. Consequently, resumes and the search for employment will never be the same, either.

RESUMES OUTMODED

The traditional, chronological, fact-filled resume that has been a standard tool for the job-seeking middle manager and executive is no longer effective and seldom gets by the initial screening level. In its place is a power resume, a cleverly written document that is a combination of sales, experience, and accomplishments that is structured to get by screeners and obtain an interview for the applicant. It is accompanied by a cover letter targeted equally well. No resume can nail down a job, but power resumes open the door.

The power resume is written and constructed to take the changes in human resource departments (once known as personnel), as well as resume screeners, into consideration. Where there were once 30 applicants for a job, there are now 300. Add to this the time crunch that most interviewers are under and the applicant will see that resume screeners do not have enough time to read everything. They look quick and read less. The old-style resumes seldom get beyond the human resource screener. If an applicant does make it beyond this point, they will be in the company of at least 20 to 30 other applicants. (This is not true for *every* position. There are numerous occupations that still have a high demand.)

Job applicants can rely on one other thing aside from the hordes of resumes that will accompany their's: When a hiring manager interviews applicants, he will be more interested in their personalties and how they fit his organization than their experience. The big question the hiring manager asks is, "Do we have rapport?"

Almost as important as rapport is the ability for an applicant to come up with a referral, that is, someone within the company whose name can be used (for example, Jane Doe suggested I send my resume to you.) An applicant with a referral is virtually assured of being one of those selected for an initial interview.

The applicant can be sure of something else, too—cover letters count. But they can count for or against you depending upon how they are written. The mass duplicated, generic cover letter says the applicant does not care enough to send an original. The cover letter that is not customized for the position is equally bad. Cover letters have to sell; they are sales letters.

WHO HANDLES THE RESUME

One of the more interesting developments within the changing American employment market is how the handling of resumes has changed. Hiring managers only see the resumes that human resources sends them. In some rare instances, the astute applicant is able to bypass human resources and get to the hiring manager, but for the most part, human resources does the screening. A problem develops when the human resource director gets too busy to screen everything. Remember, he or she is hiring for an entire company, not just one department. Consequently, the director many give a list of four or five requirements and a stack of resumes to a secretary along with instructions to match them. The resumes that do not match are discarded—often by a secretary who does not have time to read or analyze them. Thus, the power resume with its unique format, becomes even more important.

The applicant who makes the mistake of using a functional instead of a chronological resume could be one of the first discarded. Although many career counselors encourage the functional resume, most human resource directors despise them. A power resume incorporates some functional elements, but it is chronologically arranged.

Two-Tiered Process

Few job seekers realize that many resumes have to go through a two-tiered process. First, if human resources is going to screen applicants, resumes have to be structured so the applicant's qualifications stand out and closely match the requirements of the job. Screeners in the human resource department are not going to read every line to see if the qualifications and requirements match. They have a sheet of paper listing three or four requirements and they examine resumes to see if those items are listed. A chronological resume may fail because it does not match the qualifications to the requirements in a manner that is easy to find.

The second tier is the hiring manager who has knowledge of the job and can look at the resume and determine if the applicant fits. The problem is he or she will never see the standard chronological resume because it does not make it through human resources. Applicants should keep this two-tiered process in mind when submitting resumes. Unless the resume is targeted and addresses the exact requirements of the job, it will never get beyond the first tier.

THE PEER REVIEW

In the past, an applicant whose resume made it through the maze could count on one, perhaps two, interviews before being hired. Today, it is common for applicants to be interviewed for three or four one-hour (or more) sessions before being offered a position.

Bernadette Senn, who interviewed nearly 2000 applicants last year, says her firm often runs a management consulting candidate through three, four, or five one-hour sessions. The multiple interviews are because firms often have more than one location. For example, Senn may interview in California for a subsidiary in New York. Ultimately, the applicant is going to be interviewed by the New York hiring manager but before getting there, the applicant is screened by human resources (Senn) and local (California) managers. There are many multinational U.S. firms that interview in a similar manner.

One of the newest interview techniques is peer interviewing. "A firm," explains Rudoloph Dew, who runs a long-established West Coast outplacement firm, "will insist that members of the group the candidate is going to join interview him as well. The team may not have the ultimate decision, but they have input. The hiring manager asks for their opinions. Do they like him? Do they think they can work with him?" This technique also takes part of the responsibility off the hiring manager. If he makes the wrong decision and the applicant turns out to be a poor employee, the hiring manager can share the blame with his group.

MEETING THE NEW DEMANDS

To meet these new demands, resumes must have a certain look, length, and content. To understand why resumes have changed both in appearance and purpose, it helps to look at the job market, U.S. companies, and how things were a few decades ago in comparison to today.

During the fifties and most of the sixties, "paternalistic" feelings between company and employee were at their height. Managers went to work for a corporation and never expected to leave until they voluntarily retired. Loyalty was to the firm. Pensions and retirement were a way of life. It was common to see workers retire with 30 and 40 years of service. This loyalty could be traced to a generation that grew up during the Depression (1930s) and believed that having a job was a goal in itself. If a person was fortunate enough to find a job, they were considered a fool to even contemplate leaving. This attitude carried through World War II, into the fifties, and throughout the sixties.

The seventies saw the beginning of change. Energy shortages, inflationary pressures, and imports changed the way America did business. The recessions that took place during the turbulent period from 1971 to 1981 changed the way America's managers thought. They saw fellow workers, many with years of tenure, being laid off. Companies that survived the recessions cut back on everyone from temporary hourly wage workers to high-salaried executives. Middle and upper managers discovered there was no such thing as "job security."

The children of these managers saw their fathers laid off after devoting years to the job. For most, the thought of ever being loyal to a company was a thing of the past. Their goal was not to get a job but to get ahead. If that meant switching employment every two years, so be it. A job was no longer forever.

With the change in industry, came the revolution in the personnel field. To survive, companies cut back, sometimes using reasoning that made employees unhappy. As a result, workmen's compensation and other lawsuits became commonplace. Litigation over stress and other job-related illnesses mounted.

Management turned to personnel departments for guidance. That meant upgrading these departments and bringing in more qualified people to handle employee relations. Personnel became human resources and management began to take their advice on everything from hiring and firing to benefits.

Outside Help

Outplacement firms, or companies that specialize in helping fired, laid-off, and displaced middle managers and executives, were nonexistent during the late sixties and early seventies, but by 1975, they could be found in many areas of the country. Outplacement developed as a stopping-off point for these middle managers or executives. The outplacement firm came in and counseled company management on how to fire and *what* to say. In many cases, the company hired outplacement firms to take in these displaced employees, counsel them, help them write resumes, provide them an office and/or telephone, give them moral support, and get them started back on the road to employment—with some other company. Here was a way for companies to assuage guilt and, hopefully, avoid lawsuits.

By 1980, outplacement had become one of the fastest growing segments of the employment field. Major companies trying to ease the impact of a firing or layoff of long-term employees flocked to them for help. With the metamorphosis of U.S. industry and its hiring practices, outplacement developed into one of this country's growth industries.

The paradox is that in today's employment market, two of the fastest growing segments are outplacement (to counsel unemployed workers and set them on the right path) and executive search (companies specializing in finding the right executive for a job opening). One reason for this odd pairing is the frantic pace of American industry. Part of that tempo is due to the takeover and leveraged buyout mania that swept industry in the late 1980s.

Thirty-nine-year-old John Simon knows how that pace can impact someone's life. He was a fast-tracker running a rapidly growing restaurant company on the East Coast. Under his guidance, the firm had tripled in size.

Another company, eyeing the growth of Simon's firm, approached him and asked for help in convincing the owners of his firm to sell. John listened to the plans and advantages the takeover firm would offer through expansion and capital.

Eventually the company persuaded him that the buyout would be beneficial to everyone and he agreed to help in the takeover effort. He met twice with owners of his firm and they agreed to meet with the company proposing the buyout. Four months went by before the price and terms were settled, but the firm was sold and on February 1, 1989, Simon found himself working for new owners.

On February 21, Simon was asked to leave. He had only met and talked to the new chairman once. Unfortunately, once was all it took.

"I never realized," he said after losing his $250,000-a-year position, "how important relationships were within a company. I always figured if you did your job and showed results that was it. It isn't. Politics are critical in any organization . . . that is, if you are going to have a position and not just a job."

Politics impact more than the $250,000-a-year manager. There is one company that is well-known for its tendency to favor employees who put in long hours, and it holds back others who do not— regardless of their productivity. The company is obsessed with the amount of hours executives put in each day. Astute managers arrive early (usually by 7:30 A.M., although the office does not open until 8 A.M.), and they stay until 5:30 to 5:45 P.M., 30 to 45 minutes after quitting time.

During the pre- and post-work hours, they walk through certain areas of the hallway, making sure that senior management sees them after hours. Almost without exception, the managers who arrive early and stay late (regardless of productivity) are those who have been promoted and given the highest raises. Politics? Favoritism? Possibly, some of both, however, managers should recognize that every company has its culture and habits. To play by the rules, often means a promotion and raise. To ignore them may mean unemployment, as in Simon's case.

The $100,000 Manager

By the beginning of the 1990s, outplacement firms had interviewed, counseled, and aided a record number of higher priced managers such as Simon. Although many were not in Simon's $250,000 bracket, there were a good number in the $100,000 plus category. McDonald says that executives in Simon's position are becoming commonplace:

> Managers should realize that industry has been in a constant state of change. It's no secret that we are going from a manufacturing economy to one based upon service. The key, however, is for employees to look at their companies and industries and ask how that switch is going to affect them.

POWER RESUME DEVELOPMENT

Although unemployment figures have certainly been higher, there is an inordinate number of middle and upper level managers out of work. The increase in their numbers sparked the growth of outplacement firms and made job seeking more logical and scientific. It also brought on the power resume.

Part of the credit for development of power resumes goes to outplacement firms. They had the benefit of seeing both sides of the coin. That is, they were hired by the firm that was about to layoff, fire, or "early retire" employees. They were able to see why these managers were being released and what, if anything, could have prevented it. They also saw why some managers were cut while others were saved. They saw exactly what the company under pressure was looking for in an executive. Consequently, when they provided counseling, they were able to tutor job seekers and target resumes better than ever.

For example, in the past, a resume similar to the resume in Figure 1 was commonplace. It was all that was needed to get an interview. But with the change in corporate attitude, this resume became a loser.

Similar resumes are still being used by applicants. The resume in Figure 2 was recently received by a personnel department. It may

Figure 1   Resume That Was Adequate in the Past

PROFESSIONAL OBJECTIVE

A challenging and responsible position with a growth-oriented company which would effectively utilize prior experience, demonstrated expertise and personal abilities in the Real Estate and Construction Industries. Position should offer the opportunity for continued professional growth and advancement with compensation commensurate with qualifications.

SUMMARY OF QUALIFICATIONS

Experience: Successful background encompasses comprehensive professional experience, with responsibilities, skills and competencies in the following areas:

. . . Significant experience in the Real Estate and Construction Industries, including project development, construction supervision, sales, marketing, public relations and management.

. . . Establishing, implementing and enhancing administrative systems and operational procedures to achieve maximum efficiency, productivity and profitability.

. . . Conducting site and market analyses to determine feasibility of purchasing land for development; negotiating contracts and lease agreements.

. . . Functioning as an independent Real Estate Broker and working directly with developers to effective market properties, including setting up model centers, interfacing with advertising agencies, staffing and supervising sales force, creating marketing strategies and advertising programs.

. . . Recruiting, training, supervising and evaluating marketing/sales and support personnel; conducting sales, motivational and real estate courses and seminars.

. . . Developing and maintaining good customer/public relations; finding innovative ways to close sales and enhance company image.

Strengths: Excellent management, organizational and communication skills . . . innate ability to handle people with and enthusiasm that generates confidence . . . adept at planning and administration . . . able to assume and delegate responsibility . . . sustained record of growth, achievement and advancement . . . a highly qualified and goal-oriented individual.

EDUCATION   EASTERN MICHIGAN UNIVERSITY, Ypsilanti, Michigan
Postgraduate studies toward Masters Degree (one year).

INDIANA UNIVERSITY, Indianapolis, Indiana
Postgraduate studies on Masters and Law Degree (two years).

INDIANA UNIVERSITY, Bloomington, Indiana
Bachelor of Science Degree
Major: Real Estate Administration
Minor: Marketing & Advertising

PROFESSIONAL EXPERIENCE

1981–Present
Company Name
Real Estate Broker/Director of Sales & Marketing/Consultant
Responsible for establishing, managing and operating real estate brokerage firm specializing in handling projects for various developers. Instrumental in launching the _____ single family development in southwest Orange County and negotiating the sale of the entire tract to Company Name.

Following completion of that sale, accepted position of Director of Sales & Marketing for _____, a luxury single family subdivision located in Windermere, Florida. Currently _____ features homes ranging from $150,000 to $725,000 and has completed an eighteen hole golf course with lots ranging from $60,000 to $185,000.

In addition, served as Consultant to Company Name for sales of their residential properties. Hold an exclusive listing on the balance of their _____ condominiums in Orlando. Also hold an exclusive listing for ____ single family development featuring homes on lots of 1 to 5 acres. Development has 400+ acres, with homes ranging from $115,000 to $300,000. In charge of marketing, advertising and all sales functions.

1975–1981
Company Name
Director of Marketing
Responsible for establishing and operating a full-service real estate organization and advertising agency for this planned unit development of 1,000 single family and multi-family homes. Involved in all facets of project development, construction supervision, public relations and management.

1973–1975
Company Name
Director of Marketing
Responsible for supervising and directing marketing activities for condominium development in the Central Florida area. Position entailed site selection and analysis, advertising and operation of sales organization.

1971–1973
Company Name
Director of Marketing
Functioned as Director of Marketing for condominium development for a California based company. Held total responsibility for site selection, market analysis, staffing of sales organization and assuring productive daily operations.

1970–1971
Company Name
Mid-West Coordinator for Dealership Real Estate
Responsible for performing site and market analyses to determine the feasibility of purchasing land and constructing dealership facilities for Company. Following construction, responsible for obtaining leases from the dealers and managing the properties.

1969–1970
Company Name
Vice-President of Land Acquisition
Served as Vice-President of Land Acquisition for Corp. "R," a subsidiary of Company Name with responsibility for site and market analyses for the purchase of land for mobile home parks and apartment complexes nationwide.

Figure 2   Resume That Is No Longer Adequate

Name: Lawrence
Address: 1222 Hinds Avenue
City: Toluca Lake, CA 91335
Telephone: (213) 555-1438

OBJECTIVE: A challenging position in finance or MIS, which will utilize my
                quantitative, financial and managerial skills to the fullest.

EDUCATION: Brown University
                Graduate School of Management
                MBA, May, 1988, GPA 3.75.
                Emphasis in management.

                Massachusetts Institute of Technology
                Bachelor's Degree in Engineering, Sept., 1986.
                Bachelor's Degree in Management Science, June, 1986

WORK
EXPERIENCE

5/87 to Present _____ Foods, Inc.
                *Performed primary research on consumer preferences concerning
                specialty products.
                *Interviewed store personnel, distributors, sub-distributors, purchasing
                agents, consumers to collect information on consumer buying patterns.
                *Made recommendations based upon research for new marketing
                opportunities.

6/84 to 5/87 _____ Dairies, Inc.
                *Responsible for inventory and administration of multi-unit retail
                operation.
                *Assisted in development of UPC pricing and inventory system.

6/83 to 6/84 _____ Warehouse, Inc.
                *Designed and maintained inventory control system for retail outlets
                and warehouse unit. *Selected software to assist in daily administrative
                functions.

OTHER SKILLS

                *Proficient in use of dBase III, SAS and LINDO. Programming
                experience with BASIC, LISP, FORTRAN. Worked on VAX/VMS,
                IBM-PC and Unix systems.

appear to be adequate but it contains glaring deficiencies that will become more apparent as we go along.

In today's—and tomorrow's—job market, resumes have to be targeted because there are more candidates than ever.

MIDDLE MANAGERS—ENDANGERED SPECIES

"For the most part," theorizes Dew, "the middle manager is the vanishing American. His role has been to gather, collate, and disseminate information. The computer has come on the scene and is replacing many of these people. At larger companies, he is the middle manager, at smaller ones the senior manager." That does not mean the employee being impacted is necessarily involved with computers. In some cases he is, however, in others the middle manager is merely a buffer between top management and supervisors. Larry Senn has examined the contemporary corporation and says "the tendency for corporations to flatten out is not just a matter of saving dollars. The thicker the management layer the more bureaucratic and the less individual initiative."

Many U.S. companies have already thinned. There is, however, more to come. "Someone," explains Izzo, "has to go if the thinning is to continue. That someone is the middle manager or executive who is earning from $80,000 to $150,000."

Senn and Dew say cuts also hit managers earning as little as $30,000 a year. "Typically, the larger the company, the higher salaried the middle manager," says Senn.

For managers wondering if they fall into the targeted group, Izzo offers guidelines. "In the typical organization, the president or chief executive officer (CEO) has a level reporting directly to him. That level is safe. The level beneath that is in danger. This level— and any between the foreman or supervisor of hourly workers—is in danger."

Senn divides the endangered middle managers into functions. "Usually it is the person in planning or finance. That is, employees who have become buffers between top management and production. For example, I may be president of a division and report to the company president. Everyone in my division has to go through my staff before they reach me and I have to go through additional staff before I reach the CEO. A buffer has been created around the CEO and it makes decision making slower. Companies can no longer tolerate this slowdown."

One reason is because of takeovers. Speculators are taking over billion-dollar conglomerates with leveraged buyouts or other techniques. Management in many firms is trying to block the takeovers.

By restructuring, they are not only able to respond faster to changes in the marketplace, but lower labor costs improves the bottom line.

"If a company is going to be strong, it has to be lean," says Izzo. "If they are making good profits and are distributing that wealth to shareholders as well as reinvesting, they are healthy and they may not be facing disgruntled shareholders or takeover bids."

The restructuring moved into high gear during the early eighties as companies went through a recession and, at the same time, became entranced with the operation of the typical Japanese firm. Top executives read one story after another about Japanese companies with flattened structures and self-managed work teams.

Although the enthusiasm for the Japanese management style has waned, the flattened structure has not. The restructuring may hasten an end to the specialization phenomena that has dominated U.S. industry.

For years, companies have been caught up in the desire for specialists or workers who had only one specific skill. The flattened corporate structure requires generalists, not specialists. For example, suppose a manager oversees four supervisors. In an effort to reduce costs, the company lays off a manager and gives the remaining manager four additional employees and or departments to supervise. A manager who is a specialist may not have the ability to handle the additional areas. The company may decide to let him go and hold onto another manager who is more of a generalist; someone who can handle the additional areas.

That is, in fact, what is happening. This trend is not going to reverse the rush towards specialization that is prevalent among U.S. retailers. Tune-up shops, cookie stores, and baked potato stands will continue to thrive, but within companies, the generalist is making progress.

HOW TO SWITCH INDUSTRIES

"An executive," says Dew, "who has good managerial skills may find himself in demand by an industry that he knows nothing about. Many companies are no longer searching for an executive with 'food' or 'clothing' or some other experience. Ideally, they would like to find someone with those skills, but if they cannot they will go for someone who has proven himself as a manager in another industry."

Not everyone agrees with Dew's assessment, however. McDonald feels it is not that easy in today's market for someone to switch industries. "It can be done, but hiring managers do not like to take time to train someone in a new industry. They may be a great auto parts sales manager but in switching to the computer industry they may find themselves with a manager who wants them to master things without instruction. That can be a problem.'

Still, the job seeker who was a long-time employee in a shrinking industry, does not have to feel that his only opportunity for a position is within the same industry. Good managers are in demand from all industries.

In today's market, administrative and management skills are valued by many companies. They would like to see similar (or same) industry experience when hiring, but that desire does not prevent them from hiring from outside. Applicants who are successful in switching industries have put together power resumes that stress accomplishments rather than industry experience.

For the manager who is concerned about his future and his firm's plans, the best time to move is when he is employed. Townsend, who we discussed earlier, waited too long. It is easier to place someone who is employed. The fact that a manger is working is a positive factor in the eyes of the hiring manager.

The Three-Strike Syndrome

The categories of managers who find it most difficult to find positions are: (1) those who have been fired, (2) those who have been laid off, and (3) those who are out of work and who are perceived to be too old for a particular position. In fact, most search firms will not touch anyone in these categories. They go after the employed manager.

For the employed—or unemployed—job seeker, there are several different "players" in the employment field. From the standpoint of recruiting, there are three types of search firms. The first is a *retained* executive search firm. They are paid a fee (usually 20 to 35 percent of the manager's annual compensation) by the hiring company to find an applicant. They get paid whether the applicant is hired or not. However, if they do not have a good track record they will not be around long. There are large search firms such as Korn-Ferry, and smaller ones, such as Executive Career Services.

The second type of search firm is the *contingency* search firm. This company works on a contingency basis, takes job orders, and tries to help the company find the employee. They do little screening and, for the most part, send resumes directly to human resource departments. They get paid upon placement; consequently, they do not want to eliminate candidates. They prefer the human resource department to see as many candidates as possible.

The third type of search firm is the employment agency. Years ago, these firms found jobs for people and the candidate paid the fee which was usually a percentage of his salary (such as, 10 percent). Today, most employment agencies search for applicants under the $30,000 yearly salary range. The contingency firm looks for people in the $30,000 to $60,000 range and the retained firm covers applicants from about $45,000 on up.

In addition to search firms, there are outplacement firms, both wholesale and retail. The wholesale firms are retained by companies to handle dislocated managers and executives. The fee is paid by the firm. The second type of outplacement firm, the retail career counseling firm, takes people off the street and counsels them for a fee. They help with resumes and counseling, much as the wholesale firm does. Neither actually gets the applicant a position but they steer him or her in the correct direction.

Nearly all of these firms are involved in relocating managers and appear to be headed for even busier times as the thinning of corporations continues.

HOW TO STAND OUT

Despite the cutbacks, Senn says there are ways managers can keep their positions or, if they are unemployed, protect the next one they get. "Be a top performer," he advises. "People think they may be protecting their position by being cautious. That is not true. You can get a ticket on the freeway by going too slow as well as too fast. In today's competitive environment, you need to take risks." This is the time to "star," he says.

Larry McGraw was a middle manager who knew the value of starring. He had been with his company for just over two years, and he could see the changes coming. The industry was changing and competition was increasing. Larry's company was a franchise firm that made its money from a percentage of the sales that the franchisees made. In turn, the franchisees were supplied with training materials produced by the franchisor. Larry's department produced those materials.

Larry, however, was an astute middle manager. He could see the day when the franchisor would take a long, hard look at the large training staff and the salaries and benefits they were given. Larry knew it would not be long before senior management began to scrutinize training, and in doing so they could decide to cutback. On more than one occasion, he had heard several of the vice presidents discuss the possibilities of buying training programs from outside consultants or other companies.

Knowing the possible direction his company might take, Larry decided upon a strategy. Each morning he arrived early, with cup in hand he headed to the coffee room that he knew would be occupied by one of the senior vice presidents. The two began to chat on a regular basis about the company, and the theory Larry had about how the company could save money by purchasing training materials from outside sources.

Before long, Larry had even produced a pro forma, showing a 12-month training budget, and how much could be saved via the outside services. He also did projections on how more profits could be made by marketing these materials than producing programs internally and selling them to franchisees.

Within six months, Larry was named a vice president in charge of training, and the department was reorganized with the new thrust being to purchase outside materials for sale within the organization.

Larry took a chance. "But," says Senn, "he had studied his company well and knew what they were after." If an organization sees and recognizes an outstanding performance, the manager has a much better chance of survival. There is no guarantee, however, that top management is going to see or take note of performance by a middle manager, especially if they are insulated by layers of other managers.

Senn and other consultants say this is where communication is of prime importance. "Learn how to blow your horn and make sure it shows. Go after a higher profile, take on things, volunteer for projects with broader ramifications." This is especially true if the manager is involved in an area that does not generate sales. These consultants recommend that middle managers ask questions. How am I doing, what can I do better? Force your boss or manager to coach you more.

Dew put it succinctly, "One reason for an employee's demise is they did not find out what priorities their boss had. You may have done your job, but if you do not know what is most important to your boss then how do you know you are doing your job?"

Some managers may do twice the work of others but they fail to find out what is most important to their boss. By not communicating, they provoke the ire of the boss and soon find themselves out of work. "That's when they wonder what happened," says Dew. "I tell them there is no reason to ponder. They blew the position when they failed to listen to what their boss was saying."

Managers should also be more attuned to what is happening within the company. "Understandably," says Senn, "middle managers value their technical skills. In today's corporate environment, however, an employee has to be seen as a good manager and leader. A manager who is a leader aside from knowing his job, can always be shuffled to another part of the company if there is a layoff. A specialist who cannot see beyond his own department, cannot."

Those who have been unable to avoid the layoff or firing, find that the cutbacks have had significant impact on the way they are treated when they apply for positions. First, there are the numbers to get around—as many as 300 candidates for a job versus 30 to 50 a decade ago. Human resources will screen the applicants to a more reasonable number, perhaps 20 to 30. Does the supervisor, vice president, chief executive officer, or whomever is doing the hiring talk to that many? Seldom. He will do additional cutting and not go beyond 8 to 10.

For those who do not make the interview, the treatment is quite different than in years past. Previously, candidates who did not make the final cut were always notified. Today, a resume and cover letter may never be answered. There are cases where an applicant has received a "thank you but no thanks" letter from human resources three months after they applied. And there are other cases where applicants receive word that they are "being considered" five months after the ad was placed and the resume sent.

In part, delays are because the applicant ranks have swelled, but there are other reasons, too. Both human resource people and applicants have become more sophisticated. The smart applicant no longer just sends a resume with a cover letter; they usually find someone within the company that they can use as a reference. With a well-written cover letter, a targeted power resume, and a reference from within the company, it is hard to get rid of a candidate.

THE HOTTEST JOB MARKETS

Which industries and companies should job applicants be targeting? There is no way to accurately forecast all the good and bad industries of the next 10 years. However, by taking what exists today and projecting it into the future, there are some obvious winners and losers—some industries that are ripe for opportunities and some that are not.

There are several factors that job seekers should take into consideration: the population is aging, computers are universal, service industries continue to grow, and manufacturing is in a decline. Some forecasters even project as many as 85 to 90 percent of all U.S. workers will be in the service sector by the year 2000. The job seeker who comes from the manufacturing sector should examine and think about those figures before jumping back into the same dead-end industry.

Perhaps the most significant impact on employment will be the computer. It has already eliminated millions of low-level clerical jobs, and now it is impacting white collar management positions. While computers will make many positions obsolete, they will also create openings. In fact, it already has done so in areas ranging from computer programming and systems analysis to repair.

There is a population shift, too. Workers and managers are still moving to the Sunbelt. States with diversified economies (such as California) offer more opportunities than those with one- or two-dimensional economies, and companies within those areas will be more recession-proof than those that do not have the benefit of diversity.

With an aging population, an industry that will boom is nursing. That does not mean hospitals will thrive. With the cost of health care rising daily, insurance companies are looking for alternatives —and home care is it. For the unemployed manager with an administrative background in hospitals, the projected growth in nursing during the next decade is encouraging but the inefficiencies and high costs of hospitals is not. The unemployed hospital administrator would do well to look at another related occupation if interested in long-term employment.

Legal services is another occupation undergoing change. Society is becoming increasingly litigious and the demand for legal services is growing. Employment in a legal profession is promising but the industry has problems—mainly cost. Like health care, the price of legal care is rapidly rising. Society is searching for methods to cap costs. The answer may be the *paralegal,* the person who can perform legal services for attorneys and others at a lower cost. Of all service occupations, the paralegal is projected to be the fastest growing in the next 10 years. Demand for attorneys will grow but will not be anywhere near that of the paralegals.

Related to downsizing is the effort by many companies to cut other internal costs such as fringe benefits. One solution has been to hire temporary personnel and avoid paying fringes. As a result, one business that shows rapid growth is the part-time or temporary help business. The growth is being spurred by two factors. First is the obvious cost savings to the client company. Second, there are growing numbers of workers who do not want to work full-time. They may be older, have partial or full pensions, or other income, and they prefer to work 20 to 30 hours per week, rather than 40.

In the next decade, there will be a 30 percent increase in demand for sales personnel. That means sales managers will continue to be in demand. As is the case with other skills, sales applies to a myriad of industries.

Also, above average growth is forecast for occupations ranging from electrical engineers to waiters and waitresses. Each category has meaning for the manager seeking a new job or job change.

There are some occupations and industries that are clearly headed downward insofar as employment opportunities. They range from architects (architectural firms) to bookbinding. Commercial building is not expected to keep pace with the early 1980s, consequently, there will be less demand for services. Bookbinding is another industry impacted by automation and labor savings. Both translate to fewer workers and managers.

In general, any industry or company that can save consumers or customers time and provide convenience is heading for growth.

Families with both partners working will generate increased growth in the convenience sector. Convenience includes everything from industries specializing in frozen "meals for two" to day-care centers.

Convenience stores are thriving even though they charge a premium for products. Nearly every fast-food establishment has installed a drive-through window for additional customer convenience. Markets are experimenting with the same concept and several major chains are installing "mini" convenience stores within the market. These mini-stores enable customers to stop at the market, pick up a few basic items, and be on their way. The markets are hoping to sell consumers on the concept because these minis—in contrast to the typical convenience store—do not charge premium prices.

The fast food industry will slow down. The industry's prime customers (the young) will decline in numbers. Adult customers will have other choices such as frozen foods that can be microwaved and which lend themselves to a healthier diet. To compete, fast-food restaurants will expand and change menus. An additional complication for the industry is hired help. In some sections of the country, it is virtually impossible to find part-time employees who want to work behind the counters. Wages are increasing and that will push fast-food prices up.

Convenience refers to more than the fast-food industry. In the real estate industry, computers are being installed that will enable homebuyers to "one-stop-shop" for loans. That is, once the consumer picks a home, all they do is return to the real estate office, sit down with a computer operator, and enter their financial qualifications on a computer terminal. The computer will prequalify the buyer, select a best-fit lender, and submit an application. All of this can be done in less than an hour.

However, for every new job that technology creates, there is usually one that it eliminates. In the case of the real estate loan procedure, it may affect the mortgage banking industry. Mortgage bankers typically act as middlemen between the real estate broker and the homebuyer. They find and arrange for the loan. With a computer, there may not be a need for the mortgage banker.

With time a precious commodity, mail-order businesses will increase as will the diversity of products being offered. At present, everything from clothing and jewelry to high-tech equipment and insurance can be purchased through the mail. In the next decade, the product line will diversify and increase.

Government and private sector firms have forecast the following for the years between 1990 and 2000:

1. The growth in the number of parents who both work, will continue. This is going to raise demands for day-care, baby-sitting, and housekeeping services. In the future, however, the individual entrepreneur who provides these services will be taking a backseat to contract firms. These firms will need managers.

2. Mining and energy-related industries are questionable. Although there will be increased demand for energy, more efficient systems of delivery and usage are on the way. Declines in nearly every domestic energy operation are forecast. Therefore, the demand for managers in these industries will continue to decline.

3. Housing and construction will grow but not at the levels of the early 1980s. Costs and a slower population growth will contain the industry. The exception may be America's transportation and roads. Many highways are in dire need of repair. The funds will have to be appropriated. Population continues to move to urban from rural areas. This movement will put pressure on existing (and non-existing) city transportation systems and roads which will have be to built and/or replaced.

4. There will be significant growth and opportunity in the communications industry. Every sector of society is becoming increasingly dependent upon relatively new innovations ranging from car telephones to sophisticated digital paging systems.

5. The continuous change in tax laws make accounting and auditing an industry destined for growth. Complex laws will open the doors for more specialized accounting services. With a growing segment of the population living on pensions and retirement income, these people, for the most part, will not need sophisticated accounting services but will give

impetus to growth in seasonal accounting firms that open in retail locations during tax season and close immediately afterwards.

6. Mass communications and advertising growth is expected. Businesses will spend more in an increasingly competitive environment. Additionally, there will be "delivery" systems beyond print, radio, television, and mail order.

7. The security industry will grow at a rapid pace and benefit from overcrowding and crime in urban areas. Security will range from in-house alarm systems to personal bodyguard services.

8. Entertainment expenditures will increase and diversify. With the population aging and the work week shortening, there will be more time for leisure. Traditional movie-going will not be the only facet of the industry to benefit. The growth of cable television will put increased demands on the industry for programming. The demand for new motion picture theaters, however, will be flat. Most movie-goers are younger (such as under 40 years of age), and this segment of the population will not grow as rapidly as the segment of people who are over 50 and more likely to watch a show on cable or commercial TV.

9. Equipment rental and leasing depends largely on tax laws. Although many businesses will continue to rent, the financial advantages of leasing will not be as significant as they once were.

10. The banking industry is undergoing a shakeout via its savings and loan problems. Licensing of new institutions will be more difficult as will be obtaining federal insurance. Existing banks may find themselves with an increasingly larger share of the market because proposed owners of new institutions will find it more difficult to enter because of government requirements. Demand for automatic teller machines (ATMs) and other customer service machinery will increase. Aside from ATMs, banks are trying to automate in other ways. With the difficulty of opening new institutions and the banker's desire to automate wherever possible, this area of the financial services industry does not offer good prospects for managers.

11. Automation will impact industries including knitting, floor covering mills, textiles, and apparel. That means less labor and, consequently, fewer supervisors and managers.

12. One of the most promising industries is the drug/pharmaceutical area. Once again, an aging population will provide a wider customer base. Progress in genetics and genetic engineering will lead to more products as well.

BEFORE THE RESUME: ASSESS YOUR SKILLS

Being part of one of these shrinking industries does not spell doom for the job seeker. Dew's outplacement firm has counseled hundreds of managers who come from declining industries but want to stay in them.

Even in industries that are declining and extremely competitive, it is possible to find good management jobs. But before the unemployed manager starts sending out resumes, he should sit down and assess his skills and desires. He should also look at the company that let him go and ask himself why.

"I know to the out-of-work executive that sounds like so much B.S. It isn't," says Dew. "I see hundreds of executives who were right for the job and the company when they started. But after 5, 10, or 20 years things change. Companies change.

"What unemployed managers should understand is that companies have personalities. Personalities change. A once entrepreneurial, open, shoot-from-the-hip firm, grows and becomes more solid. It becomes structured and rigorous. The entrepreneurial executive does not fit into this mold. Most of the time that is why he was let go. To find another similar company can be disastrous."

Before the Resume . . .

Before sending out a resume and cover letter, take stock of yourself. Assess your strengths and weaknesses; objectively look at what you want and what makes you happy. Many are doing exactly that according to McDonald.

"I think the firings and layoffs have brought many things to a head," he says. "Many managers realize they have to change careers because they cannot put up with the same environment they just came through. A good number say they do not want to go back. They want to do something else . . . and they can."

In Chapter 2, we will examine how managers can utilize their skills to not only do something else, but with the correct approach, they can even change industries.

2

ANALYZING COMPANIES—

DO YOU FIT?

Jeffrey Regal could never be called anything but a fast-tracker. A graduate of a local university, he majored in business and was determined to make banking a career. His enthusiasm and desire to learn landed him a job at Commonwealth National Bank, a young, aggressive, independent bank.

From the time he started, it was obvious that Regal was going to be more than a loan officer trainee. He dedicated himself to the job. He spent hours after work studying the bank's operations and its new computer system. When he left work, he took home banking trades and read them from cover to cover, searching for promotional ideas and new techniques that could be implemented at Commonwealth.

In less than three months, Regal had proposed three ideas. Two were money-saving ideas and were executed immediately. The third was a suggestion as to how Commonwealth could become more involved in the community and build a bigger customer base. Although the bank's managers liked the suggestion, they did not have the staff to work on it. Regal volunteered. He said he would put the program together during his spare time, and he did.

Regal's innovative suggestions did not end there. Almost monthly he came up with another new idea that would either enable the bank to save money or generate additional customers. His efforts were not without reward. By the end of his second year, he was named vice president. After four years, he was given the post of executive vice president and assistant to the president, the second highest managerial position in the bank.

Commonwealth's board of directors recognized Regal's contributions to the institution and did not want to lose his enthusiasm or ideas to a competitor. Consequently, he was named to the board on his fifth anniversary with the bank. Commonwealth had tripled its assets since Regal had joined the bank and its profits were at an all-time high. It was the perfect candidate for a buyout.

The offer came from a large, established eastern bank which saw Commonwealth as a solidly entrenched, local institution that could provide entree into a new market. After four months of negotiations, the shareholders agreed and Commonwealth was sold. With the sale, the president of the bank retired. In a surprise move, the new board, of which Regal was not a member, did not name him to replace the outgoing president. Regal was angered and puzzled. He continued to do his job and even more than what was asked. He retained his enthusiasm and his ideas failed to slow. He found, however, the new president was not as anxious as his predecessor to hear about innovative ideas. He would listen, nod his head, and tell Regal "I'll get back to you," but he never did.

Four months after the bank was sold and the new president installed, Regal found himself caught in the midst of a reshuffling. His title was changed from executive vice president and assistant to the president to senior vice president. A new executive was brought on board who became assistant to the president, forming a buffer between the new president and Regal. Regal found his access to the president restricted and his duties diminished. His ideas were being completely ignored and he was disturbed by his lack of insight into the bank's long range plans.

Regal began to feel like an outsider. In the past, even before he became a board member, he and other officers at the bank knew immediately what had transpired during board meetings. There were no secrets. However, the new owners had board meetings that were conducted 2000 miles away, at the parent company's offices.

As each day passed, Regal's frustration mounted. He had devoted years to the institution and had once thought about spending his entire career with the bank. Finally, his patience wore thin and he asked for a meeting with the president. That afternoon Regal sat down across the table from him. What was said in the next five minutes Regal never clearly remembered. The one thing that stuck in his mind was the president saying something about "this not being the right environment" for you. The rest was blurred. He recalled the president saying everyone appreciated his efforts and enthusiasm, but they were going to waste at this bank. The board thought it would be best if Regal found

Figure 3 Regal's Resume That Lacked Content

RESUME

Name:	Jeffrey Regal
Address:	128 South Ridgely Drive, #230
Telephone:	555-1287

OBJECTIVE: To find a challenging position in the banking industry in which I can use my creative, innovative ideas.

EDUCATION: Salem University, Salem, MA
Graduate, BS, Business Administration. Concentration in Finance.

Harvard University, Cambridge, MA
Attended graduate school. Awarded MBA in special Executive Management Program.

Claremont High School, Salem, MA
Graduated, June 1977. Majored in business with college preparatory courses.

WORK
EXPERIENCE: Community National Bank, July 1981 to June 1988
Hired as loan officer trainee. Promoted to loan officer in August 1981. Promoted to vice-president in July 1983. Promoted to executive vice-president and assistant to the president in July 1985. Named member of the Board of Directors in July 1986. Responsible for bank's community relations and high school trainee programs. During tenure, bank's assets tripled and earnings doubled.

Kelsey's Pharmacy, June 1977 to July 1981
Started as stock boy and clerk while going to Salem University. Promoted to head clerk in February 1978, assistant manager in July 1978, and store manager in September 1978. Developed store's annual Christmas promotion as well as a half-dozen other programs designed to increase sales.

OTHER
ACTIVITIES: Member Rotary International, chairman of Program Committee. Member YMCA Board of Directors. Chairman YMCA membership committee. Member, Planning Commission, city of Salem. Member American Management Association (AMA). Membership chairman of Massachusett's Bankers Association (MBA).

PAST
ACTIVITIES: Member Pi Rho Delpha, college fraternity.
Chairman volunteer merchandising committee, college bookstore.

other employment, a company that could better use his innovative talents.

Sound familiar? Al Adamo, a human resource director with more than 25 years in the field, shakes his head in disbelief when he hears the Regal story. "It is the classic example of an executive refusing to recognize what is going on around him. None of us want to admit things are going wrong. We tend to hide them and before we know it, we've been fired."

Hearing that you are being fired or laid off, even for a young executive like Regal, is not easy. Large companies, to ease the impact, often offer the services of an outplacement agency. Commonwealth did that with Regal. The bank also gave him the opportunity to resign instead of being fired. Although he was bitter and angry, he decided to take the offer—a wise move. The next four months were the longest of Regal's young life.

Regal's demise at the bank took place more than five years ago. Today, he is senior vice president at a small toy company located about two miles from his old employer. His salary is nearly double what it was at the bank. Interestingly, he obtained the position without ever answering an ad, visiting a headhunter, or mailing a resume. Regal did, however, put together a resume. In fact, it was the first thing he did the morning he woke up and realized he was unemployed (Figure 3).

Years later, Regal stumbled upon his resume and laughed. The reaction was similar to that of the placement specialists who saw the document. Although the resume looked good, it lacked content. He sent it to a search firm that he knew specialized in placing bankers, waited about a week, and called. A polite, well-meaning secretary asked for his name, told him no one was available and said they would call him back: They never did.

HEADHUNTERS AND JOB SEEKERS

Rudolph Dew says the treatment was nothing new. "Less than 2 percent of a search firm's applicants are going to come in over-the-transom. Such firms are usually not interested in resumes that are sent blindly. They want to dig up their own candidates and they prefer those who are already employed. Couple that with the poor construction of Regal's resume and you can see why he was never contacted."

How did Regal ultimately find a new position? Admittedly, he says it was not with that resume. Regal's road to a new position started a few days after he was fired. It was the day he began to objectively analyze what had happened to him at the bank.

Regal's awakening started with his visit to an outplacement firm. He was sad and depressed, and wondered what he had done to warrant such shabby treatment from a firm he had been dedicated to for five years. At first, his reaction to the outplacement interview was similar to that of many executives. His prime concern was to get another banking job as quickly as possible. He was anxious to prove to his previous employers that they had made a mistake.

Sound familiar? It is a reaction that many unemployed managers and executives experience. Lee Iaccoca had the same reaction when Ford fired him. He never understood why, especially when Ford's only comment was that "he never cared for him."

The other problem is the anxiety of the job seeker. Obviously, he suffers financial hardship and he is willing to take almost anything to compensate and get back on the road. "At times," says Dew, "the job seekers have blinders. They can only see the industry and the company they came from. They want the same environment which can be a mistake."

Outplacement counselors discourage this "rush to another job." John Scarlatti, who heads an outplacement firm in Washington, DC, says "the anxiety to find another position—fast—can hinder someone from finding a position instead of a job."

Dew maintains that any fired or laid-off executive should analyze the company and industry, and determine what went wrong. This analysis enables a job seeker to do more than discover why he has been fired. "Most importantly," says Dew, "it enables the job seeker to discover the kind of environment he should be working in when he applies for a position. It shows him what went wrong and how to prevent it from happening again."

THREE KEY COMPANIES

In Dew's analysis, there are three possible organizational "types" to work for today. Every company fits into one of these three categories and every manager can find his company within these categories:

1. Entrepreneurial and developing organizations
2. Growing and professional organizations
3. Mature and administrative organizations

There are also three types of managers who can be found in these companies:

1. The entrepreneur—a strong, individual contributor
2. The outstanding, integrated team player
3. The organization person—the spoke in the wheel

The three types of managers correspond to the three categories of companies. That, however, is the ideal. Typically, managers get into trouble because either they or their company have changed. Or, perhaps, a job seeker picks the wrong company because he sees himself as he would like to be rather than what he actually happens to be.

"All of us," says Robert McDonald, "gravitate towards things we are least capable of doing. It is like an alcoholic who denies he is a drinker. We want to do it so bad we keep at it. An over-whelming number of job seekers fit into this category. They do not want to admit they no longer fit."

WHY FIRINGS OCCUR

Companies are not static. They are moving all the time and most of the firms that fit into the first two previously listed categories are usually heading upward. The firms fitting into the last listed category are stable and do not change as much as the first two. The cause of many terminations is when a company changes from one type firm to another and the manager stays put. In fact, the Hay Group, a national management/employment consulting group estimates that 25 percent of all terminations are caused because the company moved and the manager involved did not.

Ernie Smith is a case in point. He was named vice president in charge of data processing for a young franchise company. Ernie's 25 plus years should have given him sufficient expertise, but he had never worked under entrepreneurial conditions. Ernie was used to someone telling him what had to be done; he did not have the ability to look at the problem and solve it without direction. Consequently, when Ernie designed the firm's data processing system, he utilized tried and proven techniques; methods he had learned during his previous years in the business. He failed, however, to take into consideration the problems that this new company might have. He failed to evaluate the needs that the new franchisees might have. Thus, the system he designed—and spent millions on—was inadequate.

For nearly two years, Ernie survived. The complaints from those in the field grew and Ernie continued to ignore them. He had more than one opportunity to remedy the problems, but he never did. Finally, one afternoon he was called into the president's office, and told he would be given three months severance pay.

Today, Ernie is still bitter. He feels the company treated him unfairly, milked him for his expertise and then dumped him in order to hire a younger, less expensive executive. Although that scenario certainly does happen, it was not the cause of Ernie's failure.

In Ernie's case, what happened was obvious to everyone but Ernie. The same was true in Regal's case. When Regal joined Commonwealth, it was an entrepreneurial, developing bank, and he was an entrepreneur; a strong, individual contributor. When the bank was sold, however, it changed characteristics. It went from entrepreneurial to professional. Regal did not move from entrepreneur to team player. Remaining an entrepreneur in an organization that disdained that type of thinking proved to be disastrous.

Management consultants Larry Senn and Joseph Izzo maintain that failure to see a company change is usually one of the prime causes of a manager's ouster. Matt Belzano says there are usually one of two things that happen to a successful manager that cause his demise.

"We recently had a case," he says, "where the human resources department of a company called us and said the president and vice president of marketing could not get along. The president said the vice president was not doing the right job. The vice president said he was. In a way, they are both right but you know who is going to win the argument.

"The vice president had been with this company for five years. During that time, he had been given an extensive amount of freedom. Then, suddenly, the president became control-oriented. He wanted to know about everything before it was done. The vice president objected. In this case, it was easy to see who was going to win. The question is, why did the president suddenly change? I never found out but it could be for a variety of reasons. Perhaps the company took a dip; maybe the president became more control oriented as time passed; maybe the president met an old friend whom he thought could do better. You never know. The fact is the situation changed.

"The vice president refused to give in and submit to the control so he was let go. Even if he had buckled under, chances are he would not be around. Once the wheels are in motion, it is hard to stop them."

The second scenario is one that fits Regal. You might have two executives who have worked together for a long time, such as Regal and his boss. Suddenly the boss gets promoted or leaves. There is a new boss. He wants something else. He has a different style. You try to adjust but seem unable to do a satisfactory job. Sooner or later you are out. Why? Once again, it could be for a variety of reasons. The new boss might have even had a "hidden agenda." That is, perhaps there was someone at his old company that he wanted to hire in Regal's place.

Regal never determined the reason but there were signs that should have warned him. Usually, the most telling prior to a firing or layoff is a lack of communication. There are others, too. For example, there may be strange faces around the office and you are never introduced to them. The boss who has been confiding in you no longer tells you what is going on. His frequent stops at your office no longer occur. You no longer get copies of memos from the president or other key executives. You are no longer invited to planning or other critical meetings.

Firings/layoffs do not come out of nowhere. The clues are there; the employee must not only be astute enough to pick them up, but they must also be willing to admit to themselves what may happen.

Regal never did. When it happened, his focus was not on why, but only on getting another banking job. Certainly, few people can afford the income cutoff nor can they tolerate waiting months before they go after another position. In today's environment, however, counselors unanimously advise job seekers to determine what happened so the same mistake is not made again.

"Look at your past positions," advises Adamo, "and ask yourself why you were laid off, fired, or asked to take early retirement. Maybe it was an across-the-board, 10 percent slash. Even if it was, ask yourself why you were in the 10 percent and not the 90 percent. Those are tough questions to answer. They involve your ego but they mean a great deal when you are searching for another position. If you answer honestly, the answers can prevent you from putting yourself in a position where you might be let go again. They are also questions that a hiring manager may ask of you during an interview."

In his anxiety to get another banking job, Regal failed to answer any questions. In fact, if not for the outplacement counselor, Regal might well have gone to work for a bank that fit into the professional or mature category and, once again, he would have found himself to be a square peg in a round hole.

"Don't get involved with another company," says Dew, "until you analyze your situation. The most difficult thing is to convince a manager not to take the first job that comes along. The problem is the manager. He or she is usually a high achiever and they do not want to sit around and wait."

PUTTING COMPANIES IN MEASURABLE CATEGORIES

Waiting can pay off. It did for Regal. He agreed to spend time analyzing his company and his industry before he sent a resume anywhere. In doing so, he discovered that his bank was one of those organizations that moved from entrepreneurial to professional. Industry is loaded with similar examples. Some, in fact, move from entrepreneurial to mature and back again. A good example is Chrysler.

In pre-Iaccoca days, Chrysler was a company that had moved into the mature category. It had problems, but when Iaccoca came aboard the entire organization changed personalities. Iaccoca was an entrepreneur; a strong, individual contributor. He moved Chrysler the same way. It went from mature to entrepreneurial. As a result, many of the managers who were with the company no longer fit. There were massive replacements of key executives who were unable to contribute to an entrepreneurial type company.

Now that Chrysler has recovered, it may move to the professional or even mature category or Iaccoca may keep it entrepreneurial. Entrepreneurs prefer to keep a company entrepreneurial but that does not always happen. Frequently, the founding/owner/entrepreneur brings in a professional, mature type management once the company is established. These managers steer the company in their direction and as a result, many of the existing managers no longer fit.

American industry is rife with similar examples. Chase Revel, the founder of *Entrepreneur Magazine,* had a management style that was definitely entrepreneurial. Once the magazine went public, he brought in managers. Revel took a back seat while the new management steered the company. Within months, the company was a professional type. A number of executives who fit well with Revel found they could not with the new managers.

In every industry and occupation, this categorization works. Take the military, for example. General George S. Patton was the military's equivalent of the entrepreneurial manager. He was a headstrong individual with his own ideas which were often implemented. Patton was a rebel who got things done in the field. On the other hand, General Dwight Eisenhower was the outstanding, integrated team player. He was a professional type organization man who could work within the structure. Imagine Patton instead of Eisenhower planning D-Day and having to work with generals from other countries who each had their own ideas and egos. The invasion, under Patton, might never have occurred.

When an entrepreneurial individual finds himself in a professional or mature environment, the results can be disastrous. A well-known executive was named director of marketing for one of the country's largest airport food, beverage, and merchandise firms. It was a well-established company with set procedures—a definite mature-type firm. Although the marketing director contributed valuable ideas, he did not fit in the organization's culture and within a year, he was asked to leave.

In corporate life, there are examples as well. Entrepreneurial companies, aside from Chrysler, might be Pepsico and EDS. They are both innovative and do surprising things. They have top executives and managers who think the same way. In almost every case, the developing, entrepreneurial organization has an outspoken, well-known chief executive officer (CEO). Contrast this with the CEO from a mature company; for example, IBM. This is not always true of mature-type firms. The President of the United States is certainly well-known, but for the most part, nonpolitical governmental figures enjoy anonymity. Developing/entrepreneurial companies are flashy, and do things that make headlines. They require managers with flair. They look for the Regal's of the world. On the other hand, organizations that are growing and professional have an entirely different philosophy and manager. General Electric, Apple Computer, and 3M are companies that fit in this niche.

While entrepreneurial companies succeed through strong, individual effort, plus unusual and nontraditional skills, the growing, professional organizations succeed through discipline, traditional hard work and less flash, good planning, and a healthy balance between the individual and the team.

The final category, the mature organization, is one typified by years of experience. For example, there is Sears, AT&T, General Mills, and the government. These organizations are well-oiled machines and their managers know they have a subordinate role in the organization. Managers within these companies do not institute change or make waves. Their leaders operate a finely tuned corporate machine. They come from within the ranks and are replaced from within the ranks. There is little crapshooting in these companies.

The differences in companies and operating philosophies is clear. That clarity should help anyone seeking a job see where he should go and where he should stay away from. There are some managers who can fit in more than one of the corporate environments. But the manger who does opt for more than one, should be able to handle either equally as well.

A headstrong, innovative manager such as Regal is not going to feel at home in anything but the entrepreneurial organization. He understands that his fellow employees will cross departmental lines, be more free-wheeling and less structured. For the person who has spent 25 years with a mature company, to join an entrepreneurial company makes little sense regardless of the opportunity. Sooner or later, the hostile environment will lead to an ousting.

GROWTH AND THE JOB SEEKER

Each of these organizations have a lifecycle and marketing approach. The entrepreneurial company experiences rapid growth in comparison to its competitors. It is fast paced, unorthodox, and often rewrites the rules in order to obtain that growth. There is no better example than McDonald's in its early years under Ray Kroc.

The growing/professional organization has disciplined growth, plans to dominate the market, and is customer oriented. This is where McDonald's is now.

The mature firm is either fully developed or in a slow decline. It may trade market share for profits, shrink product lines, or try to maximize the cash value of the company. American industry has had numerous companies that fit this category; companies that were either taken over or purchased. This is where McDonald's hopes it will never be. The question is, which one fits your management style?

Each of the firms in these categories has organizational structures. The entrepreneurial firm is flexible and influenced by certain functions that are necessary for its success. They are dominated by one individual who makes the decisions. Numbers mean little because the company is battling for survival. Accountability is not clear cut. Plans can change from day to day and today's goal may become obsolete because of a new idea.

Those who prefer more traditional structures and accountability may find it with the growing, professional company. Since it is usually divided into business units, its structure depends greatly on teamwork, and there is much negotiating and persuasion going on between departments. The managers are accountable for more than just a profit and loss statement; they are often judged by how well they work together.

In the mature firm, the structure is rigid, there is little relationships between departments, and accountability rests solely on a department's ability to make the forecast or budget. Think typically of governmental agencies and the rigidity under which they operate. They have a specific budget and that budget must be spent regardless of how senseless the expenditure.

Every manager has a comfort zone. For those who are self-starters, people who have the ability to take the ball and run, there is nothing better than an entrepreneurial firm. There is little tolerance for failure and getting ahead usually means "up or out." But the rewards are there for the entrepreneurial manager who enjoys the environment.

With growth-oriented companies, there usually is a development system for managers. These companies seek problem solvers and competitive executives. There is a career ladder and several roads one can take to climb it.

A more structured environment is the mature firm. The managers who thrive in this environment are those that can accept discipline and promotion in a stable, arranged atmosphere. There is no room for rattling the corporate framework.

Each organization fosters a different management style as well. The manager seeking employment in the entrepreneurial firm can expect a loose structure, no clear direction but opportunity to implement anything—as long as it works. To function in this environment, takes someone who can work without direction and make decisions on his own. Contrast this with the constraints of growing professional organizations that may have definite goals and objectives, and expect managers to work together as a team. In the mature organization, the manager must work under strict discipline and directions from the top. There is little pressure or leeway to do things differently.

WHERE THE POLITICS ARE

The most revealing aspect of why Regal was fired is unveiled by examining the culture/climate of these three types of firms. In entrepreneurial companies, there is immediate, high response to change. There is freedom to act, take a chance, and performance is evaluated on what you have done lately.

The entrepreneurial manager can act now and get approval later, and the organization is highly responsive to any suggestions for change.

The growth-oriented company relies on teams not individuals. Decisions are the result of planning, not impulse or chance taking. In this environment, Regal found responsiveness to new ideas was lukewarm. Managers in this environment find their performances are more dependent upon what people think of you rather than what you actually accomplish.

In growth-oriented environments, internal politics come into play. For those not accustomed to the game, this company can be extremely difficult to handle. Managers who can trace their firings or layoffs to subjective criteria, would do well to think twice before they entered the growth-oriented environment again. It takes special talent to thrive and advance in a company that values politics as much as innovation.

Politics come into play in the mature organization as well, however, performances are typically measured against return on investment rather than who influences whom. Planning dominates the organization. For example, inventory is tied to the sales forecast.

Managerial success is not related to which category a company fits but where the manger fits. Iaccoca is an entrepreneur as was Steven Jobs (one of the founders of Apple Computers), and the renowned pilot, Chuck Yaeger. All had to do things their way. Jobs wound up leaving Apple and starting another company. Yaeger, a World War II ace and one of the most talented fliers in the history of the Air Force, never fit into the military's rigid structure. He made his mark as a fighter and test pilot, two skills which depend greatly on the individual and not a team.

Entrepreneurs are going to fail (go broke or be fired) more often than others. They are born risk takers and prefer to stay that way. Age has little to do with the choice although some managers do become more conservative as they get older. If the entrepreneur never gets a second chance, he or she is going to be remembered as a failure. If he gets that second chance, he usually turns out to be an enormous success.

Regal was marked a failure from the day he picked up his severance check. He may, indeed, have remained that way if he had sent out resumes and landed a job with another growth-oriented institution. Instead, by going through a "company and job fit" matrix, Regal discovered that he belonged in an entrepreneurial environment.

Unfortunately, there were no more start-up banks in his city, but there were other companies that required entrepreneurial thinking and the type of management skills that Regal had. Thus, four months after he was relieved of his banking duties, Regal found a position with a start-up toy company where his skills were not only needed but appreciated. If not for the insistence of an outplacement counselor, Regal might still be floating around in the banking industry, drifting from one institution to another.

In today's market, it is important for job seekers to assess their skills and their industry. What kind of company did you work for? Does your resume show that you previously worked for a company in the same employment category that you now seek?

Before the right company can be found, the job seeker has to assess his or her skills. McDonald says his firm tries to get job seekers to focus on three things they do well. "Then we ask them to look at different industries. In which industries do they fit? Which will accept them? Sometimes, we wind up putting together as many as three different resumes. We are tilting the language but that is not being dishonest."

Determining the skills that the job seeker has and enjoys is the first step in formulating a resume. Every job, of course, requires skills but usage of those skills can be misunderstood. For example, a newspaper reporter not only has to be a good writer, but he should be a good listener and have the ability to ask intelligently phrased questions. Newspaper reporters are not running around covering stories all the time. They are nearly always at their desk, rewriting stories that have been given to them by the editor. Thus, if a person enjoys writing but lacks listening and rewrite skills, he may turn out to be a terrible (and unhappy) reporter. Salespeople who enter real estate have an opportunity to earn huge sums of money but to do so, they have to be outgoing, involved in the community, and give up their nights and weekends because that is when most home-buyers do their shopping.

TWELVE KEY RESUME SKILLS

Which skills do you enjoy using most? Whichever ones you pick are those that should be of prime importance in whatever job position you select. Examine the following twelve skills:

1. Selling
2. Leading
3. Training
4. Analyzing
5. Designing
6. Operating
7. Producing
8. Repairing
9. Filing
10. Calculating
11. Typing
12. Organizing

On your last job, which of these skills did you utilize? Which did you use the most? Least? Which do you enjoy the most? Least? In the position you are pursuing, which does the company deem most important? Does it match your choice? Look at the position for which you are applying. If it requires extensive analysis and calculating and you prefer selling and leading, you are heading for the wrong position.

Analysis is that simple. Put the following six categories in order of preference, and ask yourself if the potential position matches your preferred order:

1. Family growth
2. Physical comfort
3. Intellectual challenge
4. Creativity
5. Financial security
6. Personal power

Traveling salesmen may obtain financial security and physical comfort, but they spend little time with their families. CEOs usually enjoy personal power and financial security but they do not have an abundance of time for family, intellectual challenge, or creativity.

There are tradeoffs for every position. None is going to be ideal. The key is to pick the position that fits best, utilizes your favorite skill the most, and enables you to obtain the most important goals in your life.

Few job seekers stop to analyze the position and how it will impact their lives. They are preoccupied with finding work and bringing in a paycheck. That is understandable, but jobs will never substitute for positions, nor do they last as long.

TWO KEY CONSIDERATIONS

Job seekers are usually overwhelmed by two considerations: How much am I going to make and when do I start? They fail to analyze and, consequently, end up as a job seeker, once again.

Dew recalls a case where a middle-aged manager was sent to outplacement by a thriving, young entrepreneurial company. For more than a year, he had been acting CEO for a firm that had more than doubled in size. Suddenly, he was let go and did not understand the board's decision. He was bitter and angry over the loss of the job. To compound matters, in accepting the position he had closed his own firm, an eight-year-old organization that had done well. Before that, he had worked for a company where he had total autonomy over a department. It was an entrepreneurial type organization.

In analyzing the ex-CEO's past, Dew discovered that everywhere he went in which he had total autonomy, he did well. He was bright, innovative, and not afraid to take chances. The perfect entrepreneurial executive. Still, he was fired. What happened?

After extensive interviews and counseling, the former CEO admitted that he "knew something was going to happen." Communication with his boss, the chairman of the board, had been virtually nonexistent for more than two months. This happened despite the fact the chairman began to spend a great deal of time at the company.

About three weeks before the CEO was let go, the chairman came into his office and introduced an "efficiency" expert who was going to study all facets of the organization and make suggestions. The CEO was urged to cooperate and give him anything he needed.

(Efficiency experts or people entering a department to make a study of it, can be another clue that management is about to make a change. When someone studies a department, it usually means things are not going well. They want to learn everything. Why? Typically, they are learning in the event the department head is let go.)

It took about three weeks for the efficiency expert to absorb the procedures of the CEO. Then, one morning, the chairman came in, closed the door, and fired the CEO.

Outplacement counseling made the former manager aware of several things. He was an entrepreneur running an entrepreneurial company with another entrepreneur looking over his shoulder. Seldom does this work. If the entrepreneurial/founder of an organization is going to continue to come into the office, delve into things, and offer suggestions after he has retired, the incoming CEO is going to have difficulty.

The lack of communication stood out as well. In studies of executives who have been laid off or fired, one glaring weakness is that they fail to communicate. They may talk to their boss and tell them what is happening (in general terms) but they fail to keep them informed on a regular basis. Communication in any organization is a key to keeping a job.

Occasionally, a fired manager will say, "We did not have any communication problems at all. I asked my boss if he wanted a regular weekly report and he always told me it was not necessary." This is a mistake. Give it whether the boss says it is necessary or not. Even if he discards it, the information tells him you are doing something. It also keeps him from being embarrassed. There is nothing worse than having a department subordinate working on a project and his boss knowing nothing about it.

ROLE OF COMMUNICATION

Communication is the heartbeat of business. If a CEO fails to let the chairman (and board members) know what is happening, they begin to wonder. The entrepreneurial CEO who found himself out of a job was noncommunicative. No one can afford to neglect communication, not even the chairman of the board who ultimately has to communicate with shareholders (unless he owns the firm).

Where does a former CEO and top manager go? Where does he find a job? This CEO had the option of opening his own business once again or going to work for another firm. The former CEO realized he did not want to open his own business nor did he have any desire to become CEO of another company.

Through analysis of his skills, he discovered that the happiest time of his working life was when he worked for someone else, headed a department, and did as he pleased—as long as the results were obtained.

His goal was to find an entrepreneurial company that would be willing to hire him in a lesser position (department head). It took more than four months before he found a job, but he did thanks to the aid of a power resume, three interviews, and a critical referral.

CHALLENGE FOR THE FIFTY PLUS

The ultimate challenge for a 50-year-old seeker is finding and obtaining a job of lesser title that pays less and that he prefers more. This CEO was able to do it. Some of the techniques he utilized will be covered in the following chapters of this book. Whether it is a 50-year-old former CEO looking for a position or a 25-year-old fast-tracking sales manager, they must fit before they can be assured of a long-lasting position. Fit means more than having the qualifications on a resume.

When someone is fired, associates assume the person was not competent. Nothing could be farther from the truth. Certainly, in some cases people are fired because they do not perform, but in most managerial situations the end comes because the person does not fit. Fit means things as simple (and often overlooked) as *small talk.* If you cannot small talk with the boss, it does not mean you will be fired but it does mean you have a greater chance of termination than someone who can. An inability to talk about things other than the job means there is a communication gap.

How does an applicant find the right fit and what does he or she do once they have? We will answer those questions in Chapter 3.

3

THE HIDDEN

JOB MARKET

A mong his friends, John Stewart is known as congenial, outgoing, and generous. To his employees he is a hard-driving, tough entrepreneur who founded his business more than 30 years ago and built it into a multimillion dollar insurance agency. Stewart's hard work paid off. He has a winter home in Palm Springs, a summer house in Newport a few blocks from his office, and a townhouse in New York City.

For the past few years, he has been trying to take time off, travel, and delegate duties to others in his office. Yet, every time he does, he returns to find chaos. The disorder no longer disturbs Stewart thanks to Harold Simpson, a young, bright, aggressive accountant that Stewart started using a few years ago. Simpson comes in, spends a week or two straightening out the books, and gets the company back in order.

Despite their age differences, Stewart and Simpson have become close friends. Once a week they play golf and their families exchange gifts at Christmas. Once or twice a month, the two discuss Stewart's business, toss around expansion plans, and exchange views on the industry. Simpson's slow, methodical style impresses Stewart who, like many entrepreneurs, is impetuous.

In the fall of 1988, Simpson noticed that during their weekly golf games, Stewart seemed detached, quiet, and preoccupied. At first Simpson did not say anything but one Friday morning as they approached the tee for the 18th hole, he asked Stewart if something was bothering him. Stewart shook his head, said nothing, and continued playing.

Stewart, however, was troubled. He had developed back problems that the doctor traced to hours of sitting hunched over his desk, studying reports. The doctor told him to get out from behind his desk, exercise more, and enjoy life. Stewart thought, why not get someone to run the business? It was established, and with a manager who had good organizational skills, the company could certainly function without him. But how would he find a manager? He thought about running ads, screening and interviewing people, but he kept putting it off.

Searching for employees can be time consuming and frustrating for executives. Many, like Stewart, know they need help but they delay it. They do not want to get bogged down with paperwork, screening, and interviewing. Human resource departments are familiar with executives like Stewart. "They know they need someone," says Hasten Roberts, "but they do not want to take the time to search. To executives, hiring is a cumbersome, tiring activity. In many ways it is nonproductive. If they can avoid it, they never put the ad in the paper."

There are exceptions. If the vice president of a department leaves and his post has to be filled or if any key position suddenly opens, an ad will be placed and the search process gets underway.

"But," says consultant/counselor Matt Belzano, "many positions within a corporation are newly created. They may be caused by growth or a new, perceived need. They are positions that the CEO or a vice president thinks about but does not establish. A CEO may say to himself 'We should have a vice president in charge of planning. When I get some free time, I am going to sit down with human resources and map out a job description.' The CEO never gets the time. Or, you might have a vice president saying the company needs a data processing specialist to head the new computer department. That never happens either. In both cases, the company has been running without those positions. They are not critical."

Stewart, however, did find a way to solve his executive search problem without putting together a job description or consulting human resources. One afternoon, Simpson came by with several forms for Stewart to sign. In the course of the meeting, John told him what he had been thinking—he needed someone to take the burden and run the office. "I need someone with your patience, thoroughness, and expertise." Almost immediately, the answer came to Stewart. He looked at Simpson, smiled, and asked "How about you?"

Two months later, Simpson was named chief operating officer of Stewart's company. This process illustrates what happens nearly 50 percent of the time when it comes to finding people to fill positions—an ad may never be placed and the position is created and filled because the executive doing the hiring "knows someone."

WHERE OPENINGS DEVELOP

According to a recent study of professional, technical, and managerial workers who had recently found jobs, nearly 44 percent had new positions created for them. The study, done by sociologist Mark Granovetter of Harvard University, points out how executives like Simpson find positions—positions that never appear in any advertisement.

Some would say that Simpson just happened to be in the right place at the right time. True, but Simpson did something that all job seekers should be practicing—networking. Webster defines "networking" as the "exchange of services or information among individuals or groups."

In the employment field, networking is the single most misused and abused word. To many, networking means taking advantage of the contacts you have made in business, someone you know who might be able to steer you to a new position. Nothing could be farther from the truth. If a job seeker calls a friend or acquaintance and tells him he is "looking for a new position," the contact immediately becomes uncomfortable. He feels put on the spot and asked to produce. No one enjoys being placed in that situation.

How and why should networking be used? The answer: by following Webster's definition. Networking should be used as a vehicle for an exchange of ideas, information, and advice.

ADVICE VERSUS ASKING

Call anyone and ask for advice and the reaction differs markedly from asking if they know where you can get a job. Ultimately, networking is going to lead to a job, but its prime purpose is to make contacts, talk to people, find out what is happening, and to let them know what you are doing.

The temptation is great for the job seeker to call a Rotary or Kiwanis acquaintance and ask if he knows of any openings. Usually, the answer turns out to be a hesitatingly, uncomfortable "no . . . but if I hear of anything I will let you know"—sound familiar?

As young as he was, banker Jeffrey Regal knew better. The first thing he did was sit down and list friends and acquaintances who dealt with people. Rudolph Dew divides those with job information into three categories:

A. Those people with whom you feel most comfortable. You know them and they know you. They can be counted on to supply you with additional names and contacts. Close friends and acquaintances would be in this category.

B. Those people you know through work, associations, or other activities such as community or volunteer groups. They have knowledge of you as a person and professional and have information or advice.

C. Those people less known to you but who have information that might be of use. They also may have contacts that can be utilized. They are usually people with whom you have had infrequent contact.

Names from each of these groups should be compiled. The names can come from a myriad of sources ranging from your business card file to your Christmas card list. Other sources include:

- Club directories
- Church rosters
- College alumni directories
- Executives in your (previous) company
- Previous interviews
- Industrial directories
- Your rolodex—at home and work
- Professional acquaintances such as lawyers, doctors, bankers, brokers, dentists, teachers, politicians, and consultants
- Suppliers and salesmen
- Small business owners

In the days following an employment severance, a job seeker may find it difficult to think of all the possible contact sources. Some questions the job seeker should ask that may make it easier are:

- Whom do I know from my family or my old job?
- Anyone from the last seminar or special school I attended?
- What about people I met on the golf course or at sporting events?
- How about those I know because of their children and mine?

We all know dozens of people—networking contacts. But the lists must be compiled before any hidden jobs can be found. The natural inclination of the job seeker is to make appointments with people from the A list. That, however, is a mistake. Tackle the C list first. Test your interview and marketing skills with these people, and remember, each person on the C list (or the A or B) know others. Regal's list was a long one—bankers, insurance salesmen, real estate brokers, doctors, lawyers and, dentists.

Picking up a telephone and calling someone is tough when you are out of work. The job seeker is already suffering from doubts and questions relating to his ability. Pride and self-image can be damaged again. What the job seeker has to keep in mind is that he must become a salesman. He is selling his ability and it must be sold before he gets the position he is after. There will be people who will turn him off, turn him down, and refuse to see him, but there will be others who will not. From one of these can come a lead that is worth a hundred refusals.

FINDING POSITIONS WITHOUT COMPETING

The job seeker should keep one other thing in mind: networking affords someone the opportunity of finding a job without competing against hundreds of resumes. One of those calls and visits could lead to a situation and job similar to the one Simpson found. The effort is worth it.

A job seeker has several options in approaching names from the C list. First, he can place a call to the person and attempt to get an appointment. If the job seeker knows someone who is acquainted with the C list person, he can drop that name. "Phil Jones suggested I talk to Mr. Smith" is a more potent line than "I would like to speak to Mr. Smith." Whether he has a reference or not, he has to get by a secretary.

Typically, secretaries are a barrier when trying to reach middle-management (and above) executives. They will screen the call and attempt to shortcut it. The questions they ask could be:

- What is this call in reference to?
- He is in conference, can I have him call you back?
- Is this in reference to employment?

Each question takes a different approach. For example, the first question can be answered with, "I am calling at the suggestion of Phil Smith." If there is no reference, the answer could be, "this is in reference to a marketing project I am involved in." Never should the job seeker indicate that he is unemployed, looking for job advice, or searching for a position.

If a job seeker is hit with the second question ("Can I have him call you back?") he should decline. If the job seeker is at home, he does not want a business call coming to a nonbusiness line. Aside from it sounding unprofessional, it will make the executive wonder, "What small time operator am I calling?" The job seeker should always say he will call back. He should tell the secretary he is on the road and it would be much better if he made the call—"Is there a good time to reach him?"

If the job seeker continues to have problems reaching the contact he should try early in the morning or later in the work day (that is, 7:00 to 7:30 A.M. or 5:30 to 6 P.M.). Most secretaries are gone by then and many executives either come in early or stay late. They also pick up their own telephone.

Another dialogue suggestion: Ask for the secretary's name if you have to call back. When you do and she gets on the line, address her by her first name. It makes the call more intimate and brings the secretary closer to your "camp."

Once the executive gets on the line, the conversation should be brief and to the point. Let the executive know what you are after. For example:

> Mr. Smith, John Jones suggested I give you a call. He says you know the (whatever) industry well, and you might have about 10 to 15 minutes in which you could give me some advice. I recently left (name of company). Incidentally, this is not to ask you about a position. That is not the reason I am calling. I am looking for some insight and advice as to the career options I am considering.

The executive can react in several ways. He might immediately give you a time he wants to talk or he could try to do it over the telephone. "I am free, ask me now." Do *not* ask. There is nothing that replaces face-to-face contact. If the executive asks about the telephone, answer with something like:

> I would really appreciate talking to you in person. I know you are busy, but his will not take longer than 10 to 15 minutes. I will be in your area next week. Is there any day and time that may be convenient?

Most executives will assent if the objections are handled as outlined. Job seekers have one other option. They can send a note to the executive asking the same questions and saying they will call "next week" to see if a convenient time can be scheduled. If the job seeker has a referral, he should telephone first and forget the letter. If he does not have a referral, or if he cannot get the executive on the telephone, he should send the letter and follow it up.

Regal wrote letters to several people on his C list. His letter was similar to the one in Figure 4.

Flattering? Of course. Most people love to give their opinions. One of Regal's initial letters went to Sam Henderson, owner of the largest insurance agency in town. Regal had only met Henderson once or twice, but he did know that Henderson specialized in corporate accounts and could offer insight into every major company in town.

By meeting with someone from his C list, Regal would be talking to an individual who was not a personal friend and therefore he might be more willing and honest insofar as giving an opinion as to Regal's resumes. Friends may be great to talk to, however, if they know you have been fired or laid off, they may not want to say anything critical. They know you have already been hurt.

Close friends may not be the best source of networking, either. In many cases, the job seeker knows the same circle of people as his friend. Those from the C list may have a much wider circle.

Preparation for a meeting is a necessity. The job seeker should have familiarity with the contact's business and industry. He should have an understanding of it and be able to exchange ideas. The dialogue in a networking session should not be one way. The job seeker should be able to exchange views even though there is no position in the offing.

Figure 4   Letter to an Infrequent Contact

Dear _____:

I recently parted company with Commonwealth Bank and I am in the process of embarking on a new career direction.

I have always respected your opinions, and I would like to take 10 or 15 minutes of your time for some input on my resume as well as advice and recommendations on business in the industry.

I am not, incidentally, looking for a job with your company. I am primarily interested in your knowledge and suggestions.

I'll give you a call next week to see if there is a convenient time we can get together.

Many thanks.

Sincerely,

PRESENTING THE RESUME

When the meeting opens, the contact should be reminded as to why the job seeker is there and the contact should also be thanked. "I have a high opinion of you" or "Joe Jones has told me much about your company and I think you could offer valuable advice."

The job seeker should also make it clear, once again, that he is not in the contact's office looking for a job. Still, the job seeker may find the contact cautious. He may even find the question asked, "What position are you looking for?"

If that happens, the job seeker has the perfect opportunity to present the contact with a resume. He might say something like, "Well, one in which I can utilize my strengths. I do not really want to take up your time describing my background and experience, so I brought along a copy of my resume. I think it will give you some insight into my abilities."

Robert McDonald suggests a line such as, "Well, Mr. Jones, I would be delighted to tell you about my background but the simplest way may be for you to take a look at my resume." The job seeker then pulls out the resume (which is folded in his coat pocket), opens it, and slips it across the desk. "I will just sit here for a moment while you are looking at it, and if there are any questions I would be happy to answer them."

The job seeker should remain quiet and give the contact a chance to read through the resume. "Do not," cautions McDonald, "say another word. Let him open it up. Too much talking can get you into trouble. Let your resume trigger the questions and his response."

That response may go all the way from "It is impressive" to the contact suddenly thinking to himself "We have needed a good corporate planner . . . now, suddenly I have one who has all the qualifications." It may trigger other responses, too. The executive may have been thinking about replacing someone only he did not want to go through the hassle of running an ad and interviewing applicants. Now, he has someone in front of him who could fill the position. Networking contacts should be handled in the same manner as an interview with a hiring manager. In Chapter 7, there are procedures laid out that should be followed when visiting someone's office. They spell out how to make an interview more effective and productive, and provide some of the dialogue that should be used as well.

A position is not always going to emerge. If one does not, the job seeker should give some thought as to how he might generate additional contacts from the interview. Typical guidelines might be:

When sufficient time has been spent on the seeker's objectives and qualifications, the seeker should thank the contact and ask something like, "Based upon our conversation, I would like you to suggest the names of some people you think would be helpful for me to meet—people who might be as helpful as you—and who would enjoy meeting me."

The job seeker should not rush the contact. Give him a chance to answer. Occasionally, a contact might return the question with another such as "Like who would you want to meet?" The job seeker can offer suggestions such as, "People in a similar position to you" or "Suppliers" or "People you know at other companies."

The seeker should make sure the contact knows he will not press the reference for a job. The meeting with the next contact should be as broad—and noncommittal—as this one. Before leaving the meeting, it is critical to get the contact to agree that the job seeker may use his name in setting up the next contact appointment. All it takes is a question that is posed after the contact gives the job seeker a lead: "Do you mind if I mention your name?" Typically, the response will be, "Of course, not."

DISTRIBUTING RESUMES

At times, a contact may be so sold on a job seeker that he gets overly enthusiastic and volunteers to "distribute your resume" or "set up a meeting for you" or "talk to so and so for you." That approach has faults. The contact may cool after the job seeker leaves and never follow through. Or, he may suffer "buyer's remorse," follow through in a half-hearted manner and send a resume to someone with a noncommittal note like:

Met this guy the other day and he gave me this resume. He asked me to send it to some of the people I know.

If I can tell you anything else, let me know.

Best Regards,

A referral such as this will do the job seeker little good. Occasionally, however, the contact may be sincere and could do some extraordinary things insofar as making contact with a potential employer. In that case, the job seeker has to judge the tone and commitment of the contact.

LOADED QUESTIONS

Not all contacts are going to be overly enthusiastic. Many will be cautious despite reassurance from the job seeker. They could greet the job seeker with the following questions:

Why did you want to meet me?

A question loaded with suspicion. The job seeker may alleviate the concern by alluding to his regard for the contact: "I have respected your opinions and reputation for a long time and I would like to get some firsthand advice about some of the options I am pondering."
The contact could ask:

What kind of help do you want from me?

Among the possible answers:

I am not looking for help but advice. I have always had high regard for your opinions.

Other possible questions:

What kind of position are you looking for?

Answer:

I am weighing some options now. That is one of the reasons I am here; to get advice from someone I have extremely high regard for.

Question:

Tell me something about yourself.

This is the perfect opportunity to reiterate qualifications and outstanding accomplishments. Do not spend an hour, however, on the subject. Give the contact a summary in one to two minutes. No one wants to be bored by someone's autobiography.
Contact's response:

I am happy to talk with you but I do not know anyone who needs someone with your experience.

Answer:

That is fine. I am not looking for a job, but advice. I appreciate your time.

Question:

Why are you leaving (or left) your present employer?

Answer:

Frankly, we differed in the way things should be done. It was not a question of my being competent, however. I think Joe Jones, my supervisor, would tell you how competent I was.

Question:

What kind of company do you want to work for?

The job seeker should be familiar with his choices (that is, the entrepreneurial, growth-oriented, or mature firm). He should also know which one he fits and why. From there, this question will be easy to answer. In providing the answer, the job seeker should also mention specific accomplishments. They help illustrate how well he functions in a certain environment. Although the specifics are on the resume he hands to the contact, he should not rely on the contact remembering everything he read. Bring the points up again.

Another important question:

What kind of salary would you anticipate?

Give a figure and you lose. This is a question that should definitely be skirted. It can be with answers such as "Right now I have not even thought about salary. I am trying to determine the right direction. Once I have that and know what kind of position I am looking for, I will deal with the salary."

The contact may end the discussion with:

Give me several resumes and I will send them out to my friends.

Always go for the personal contact. Ask for the name of the friend and say you would be happy to drop one by in person. As stated previously, resumes sent out by a contact may not have any impact if the contact is not convinced of your capabilities.

If the contact says:

I will call my friend and let you know if he wants to meet you.

Too chancy. Make the call yourself. You do not want the contact to be "bothered" with making the call since he has already been so helpful. The exception is if the contact is so enthused that he wants to do it then.

Regal was ready for all questions and events when it came time for his appointment. He brought along a copy of his resume and a note pad—no sage minds someone taking down his advice. He had also rehearsed what he was going to say insofar as his qualifications and goals were. He rehearsed over and over. There was nothing left to chance.

WHAT TO REHEARSE

Most job seekers get tripped up when they fail to rehearse. Meeting a contact and looking for additional contacts is work and work takes practice. Without practice, the job seeker cannot possibly anticipate all the seemingly "easy" questions that will come his way.

The meeting should follow steps similar to the following:

1. *Lead-in.* This consists of introductions, the name of the person who referred you (if there was one), and a reiteration that you are not looking for a job but seeking advice.
2. *Ask prepared questions.* Tell the contact what your objectives are and ask what he thinks. Let him know what your major accomplishments were and give him a copy of your resume so he will be familiar with some of the things you have done.
3. *Listen.* The most important thing any job seeker can do with a contact. Aside from advice they may also drop something that is critically important.
4. *Get referrals.* This might be in the form of a second meeting with this company or with an executive from a firm that the contact mentions.

When Regal gave Henderson a copy of his resume, Regal asked him for his opinion. The answer surprised him.

"Jeff, I don't know you well, but I have heard about you. Tell me, what does an executive vice president do at a bank or, for that matter, an assistant to the president?"

"Regal," says Matt Belzano, "made the mistake that many managers do. They assume that a title coupled with duties and responsibilities explains what they did. It does not. I cannot tell you how many thousands of managers looking for a new position waste contacts and resume paper because they assume that duties and responsibilities tell the story."

"Few people," adds Rudolph Dew, "know or even care what you do (or did) on your job. If I called my mother and told her I was head of this firm and we helped people get back into the employment ranks, she would not know what I did. She would only know that I was president. President, however, like the bank's executive vice president, is no more than a title. It is impossible to utilize contacts if they do not know your specific accomplishments. That is one of the differences in a power resume versus a standard resume. It goes straight to specifics."

To most, the term "banker" means someone who loans money. But it can also mean management of the institution's investment portfolio, dealing with regulators, preparing proposals, handling personnel, working with community organizations, or designing promotions. Regal did all of those things.

POWER IS SPECIFIC

More important, however, than duties and responsibilities are specific accomplishments. In Regal's case, he designed several bank/consumer promotions that increased Commonwealth's customer base by 15 percent and its assets by 22 percent in six months. He was not just part of the promotion, he designed and ran it. These are specifics; the information a potential employer is going to want to hear; the information that belongs in a resume.

If, for example, a job seeker were in the data processing field, key specifics might be: cut processing time by 12 percent, designed and implemented special sales information and inventory status program that provided feedback to management on a daily instead of weekly basis, saved company $9,500 in department overtime by rescheduling programs and data processing runs. These are all items for a power resume.

In explaining his accomplishments to Henderson, Regal realized that his resume was incomplete. The conversation also prepared him for employment interviews because many of the questions Sam posed were similar to those he would be asked by a potential employer: What did you do specifically? What were your accomplishments? How did you increase business or add to profitability? What were your most valuable contributions? These are all potential human resource department questions and the answers should be on every resume.

Regal listened, too. Whether talking to a contact, human resource director, or potential supervisor, hearing what someone says is critical. They may mention something that can be the opening for a position or they may say something that enables the seeker to "score points" or open another door. Henderson did. He mentioned a client who had run a promotion similar to the one that Regal ran at the bank, though the results were below expectations.

The mention of the company gave Regal an opening. He suggested to Henderson that there might be someone at the company with whom Regal could exchange ideas. Perhaps he could help them find the problem and they might offer him input as to his future.

Why not, thought Henderson? He would be doing a client a favor by introducing them to someone who could provide valuable promotion insight. He picked up the telephone and within minutes introduced Regal to the company's president. The two chatted for a few minutes and before he hung up, Regal had an appointment to see the president. None of this would have happened if Henderson thought the reason for Regal's visit was to find a job. He would have been on guard, cautious and hesitant about mentioning anyone, particularly a client.

Before he left Henderson's office, Regal began the next phase of his job search—gathering information on his next contact. He asked Henderson what he knew about the firm, its product line, sales, and other pertinent information. Regal also discovered where the company did its banking.

The next morning was a busy one. Although the appointment was a week away, Regal went to work. First, he did the most important thing any job seeker can do following a contact—he wrote the thank you note in Figure 5 to Henderson.

He wrote the note in Figure 6 to the company where he had his appointment.

Tom Hopkins, author of numerous books on selling, maintains that follow-up notes are one of the greatest sources of business. The problem is that most job seekers (and executives) do not take the time to write them or they think they are too complicated. A note is not.

A thank you note differs from a formal letter in that it is written the way one talks. It should be informal. One thing that helps make a note informal is a contraction. Notice "I'll" is used instead of "I will." The "I'll" is less formal. Notice, too, the last sentence (which is not complete) that says "Looking forward to the meeting."

Figure 5   Example of a Thank You Note

Dear Sam:

Just a short note to say many thanks for the time you took yesterday going through my resume and talking to Mr. Brown of _____.

I appreciate your interest and help and will let you know how things turn out.

Once again, many thanks.

Sincerely,

Figure 6   Example of Letter Confirming an Appointment

Dear Mr. Brown:

Just a short note to confirm our appointment on Friday the 29th, in your office at 3:00 P.M.

I'll bring some of the promotional plans and thoughts we utilized that I think will be of interest.

Looking forward to the meeting.

Sincerely,

As soon as he finished the notes, Regal telephoned one of his friends at Brown's bank. Without violating any confidentiality, Regal's friend was able to give him insight into the firm's cash flow and apparent sales.

CHECKING POTENTIAL EMPLOYERS

Not all job seekers are going to have access to a bank that will help them check out a company. They can, however, find other sources such as suppliers and sales representatives. Regal also visited the library and scanned previous copies of the local newspaper's business section for stories on the firm. He visited the local newspaper and, through its library, found additional data. Local newspapers maintain files on companies that have had stories written on them or their personnel. While some of these are actual clips, many are on microfilm and both are available to the public.

Regal called the firm's offices and had a brochure on its product line mailed to him. By the time the appointment arrived, he knew a great deal about the company. It was young, entrepreneurial, and aggressive. It fit the profile of the company that Regal was interested in exploring. It was not in the banking industry, but it could be a potential employer.

Although employment was a possibility, Regal did not attend the meeting with the thought of getting a job. If he had, the referral might have been wasted and he would have violated Henderson's trust. He looked upon the firm, as all job seeker's should, as another rung in the networking ladder.

With the information he had, Regal felt confident when he entered the president's office. Knowledge means everything to the job seeker. Imagine interviewing for a position and not knowing a thing about it and, at the same time, competing with two other people for the same job who know everything. The ill-prepared, uninformed job seeker seldom feels confident during contact sessions. By not knowing anything, they are unable to ask penetrating questions that can lead to additional networking leads or perhaps even a position.

Although Regal's meeting had been scheduled for an hour, he and the president spent nearly two and a half hours together. He impressed the president with his insight into the company and his marketing knowledge. Towards the end of the session, the president mentioned that Regal's employers were fortunate to have a man with his talents working for them. Regal smiled and told him he had recently severed ties with the bank and was in the process of selecting a new direction. He pulled out a resume, slipped it across the desk, and asked him the same questions he had posed to Sam. There was one difference, however. By this time, Regal had rewritten the resume.

Brown studied the two-page document thoroughly. Regal remained silent as he had done with Henderson. Finally, Brown looked up. "Impressive." Before Regal left, he asked Brown if there was anyone he knew that Regal might talk to who could provide additional advice. The president thought for a moment and said he had some ideas "but he wanted to check them out first. I will give you a call or drop you a note on it."

Regal knew from the president's reaction that he had more than a referral in mind. Sensitivity is part of any interview. Regal did not push for the name of an additional contact. This one, he decided, he would wait out. He would give it a week.

The next morning Regal sat down and followed his standard routine. He wrote the thank you note in Figure 7.

Two days later, the letter in Figure 8 arrived at Regal's home.

The following week, Regal met with the president. That is when he found out that Brown had been thinking about bringing in a vice president/director of marketing for six months. It was a position that had never existed in the company. It was also one that the president had known for some time that he would have to create and fill.

Figure 7   Post-Interview Thank You Note

Dear Mr. Brown:

Just a short note to say how much I enjoyed our session yesterday.

If I can supply any other information or be of help in any way, let me know.

Sincerely,

Figure 8   Possible Response to a Good Interview

Dear Jeffrey:

Your comments about choosing a new direction were quite intriguing as was our meeting.

I would like to discuss an idea I have with you. It involves our company. Would you give me a call at your earliest convenience.

Best Regards,

FINDING THE HIDDEN JOB

The president had never even taken the time to work up a job description for the position with the human resource department. The position, which was never advertised or even circulated throughout the company, was offered to Regal. Three weeks later, salary was settled, an employment agreement was signed, and Regal left the banking industry for a new career in marketing toys. Regal had found one of those elusive "hidden jobs," the near 50 percent of all positions that are never found in classified ads or in a headhunter's office.

Networking has one other advantage for job seekers: It bypasses the human resource department. If the job description for a marketing director had been put together, an ad placed, and resumes screened, there would be little chance that Regal would have survived the initial screening. Even if Regal's resume had made it through, the president would have thought twice before "wasting" his time in an interview with someone who did not have industry-related experience.

Networking also brings the job seeker and potential employer together in a more cordial, relaxed atmosphere. In that environment, the job seeker and contact are more likely to find areas of common interest and a rapport can develop. Contrast this with the "stress" of the job interview. (Techniques to avoid the stress are discussed in Chapter 7.)

Regal's success does not mean that a job seeker should forget ads and concentrate on networking. Both techniques should be used. They are equally as important in the search for a position. Networking is a shortcut and a technique that should be used along with answering advertisements. Cold-calling is not the easiest thing to do but if the job seeker follows the steps that have been outlined, the process is not difficult.

Alan Bayless, a client of Stuart Counseling Services, a Midwest outplacement company, owes much to the procedure. Bayless was a native of Minneapolis and a graduate of the University of Minnesota. He passed the CPA exam and, as is the custom, spent several years with an accounting firm before joining a large, well-known corporation headquartered in Minneapolis.

Bayless started as an auditor in the firm's accounting department, but he soon saw the impact computers were making. He utilized every spare moment to learn computerized accounting and production systems. He enrolled in night school and took specialty courses and seminars. In 1975, he was given the job of supervising the company's first data processing system. His efforts did not cease there, however. He kept up his schooling and seminars, learning the latest in information processing and technology. Two years later, his supervisor retired and Bayless was given the title of data processing director, a position he would hold for more than a decade.

By the end of the 1970s, there was a shift in the operating philosophy of Bayless' company. Its product lines, considered the best in the world, were beginning to lose market share to the Japanese and Koreans. Management worried about the losses, shareholders became disgruntled, and top executives began to fear a takeover.

In 1981, a team of senior executives from the company visited Japan and toured several factories in similar industries. What they saw astonished them and they decided to change the structure of their company. A month after their return, they brought in a management consulting team that spent the next two months analyzing the firm and how it could be streamlined.

Bayless was oblivious to the activity around him. He failed to notice that his annual job review was a month late. He failed to notice that two fellow department heads had recently been let go. Incredibly, he failed to take note of anything being wrong when the financial vice president formed a team to evaluate computerization throughout the company, and did not include Bayless.

Ultimately, Bayless found out. In January 1989, after 16 years on the job, he was fired as part of the company's move to thin and flatten its corporate structure and increase profitability. Bayless was shocked and angry. Although many in his generation had grown up without loyalty to a company, Bayless was faithful and considered the Minnesota conglomerate a "home forever"—it was not.

Bayless put together a resume and was scanning the "help wanted" ads within a week. He was not, however, a writer nor did he have the sales acumen needed to understand what another company would want. He had not hunted for a job in 16 years and he knew little about the steps he should be taking. Because he had buried himself in work, he had few friends or acquaintances within the industry.

In an effort to ease Bayless back into the job market, his company hired an outplacement firm. At first Bayless declined the services. He did not need a psychiatrist or psychologist, he said, there was nothing wrong with his attitude.

After three months of mailing resumes to blind and company ads, he found one that was, in his opinion, the perfect fit: Manager of Software Engineering (Figure 9).

Bayless answered the ad, included everything it asked for and waited—and waited—and waited. Nothing happened. After seven more weeks, he gave in. He called his former human resource department and said he wanted to take advantage of the outplacement services. A few days later he was in the office of a local firm.

He brought the ad with him to the outplacement office, slapped it on the counselor's desk, and said, "I answered this ad and did not even get a polite rejection note. I have all the qualifications for the job. If I cannot get these people to answer, what can you possibly do for me?"

Figure 9   Sample Ad

Manager of Software Engineering

Can You Make Things Happen?

We are a well-established computer products firm located in the San Fernando Valley area. Our continued growth depends on our ability to foresee new business opportunities and the timely delivery of new products to the marketplace.

Currently, we seek an individual with a BSEE or BSCS and significant management level experience in a high volume software development group within the commercial electronics industry. This should include significant data communications experience and a background in PC development. Strong leadership skills are essential.

Besides the opportunity to have a genuine impact and make things happen, we offer a competitive salary and a comprehensive benefits package. Qualified applicants please send your resume with salary history to:

Los Angeles Times Box # Z235NA

Equal Opportunity Employer

WHY SOME RESUMES FAIL

The outplacement counselor studied the ad and asked for Bayless's resume. He paired the two, smiled, and answered: "Give us one week. By the end of that time you will understand why you never received a response."

In less than two days, Bayless knew the reason. For one, his resume did not have one specific accomplishment. It contained his job titles, promotions, and responsibilities, but nothing pertaining to accomplishments. He was also attempting to switch industries and, in doing so, had sent the resume without any of the rationale needed to bypass a human resource director. A third mistake was that he knew nothing about the company and his resume (and lack of cover letter) reflected his lack of knowledge.

Bayless found himself starting from scratch. He spent time with a counselor and learned his own likes and dislikes. For the first time, he obtained an insight into the type of company in which he wanted to work, and he understood what networking meant and how it should be used.

On his second afternoon, he spent four hours compiling an A, B and C list. Initially, he had told the counselor he only knew a handful of people, perhaps one in each category. Before he was finished, he had 44 people on the three lists. The last thing he learned was how to structure a power resume. That afternoon, when he completed the resume, he started making networking calls. In the next three weeks, he scheduled six appointments, from which he met 14 other people and found himself talking to executives in three other industries.

At the end of his third week, he spent more than an hour with an executive (who had been referred) who was in the process of restructuring a data processing department. He had not gone ahead with it because he lacked the individual to head it up. Bayless and the executive hit it off immediately and the executive asked Bayless to call the following week for an appointment. Bayless knew there was a potential position in the offing; the kind of spot for which he had been waiting.

For the first time since he had been fired, he felt elated. At home he studied an invitation that he had received a week before. It was to a cocktail party. Normally, he would have passed, picked up a book, and gone to bed. But on this particular night he was too excited. He decided to go.

At the party were a number of familiar faces. The most familiar, however, was the executive with whom he had spent more than an hour. The two picked up their conversation where they had left off.

Two hours later, Bayless left the party with a firm offer for a position in which he would head up a new data processing department.

The Bayless and Regal stories are commonplace among job seekers. They are typical of people who found positions in the hidden job market. In Chapter 4, we will explore the market that is not hidden—the job market that is advertised in the business and classified sections of the daily and Sunday newspapers.

4

POWER SUMMARIES

AND ADS

T om Ahrens spent the past 15 years as marketing assistant and then as marketing director for one of the country's top 10 residential homebuilders. In the building industry, the hours are long and the work weeks consist of six and seven days. Ahrens never complained. He handled project after project and did a remarkable job. Of the six major developments he marketed, all but one were sold out within three weeks after they opened. Despite his success, his boss, the vice president in charge of development, never seemed to appreciate his accomplishments.

Ahrens was not a forceful or expressive individual. In five years as marketing director, he had only received two raises. His wife complained to him about the shoddy treatment but he said nothing to his boss. He told his wife the building business was tough and profits were not there. She countered with his track record and urged him to either say something to his boss or look elsewhere for a company that would appreciate his efforts. After her tirade, Ahrens nodded his head in agreement but said nothing. In fact, he rarely said anything to his supervisor, the vice president. Most of the time Ahrens was in the field and his boss was at the corporate office. Once every other week they met for an hour and Ahrens updated him on each project. The meetings rarely lasted an hour before the vice president dismissed Ahrens.

In five years, the two had never had lunch or even coffee together. Al Adamo shakes his head when he thinks about the Ahrens case. "It is an example of a company lacking a formalized evaluation system and an illustration of how important communication is in a firm."

The event that motivated Ahrens into action happened the morning of his scheduled meeting with the vice president. Just as Ahrens approached the vice president's door, his secretary called out and said the meeting had been cancelled. The vice president had urgent business and was called out of town. She had forgotten to call Ahrens and let him know. Ahrens suddenly realized how little he meant to the company.

That Sunday, Ahrens scoured the Sunday paper. He also read through the industry's two leading trade journals. He was tempted to send his resume to several competing companies but thought better of it. It was a small industry and one competitor might leak word to another and it could come back to his boss. Instead, he decided to confine his resumes to the advertisements he found in the newspaper and trade papers. *The Wall Street Journal* was a third option.

On the third Sunday following his cancelled meeting, Ahrens saw a small ad under Construction. It read:

Opportunity. Established construction firm specializing in residential real estate seeks take-charge marketing director to handle new developments. Industry experience desirable. Send resume to Builder, c/o the Daily Express, Box 101, Los Angeles, CA 92111.

Ahrens studied the ad. It asked for everything he had. Excitedly, he duplicated his resume at the local instant printer, wrote a cover letter listing his specific accomplishments, and mailed them. Then he waited.

One week passed, then two, and finally three. He did not expect an immediate reply, but he did count on something by the third week. When nothing happened at the end of the fourth week, he forgot the ad and went looking through the newspaper again. That Sunday he saw it once more: same ad; same qualifications. He showed the ad to his wife and told her about his first attempt. She suggested he try again. Perhaps the first mailing was lost. Ahrens tried again.

Three days later, he was in the temporary trailer that had been set up in the middle of his latest building project. It was noon and everyone was out to lunch. As usual, Ahrens was at his desk doing some calculations and scheduling for construction crews. Unexpectedly, the door opened and in came John Oldman, the company's human resource director. The two had known each other for years.

It was, in fact, Oldman who originally screened Ahrens' resume 15 years before.

Oldman closed the door behind him, smiled, and sat down. The two exchanged a few words and had a cup of coffee. Ahrens could tell that Oldman was uneasy about something. Finally, Ahrens asked what was bothering him. Awkwardly, Oldman reached into his pocket and pulled out a white envelope. Ahrens recognized it immediately. It was the envelope he had used to mail his resume and cover letter for the construction job. At first, he was baffled. How had Oldman gotten it?

"We run blind ads all the time," Oldman said, "especially if the position is filled and we do not want the current executive to know we are searching. Unfortunately, we occasionally get an executive applying for his own job. . . . I guess that is what happened here."

Oldman never said anything further to Ahrens. Nor did he say anything to the vice president who was advertising for Ahrens' replacement.

DANGER OF BLIND ADS

"That happens," says Adamo, "more than people think. An executive answers a blind ad and it turns out to be his job. It is embarrassing but the human resource directors usually keep it confidential. Ahrens was fortunate because the human resource director took a big chance in giving the resume back to him. Ahrens could have raised hell with his boss and the human resource director would have been looking for a job, too."

The lesson: Blind ads can be dangerous. Almost as dangerous as someone who does not objectively evaluate his present position and where he stands with his boss.

Why do companies run blind ads? For several reasons, Adamo says. One being to maintain secrets from both current employees and competitors. If an ad agency, for example, starts placing help wanted advertisements in a trade journal for an experienced food copywriter, the competition is going to immediately notice. If the agency seeking the copywriter does not have a food account, it signals competitors that either it is about to get one or it is about to go after one. The blind ad eliminates the disclosure.

Some companies run blind ads to save time. They may have small human resource staffs and they do not want to respond to everyone who sends in a resume. A blind ad eliminates that need. Or, perhaps they do not want candidates calling the company and asking questions.

Regardless of the reason, companies running bind ads usually have something to hide or they are being inconsiderate for a specific reason. Anyone answering a blind ad should definitely research the company if they are called in for an interview. They should also ask why a blind ad was placed. The answer can be surprising. A rule to go by: If it sounds like your job, do not send a resume—just start looking.

OPPORTUNITIES

One of the best sources of job opportunities is the Sunday newspaper. Most employers run ads Thursday through Sunday. On Thursday and Friday, they may run a shortened version of the ad or it may only refer to the ad that will run on Sunday and say something like "See our ad this Sunday under Sales."

For professionals/executives, an excellent source is *The Wall Street Journal,* usually on Tuesday and Wednesday. The *National Business Employment Weekly* carries most of the ads from the *Journal's* regional editions. It is informative, loaded with opportunities, and can be found at most libraries or newsstands.

Another place to look is in trade papers. Every industry has trades that cater to those in the industry. For example, the advertising field has *Advertising Age* and a host of others. In every issue, ads will be found that cannot be located in the Sunday newspaper. Employers utilize trade papers because they want someone from their industry or they want someone who is in a particular profession. Any job seeker contemplating a different industry, should pick up a copy of one of the trade papers that services the industry. Aside from the job opportunities, applicants can also get valuable insight into the industry that can be used in resumes or interviews. The trade papers may also provide the job seeker with information about a firm he is researching or ideas as to what firm may need his services due to expansion or even someone leaving his post.

Regardless of where the ad appears, the headlines in each can be fascinating. Often, an ad will be placed in a section or under a heading to which it does not belong. This is not the newspaper's fault, but rather the fault of the firm placing the ad. In many instances, the firm does not know whether they should put a sales management ad under sales or management. If the ad was placed under management, it would indicate that the firm is more interested in the candidate's management ability. If it was under sales, it would indicate exactly the opposite.

The confusion takes place because classified/display help wanted advertisements are a category of ads that do not normally involve outside professional advertising agencies. They are usually written and placed by the human resource department, sometimes with help from the hiring manager's department. Neither may be experienced at copywriting. As a result, the classified/display help wanted sections of the newspaper are loaded with ads that do not accurately reflect the position or its requirements. Help wanted ads contain the requirements, duties, and responsibilities but they seldom have these items prioritized. Each ad has to be read, reread, and carefully analyzed before answering it.

The aerospace marketing position advertisement in Figure 10 is a blind ad but there are signals that the job seeker can interpret for further information. The headline and first word are clues— Aerospace and Phoenix. The next line gives the applicant the type of firm: manufacturing. In one trip to the library, the applicant could determine the company name. By scanning the Standard Industrial Codes (SIC) and cross-referencing them, the seeker would soon run down the number of aerospace manufacturing firms in Phoenix. Chances are there are not too many. There are other clues as to the identity of the company. Notice the line: Precision Machinery and Fabrication of Aerospace Hardware. That line should enable a job seeker to pinpoint the firm, if the earlier information has not.

Identifying the firm is worth the effort. Once the company is known, the next step is to call and find out who the hiring manager is for that particular department. A resume and cover letter could be sent directly and would enable the applicant to bypass the human resource department. Identifying the firm also enables the job seeker to determine what kind of company it is—entrepreneurial, growth-oriented, or mature—and whether he or she could fit into it.

Figure 10   Marketing Position Ad

AEROSPACE
MARKETING POSITION

Phoenix based Aerospace manufacturing firm is seeking a person with marketing experience in the Aerospace field. Applicant should be technically knowledgeable in the area of Precision Machining and Fabrication of Aerospace Hardware, and have recent experience in direct sales of same. Position will require travel to a national marketplace.

Please send resume, including employment history and salary requirements to:

Box FQ000, Wall Street Journal

If the company is the kind the job seeker is looking for, the next question is, "What does this company really want?" Marketing is a broad, overused, and misused term. Former marketing directors would be attracted to this position but they should examine what the ad actually says.

ANALYZING THE AD

This marketing position is not one in which a person plans and directs a salesforce or sales campaign. The firm is looking for someone with aerospace experience. It requires someone with an advanced degree or an applicant who is well-versed in engineering. The line that states "Applicant should be technically knowledgeable" gives clear warning of that. It also asks for someone who knows "Precision Machining and Fabrication of Aerospace Hardware." These are specialties, not something for a marketing generalist.

When the human resource department gets resumes for this position, they are going to look for: an advanced degree or equivalent aerospace background, industry experience, and direct sales in the aerospace field of similar products.

For a family man, this job may not be ideal. Notice the travel requirement to a "national marketplace," which could be Washington, DC, or a host of other cities where procurement offices are located. If the company markets products to the government, traveling to a national marketplace could mean a half-dozen cities. On the plus side for the family man will be the health and insurance benefits. Generally, companies in this industry have superb fringe benefits.

What this company wants is someone who has direct sales experience, is willing to travel, has an advanced degree or experience in the product line, and knows aerospace. In other words, an industry-experienced salesperson. A blind ad, but it clearly spells out the kind of individual the company is seeking.

ROLE OF THE SUMMARY

When resumes are submitted, they should contain a summary of qualifications. In power resumes, the summary is always near the beginning of the first page. It enables the hiring manager or human resource director to immediately see the background and experience of the candidate. When applying for a position, applicants should customize summaries so they fit the job—if, of course, they have the qualifications.

Summaries do not contain *all* of an applicant's qualifications. They are geared to match the requirements of the ad and may only contain a small portion of the job seeker's background. The idea is to have a summary cover the requirements in the ad.

A summary that would attract the hiring manager or human resource director's eye should always involve as many key elements as possible. For example, a resume summary for the previous job might be:

> Summary: More than 10 years of sales/marketing experience in the aerospace industry with 6 years of experience in manufacturing of precision machining and fabrication.

Effective summaries mention years of experience when the time involved is substantial. Contrast this with the blind ad for another sales-oriented position: Sales Executive, Health Insurance Sales (Figure 11).

This, too, is a sales position but it is not hidden in the guise of a marketing position. It indicates the individual desired is a salesperson. The eliminator for most would be the industry experience. Note the line that says "experience in sales through independent agents." This company is searching for someone who knows the business and has worked with independent insurance agents. He is probably going to be assigned a territory and will be responsible for his own scheduling and progress—hence the term self-starter, meaning there is no supervisor close at hand.

This does not appear to be a national firm. From the descriptive first few lines, the job seeker can ascertain that this is a hospital/medical center that has a prepaid medical plan it wants local insurance agents to market. The executive who lands this job will probably find himself traveling throughout most of the Chicago

Figure 11   Ad for Insurance Executive

**SALES EXECUTIVE
HEALTH INSURANCE SALES**

Large Chicago medical center initiating new and unique prepaid medical plan for sale through independent insurance agents, needs self starter with experience in sales through independent agents. Send resume, accomplishments, and salary history to:
Box BK244, Wall St. Journal

area. The company could be a mature, conservative organization with little flexibility, but the position is asking for an entrepreneurial type. Thus, regardless of whether the company is entrepreneurial, growth-oriented, or mature, the position will be entrepreneurial. Unless the company is also entrepreneurial, the person who takes this position will not have much chance of advancing up the corporate ladder.

Since this is a large, Chicago medical center and the product is a prepaid medical plan, the medical and health benefits for the salesperson will be excellent.

When the human resource department gets resumes, they will be searching for sales experience with independent insurance agents (the top priority) and knowledge of the insurance industry. Although this is a sales job, the applicant with only sales experience is going to have a difficult time getting beyond the initial screening. A clever cover letter would help.

For those serious about this job, a little detective work would enable them to determine what Chicago medical center is involved. Although Chicago is a major city, the number of medical centers that could afford to have a "prepaid medical plan" to market through insurance agents is small. By calling a local Chamber of Commerce, major medical centers could be pinpointed. A call to City Hall could do the same thing. From there, it is a simple matter of making a few calls and asking about prepaid medical plans that are being marketed to agents.

An effective resume summary for this job might be:

Summary: Sales manager with 10 plus years experience in marketing products to independent insurance agents in the midwest.

The summary is always short and to the point. Seldom does it run beyond two sentences.

For marketing and sales positions, firms get hundreds of resumes, hence the reason for the first two advertisements being blind. The General Manager ad in Figure 12, although blind, gives away a great deal.

The body of the ad indicates that the company wants a production manager rather than a general manager. The ad stresses manufacturing experience rather than management. The company is searching for someone who has technical knowledge of equipment and processes and has the ability to quote new business. The 50 employees mentioned are all in the production end of the business.

This is an aerospace firm specializing in the sheet metal parts. With the location (Gardena is a relatively small city adjacent to several cities which are home to major aerospace corporations) and

Figure 12   General Manager Ad

★ GENERAL MANAGER ★

To manage the Sales, Fabrication and related support functions of a $5 million manufacturing division, specializing in aircraft sheet metal parts. This division is located in the Gardena area.

Your experience should include 10 years in manufacturing with at least 2 years in general management, you should have had P&L responsibilities and supervised at least 50 employees. Technical knowledge of equipment, processes and ability to quote on a new business are important attributes.

Besides an excellent salary, there will be a substantial bonus opportunity, car allowance and employer-paid medical/dental benefits. Please send your resume to:

**Box R-094,
L.A., CA 90053**

dollar volume, it would not be hard to pin down the company name through the SIC. Notice the company is a "division" of another, larger firm. That means the resume could be screened by the human resource department of the parent company. It also means the firm is probably in the mature category and has stringent rules and regulations.

The human resource department's priorities will be:

1. Manufacturing/assembly line experience
2. Technical knowledge of equipment
3. Management

For the applicant whose strongest asset is management ability, applying is a waste of time.

The ideal summary to attract the attention of the human resource department would be:

Summary: Engineer with 15 years of manufacturing and assembly line experience including designing, installing equipment for aerospace parts fabrication, costing, and pricing of products.

Unquestionably, one of the most aggravating blind ads for a job seeker to answer are those without location. The Financial Management ad in Figure 13 appeared in *The Wall Street Journal,* which is an excellent source of executive and management positions. The advertisement did not, however, identify the city where the firm was located.

Advertisements in this style—long, lengthy narratives—have to be read more than once to pick out the key elements. When this is done, the employer's goals become obvious. Unlike the previous ad

Figure 13   Financial Manager Ad

**Financial Management
Manufacturing**

Leading national manufacturer has current opening for career oriented financial professional with strong background in developing and implementing financial systems including manufacturing cost accounting. This position is a career opportunity which has exceptional long-term career potential in one of the nation's most successful corporations. Initial responsibilities are a unique mix of "hands-on" project work, coordination of division level controller functions and participation in long term strategic issues. Requirements include minimum of Bachelors Degree in Accounting plus a history of progressively responsible financial management positions in a large manufacturer. MBA or CPA is preferred. Strong background in cost accounting and exceptional leadership and communications skills are mandatory.

Compensation is in the range of $65K to $75K plus exceptional incentives. Interested individuals please send resume to:

Box ER400, The Wall Street Journal

---

where manufacturing skills were important, this ad has requirements that are not as easy to isolate. Although manufacturing is mentioned throughout, the key terms are accounting, CPA, financial management, cost accounting, and controller functions. Whoever applies for the job should have an excellent background in determining manufacturing costs. They need not have much knowledge with respect to the actual manufacturing process.

There is not a specific industry mentioned, a sign that the employer is looking more for financial expertise than actual industry manufacturing experience. The ideal candidate is going to have a cost accounting background with a manufacturer.

DEFINING THE TERMS

"Hands on project work" refers to new manufacturing projects that the company has taken on and the ability of the person taking the position to determine costs and controls.

"Exceptional leadership and communications skills" means that the job holder is going to be interfacing with management from the manufacturing end. This person will also have to aid management when it comes to cost and pricing.

"Career opportunity" sends another signal to the applicant: The company is searching for someone who is going to be stable and stick around for awhile, not someone that has a history of job hopping. This company is looking for stability, but what constitutes longevity in one occupation and industry may be totally different in another. In sales, capable personnel may move around every other year. In finance, employers expect applicants to show a more stable job record, with four to six years between moves being the norm. Anyone with less time is going to be scrutinized.

The line that says "one of the nation's most successful corporations" indicates that this company fits into the mature category. The individual obtaining this position is going to be working in a structured environment.

The type of power resume summary that the human resources department is looking for would be:

Summary: More than 12 years experience as controller in manufacturing environment with responsibilities running from coordinating day-to-day operations of three divisions to long-term financial planning.

The General Manager ad in Figure 14 is from a small entrepreneurial firm. The sales figure (one million dollars) is indicative of size. Some service companies with $1 million in sales may be mature, but a manufacturer in that category is young and entrepreneurial. With that background, the qualified job seeker has opportunities to work an exceptional salary/incentive arrangement. The company is not rigid in its compensation plans. It is interested in results as indicated by the need for an "aggressive general manager to double sales."

If someone is going to double sales, they are going to be able to negotiate compensation. But the person who earns the position is going to have to produce.

It asks for a general manager but a quick reading will convince most job seekers that the job is for a sales manager, not a general manager.

Figure 14   Misdirected Ad

GENERAL MANAGER
VALVE MFGR. CO.

Small (1m sales) high pressure solenoid valve mfgr. needs aggressive general manager to double sales and direct new product effort. Unusual opportunity with substantial potential. Prior successful sales experience essential, valve, and engineering background helpful.

Submit resume to:

Controls Corp.
P.O. Box 4325
Fullerton, CA 92631

The company is small which indicates it may not have a human resource department. The advertisement may have been written by the president or whomever is going to supervise the general manager. Notice the management duties. They consist of doubling sales with prior successful sales experience essential. It says nothing about prior manufacturing or administrative experience. Industry experience is helpful but not required. This company is after an aggressive sales manager who can direct a new product effort. The company has a new product being manufactured and it needs someone to sell it. It does not need someone to ensure that the new product is manufactured.

The hiring supervisor (vice president or whomever) is going to look for a successful sales track record, regardless of industry. If they can find someone who has valve and engineering background in addition to sales, that will be a plus. The engineering and valve background will take a back seat to sales ability.

In answering the ad, an applicant should stress:

1. Sales ability
2. New product sales ability
3. Industry background—that is, valve and engineering
4. Management skills

Anyone lacking the first two will not be considered, but those with the first two qualifications may be eligible even though they do not have the latter two.

The summary for this job would be similar to:

Summary: Engineer with 15 years experience in sales/sales management and responsibility for developing markets and channels for new industrial product lines including line of industrial hoses and valves.

SEARCH FIRM'S ROLE

The ad in Figure 15 indicates a search firm is involved. Senior management needs a vice president who will be responsible for marketing and finance. The company is young and growing. It is entrepreneurial as indicated by the sales range, five million dollars. Job seekers should recognize that this is a position that a networker often finds. The firm needs it filled but the president has been hesitant to advertise because he does not want to wade through a stack of resumes, nor does he want to make a hiring error.

Figure 15   Ad from a Search Firm

Vice President

Growing product company ($5 million in sales) in northern Michigan seeks experienced vice president to handle marketing and finance. Ideal candidate has proven track record and experience with large manufacturing concern. Vice President will report directly to President, and he will handle operations as well as manufacturing. President will retain marketing and finance responsibilities. Respond to Search Firm, Box JY222, The Wall Street Journal.

The president has gone to a search firm but he has been cautious in laying out the job qualifications, "someone with a proven track record and from a larger company." For whatever reason (perhaps he was "burned" or disappointed previously), the president does not want to take a risk. Even with the search firm around to check out the applicant, he insists on the track record. His stance is illustrated by the line that says the president will "retain marketing and finance responsibilities." The new executive will be working in operations and manufacturing, but considering the conservative nature of the president, the successful candidate could find himself in a situation where his performance is constantly being checked.

Politics enter into this position. It is going to take someone who has considerable rapport with the CEO. Anyone who does not will find himself on a short leash and with a shorter employment tenure.

The summary that appears on the resume for this job would need to emphasize a large company background, operations experience, and industry experience. Such as:

Summary: Twelve years experience as operations manager with two of the largest defense contractors in the country and 21 years experience in line management (degree).

Why some positions attract 500 or more resumes is illustrative in the Marketing Director ad (Figure 16). Call this one an *open-end* blind ad. Its parameters are broad and the duties are identical to what any marketing director should be able to handle. There are, however, some clues. Most notable is the national consumer product company. Marketing directors with nonconsumer products experience should not waste their time with this ad. The company is going to get many resumes from experienced consumer products marketers.

Figure 16   Open-End Blind Ad

MARKETING DIRECTOR

National Consumer Product Company, based in Utah, seeks Marketing Director. Requires experience in consumer product packaging, sales promotion strategy, and direct response advertising. Direct reportability to Vice President. Compensation is based on Qualification. Send resume to:

P.O. Box 10
Logan, UT 84321

The corporate structure of the company is not quite the norm. Marketing directors usually report to the president and they carry a vice president title. In this case, the marketing director reports to a vice president, but the ad does not say what kind of vice president. Most likely, the marketing director is going to report to a vice president of marketing or advertising.

There are mixed signals in the body of the ad. The position asks for someone who has experience in consumer packaging, sales promotion, and direct response. It fails to mention whether this experience is to be geared to the consumer, retailer, or distributor.

If a job seeker had to make an assumption, the safest guess would be that the company packages a product (or many products) but does not manufacture it. The products are evidently sold in retail stores and the firm is looking for someone to upgrade its packaging and displays, examine packaging for new products, and develop promotions that will generate additional display space in its retail locations. Direct response advertising could be geared to either the retailer, distributor, or both.

With the plethora of resumes this one will attract, it behooves any applicant to gather data on the firm. The location of the company (Logan, UT) is the place to start. Logan is not a giant community and the number of consumer goods firms are limited. A call to the Chamber of Commerce would probably end in a list that could be narrowed to three or four firms. With the zip code available, the list might be further narrowed. The SIC codes could be checked, too. Each firm should be called and the job seeker should ask for the marketing director. Firms that have a marketing director would not be advertising, and if the ad was meant to generate a replacement for an existing director, a city other than Logan would have been used in the address.

POWER RESUME SUMMARY

The power resume summary for the previous job would list experience in consumer products, brand management, and dealing with dealers and distributors. Such as:

Summary: Eleven years of consumer marketing experience including 5 years of brand management as well as 8 years of developing national consumer advertising plans and distributor/dealer promotions.

Occasionally, companies find that the typical ad will not work. This is particularly true when a firm searches for an experienced executive with a multitude of qualifications in an industry that does not have an abundance of applicants. Imagine, for example, a recording company searching for a CEO. It would want someone who is familiar with artists, promotion, the industry, sales, future prospects, and obstacles to the business. That type candidate is not in abundance. A record firm that ran an ad in a trade publication or the major Sunday newspapers would receive few responses from qualified candidates, most of whom would be working for another company. A candidate at X company would not send a resume to Y company for fear word would get back to his present employer in this relatively small industry.

Searches of this type usually involve headhunters. In most cases, the search firm is going to end up talking to candidates who are already employed and confidentiality is a must. The ad for General Manager (Figure 17) is an example of a vacant position that will not generate the usual number of resumes. Just as the record company executive would recognize the firm that is searching for a CEO, executives in the communications field will recognize the company that is seeking a general manager.

With middle-management employment, there are always specific jobs that are difficult for the human resource department and the hiring manager to understand. One position that is almost always advertised in the wrong section is public relations.

Take, for instance, the public relations ad for a Director of Development (Figure 18). A public relations professional is someone who works with a company, individuals, or agencies and obtains media exposure for his clients. His main qualifications would be the ability to write, contacts with the media and experience in the field.

The director of development is anything but a public relations professional. The qualifications and job requirements for this position are:

1. Conducts fundraising campaigns
2. Cultivates relationships with donors

Figure 17   Ad for a Recognizable Company

GENERAL MANAGER

Profit-oriented, energetic General Manager to manage a growing $60M, 320-employee satcom components and subsystems business located in the SF/BA. Our client and the parent is a $1+ billion diversified, well-established, and highly regarded electronics corporation.

Qualifications required include proven experience managing a multi-million dollar manufacturing, marketing, and engineering company as a significant supplier to the military and commercial broadcast (AM, FM, TV) satcom industries. Should have experience with power amplifiers, transmitters, earth stations, up-down links and complete satcom systems for the commercial and military market. Earlier engineering and marketing experience in related commercial and military systems, including a BSEE or equivalent, is required.

Our client also expects this individual to be involved in helping build the military/broadcast satcom systems business, using products and technology available from other divisions throughout the corporation. The individual selected for this position will have excellent opportunities for broader management roles in this important and growing segment of our client's business.

Boyden International, the leading worldwide retained executive recruiter, has the exclusive assignment. Address comprehensive resumes to: Boyden International,

Box FY 100, The Wall Street Journal

Our client is an equal opportunity employer.

Figure 18   Ad That Frequently Is Mispositioned

PUBLIC RELATIONS
DIRECTOR OF DEVELOPMENT

Reports to the Dean and directs all development activities for the School of Business Administration and Economics. Proposes goal and strategies, conducts fundraising campaigns, coordinates events and activities and cultivates and maintains relationships with donors. 4 year college degree and 2 years progressively responsible professional experience administering or managing development programs in a university, non-profit corporation or comparable institution. Must possess excellent communication skills. Recruitment range $3045–3715/mo. Submit a letter of application and resume by April 20, 1989. Personnel Ofc. Calif. State Univ. Northridge, 18111 Nordhoff St. Northridge, CA 91330.

CSUN

AA, EOE, Title IX,
Sections 503 & 504 Employer

3. Administrates and/or manages development programs
4. Works in university environment
5. Has a degree
6. Has experience in the area

These have nothing in common with what is required of the pubic relations professional. Someone at the university put the ad under Public Relations because there was not another category that came close. It could have gone under Communications but it would have been mixed in with ads for salesmen of telephone and radio equipment, or it could have gone under Sales. The prospective employer chose Public Relations because this category has become a catchall. Under it will be found positions for not only public relations professionals, but product demonstrators, telephone sales-people, and fundraisers like the director of development.

This overlap is an example of why it pays to scan classified ads thoroughly. Many positions that relate to one occupation may be found under another category because of the ambiguous duties.

As is the case with many professions, public relations has a num-ber of so-called specialties. For example, there is the press agent who is usually thought of as the public relations representative for those in the entertainment business; the financial public relations person who handles stockholder relations and annual reports, and the public affairs (also public relations) person who handles con-sumer and governmental issues for a company.

Each of these offshoots of public relations require similar skills (that is, the person has to be a writer, communicator, and be able to deal with the media). Yet in most cases, companies that have open-ings for a public affairs representative would never think of offer-ing the position to someone with a press agent background and vice versa. The companies have built-in prejudices. If they are seeking a public affairs person, they will always go for someone with a public affairs background. This is a shortsighted approach but one the job seeker has to deal with. Similar prejudices can be found throughout the job market.

In the Public Information Specialist ad in Figure 19, the company is searching for a professional who has, above all, experience in dealing with community groups and the public. The applicant must have experience with governmental agencies which communicate and convince the public of certain programs. In order of impor-tance, the job requirements are:

1. Public relations professional who has dealt with community groups and knows how to get the message across to them

Figure 19   Look for the "Prejudices" in the Ad

South Coast
AIR QUALITY
MANAGEMENT
DISTRICT

PUBLIC INFORMATION SPECIALIST
$2,284-$2,829 PER MONTH

Join the Leader! South Coast Air Quality Management District exercises control over nonvehicular sources of air pollution in the Los Angeles Air Basin and operates the most comprehensive air quality programs in the nation.

The Position: South Coast Air Quality Management District has an immediate opening for a Public Information Specialist to participate in disseminating information to the general public, public and private organizations, and small businesses on matters regarding the District's functions, activities, and regulations; develop and coordinate public information, public participation, and community liaison programs, and do other work as required.

Requirements (condensed):

Training and experience which clearly demonstrates possession of the knowledge and ability to disseminate information to the public, develop public participation programs, and prepare written materials for publication.

Evidence of the required knowledge and abilities may be demonstrated by graduation from an accredited college or university preferably with a major emphasis in public relations; journalism, political science, public administration, or a related field.

Desirable Qualifications: Excellent written and oral communication skills and knowledge of public participation programs and promotional techniques. Bilingual skill in English and Spanish would be useful.

The District provides an outstanding benefits program, and our employees pay no Social Security.

How to Apply: An official District application is required and must be received by March 17, 1989, to be assured of consideration. To obtain an application package and complete description of the position and minimum requirements, contact the Personnel Division or apply in person at:

SOUTH COAST AIR QUALITY MANAGEMENT DISTRICT
9150 Flair Drive
El Monte, CA 91731
(818) 572-2000

Minorities/Females/Handicapped Are Encouraged to Apply
An EEO/AA Employer

2. Public relations professional with government-related experience

3. Ability to prepare written communications

A publicity agent would be hard pressed to sell his services to this company although he has extensive experience in communicating and selling the public. The publicity agent has been selling artists and productions to the public. Would selling them environmental programs be any more complex? The same is true of a financial public relations professional who has worked with shareholders and the brokerage community. Would shareholders and brokers be any more difficult to sell than the public?

RESUME PREJUDICES

Unfortunately, companies have a fixation on obtaining someone from within their industry. Occasionally, outsiders can break into the industry but many firms prefer to play it safe and continue to hire someone from within. This is particularly true of established, mature firms such as governmental agencies. When job seekers scour advertisements, this prejudice should be kept in mind. The entrepreneurial or growth-oriented firms are willing to take chances and bring someone in from outside their industries. Mature firms seldom will.

This does not mean the professional should forget changing industries. These jobs can be obtained but they take research. They also take a summary and cover letter that concentrate on the position's requirements but never mention an industry.

The professional applying for the Public Information Specialist position should be in the library researching stories on the Air Quality Management District. He or she should find out the problems (if any) the District has had. Have they had difficulty with consumers?

With many governmental positions, there is a two- or three-step application process. Notice at the bottom of the ad: Applicants must request a package. The package will contain instructions that must be filled out and submitted by a certain date. The applications are either examined and qualified applicants put aside, or, in the case of some government positions, all qualified applicants are invited in to take a written examination. Those who pass the exam (or who are put aside because their qualifications fit) are interviewed, usually by three or four management people. These interviews are critical because candidates are scored and ranked. Usually, the top three are called back and interviewed by the hiring manager and, perhaps, one or two of his assistants. (This "team" interview process has also been adopted by some companies in the private sector.) The hiring manager can then select any one of the finalists based upon his judgment.

Answering ads in the government or public sector has pitfalls that are not always obvious. For example, applicants for the "Public Information Specialist" position would save time if they called the agency and determined if there were other people in the department that the new Public Information specialist would be supervising. Or, the applicant should find out if there is an assistant in the department. If the answer is yes in either case, applicants should realize that they will have a difficult time winning the position. The tendency in the government is to give the job to someone who is already working in the department.

If that is the case, why do we see advertisements for government jobs? In some cases, because it is required by law. In others, the agency does not want to give the appearance of favoritism. Either way, moving into a government/public sector position when others are already on-hand is tough.

JOB TITLES—HOW ACCURATE?

Titles for positions are often misleading. Look at the Marketing Communications Manager ad in Figure 20.

The title might lead a job seeker to believe this position relates to the computer or a satellite field. A quick reading reveals something else. The successful candidate will:

1. Coordinate all communications regarding marketing and sales of the company's products

Figure 20   Titles Can Be Misleading

MARKETING COMMUNICATIONS MANAGER

Reports directly to the President. Coordinates all communications regarding marketing and sales of company products including advertising, public relations, product literature, trade show planning, and communications.

We are the leading manufacturer of financial document MICR printing systems used by major banks, corporations, insurance companies and government agencies.

Successful candidates will have B.A. degree with three-to-five years' advertising and PR experience. Please send resume and present compensation data in confidence to: Los Angeles Times, Box C-278, Los Angeles, CA 90053.

We are an equal opportunity employer

2. Coordinate advertising and public relations
3. Handle product literature and trade shows
4. Have a degree with 3 to 5 years advertising and public relations experience

The word communications has been used three times. Actually, communication with the company's public and customers is what this firm wants. But with the emphasis on communications in today's work environment, this firm went too far. It is not looking for a communications manager, but rather a director of marketing or vice president of marketing who is to report to the president.

This position requires an applicant who will plan and implement the company's advertising, marketing, and public relations plans. This person will also be responsible for trade show brochures and literature as well as the company's displays at those events.

The blind ad for Corporate Director in Figure 21 is interesting in that it utilized another firm and asked applicants to mail resumes to them. Resumes would be forwarded to the employer from the second firm, which could be a search or personnel agency. This request reveals that the employer may not have a human resource department, or it does not want its human resource people burdened with telephone calls. Some companies prefer this approach.

Nevertheless, this company would not be difficult to find. It is a nationwide medical transportation provider located in Newport Beach, CA, a relatively small city. Several calls could be made to identify the firm. First, to the Newport Beach Chamber of Commerce. If the chamber failed to shed any light, some local hospital administration departments could be called. Administrators usually know what is going on in the medical community. Another

Figure 21   Blind Ad Using Another Firm

Corporate Director, MIS

Our client, a nationwide medical transportaiton provider located in Newport Beach, has an immediate need for a participative, bottom-line-oriented individual to head up its Corporate MIS function.

The successful candidate should have experience using the PICK operating system as well as being well-grounded in microbased computers (IBM and MAC). Additionally, the person selected to be an integral part of our client's management team will have a Bachelor's degree with a minimum of 8 years MIS management experience with a "system architecture" focus required. Prior health care and consulting experience desirable.

For consideration, forward a resume with salary history to: **Bentley, Barnes & Lynn, Confidential Reply Dept. #419, P.O. Box 5159, Los Alamitos, CA 90720**. *All responses will be forwarded unopened, to our client, an equal opportunity employer.*

---

source would be the SIC directory which could be found in the library.

Although this ad is asking for someone familiar with MIS systems, it is also searching for a bottom line oriented individual. That means someone with operating experience who has impacted corporate profits via his MIS ability. This search is seeking a director who has strong management skills and who is going to be interfacing with top management. The applicant's management and profit-and-loss skills should be emphasized in the cover letter as well as the resume. The requirements in order of importance are:

1. Experience with the PICK system
2. MIS management experience with "system architecture" focus
3. Experience with microbased computers, IBM and MAC
4. Prior industry experience

The Controller advertisement in Figure 22 reveals several things about the firm placing the ad. The position is new, which indicates a growing, entrepreneurial environment. The professional who earns the job will report to higher management (treasurer) and will be supervising people. There already are people in the department (should have good people skills) and, in that situation, problems can arise if any existing employee feels he or she should have had the position.

Figure 22 Learn to "Read the Ad"

★ **CONTROLLER** ★

North Orange County industry leader manufacturing company with $20 Million sales and profitable, seeks a sharp, solid accounting professional who will report to the Treasurer.

BS degree in accounting, CPA or MBA preferred, minimum 10 years professional accounting related experience. Should have good people skills, with solid cost accounting, burden analysis, computer knowledge and experience.

This is a new position requiring leadership skills and business acumen. For confidential consideration, send resume and salary history to:

_____ Smith Vice President Admin.
LA TIMES BOX R-161
Los Angeles, CA 90053

The job seeker can find out more. North Orange County is a large area, however, it would be easy to isolate cities within it. A call to various Chamber of Commerce organizations may enable the seeker to find out which company has a "_____ Smith" as its vice president of administration.

This firm expects to hire someone away from another company (for confidential consideration, send resume and salary history), however, applicants should remember never to send salary history, salary requirements, or anything pertaining to money. It is one of the catch-22s of the resume business and will be covered in depth in Chapter 7.

Contrast the Controller ad in Figure 22 with the one in Figure 23. This company is established and mature. "Shirt sleeve" always refers to a person who does part of the work as well as supervising. The environment is structured and the position requires someone with management expertise since he or she is going to be supervising employees. The applicant reports to the chief financial officer (CFO) and assumes the CFO's position in an "intermediate term." This may mean during vacations, leave of absence, or travel.

The company is specific in its requirements (that is, preparation of G/L, A/R, A/P, payroll, inventory valuation). The firm which is conducting the search will exclude any resume that does not include these specific areas. Computer knowledge is a must, as well. With the number of controller resumes that are received, the deciding factor in this position may be industry experience.

The Publications Coordinator ad in Figure 24 is interesting because it gives the reader two distinct pieces of information. First, the firm is looking for a beginner, and second it will probably be an entry level or low-paying job despite the three to five years of experience required. There are two lines that give it away: "Serves

Figure 23   An Ad from a Mature Company

Figure 24   Specific Information Is in the Ad

PUBLICATIONS
COORDINATOR

Dynamic health care leader seeks experienced writer for trade association newsletter, marketing publications and directories. Serves as in-house photographer.

Successful candidate will have BS/BA in journalism, English or related field, excellent writing and editing skills, three to five years news writing experience, working knowledge of Macintosh desk top publishing and printing specifications.

We offer an excellent salary and benefit package with opportunity for professional growth. Please submit resume with writing samples to:

HOSPITAL COUNCIL
OF SOUTHERN CALIFORNIA
Attn: Asst Director, Personnel
201 N Figueroa, 4th Floor
Los Angeles, CA 90012

as in-house photographer" and "working knowledge of Macintosh desktop publishing . . ."

Any position that requires (or suggests) the applicant be versed in photography (unless the job is for a photographer), is an indication the company cannot afford an outside photographer or it does not have one on staff. Therefore, the Publications Coordinator is required to shoot pictures, and the company does not expect the photography to be of professional quality—if it did, it would utilize a professional.

The requirement for desktop capability, means that the company puts the publication together in-house. It does not utilize an outsider designer. Design is a specialized skill, and if a company is content to let its publication coordinator design (and shoot photography as well as write the copy), the applicants can surmise that most of the job is rudimentary, beginning—and not high paid.

The responses to the ad will probably go through human resources where someone will be looking for the following, key qualifications:

1. Writing ability

2. Newsletter experience

3. Ability to use desktop, and photography skills

4. Health care experience a plus

The summary: Five years as a writer/editor/photographer of in-house, and external newsletters and brochures produced for the health care industry. Utilized variety of desktop publishing programs including Macintosh.

When submitting the resume, it would be wise to call the hospital and find out to whom the publications coordinator reports. The company (NEC) in the training ad in Figure 25 is obviously easy to identify. A second element of the ad that also sticks out is the fact the position is well-paying. Note the title (Corporate Training and Development Manager), and the request (by the company) at the bottom of the ad for "principals only" (meaning applicants only, no headhunters, please). The company wants to find the applicant on its own. If unsuccessful, it will call in a search firm but, for now, it prefers to do its own searching.

This type ad will generate numerous responses, and most will be screened by the human resource department, which NEC—and other large firms—certainly have. This is the type position where the resumes could fall in the hands of someone who is not familiar with training or the position. Consequently, they may simply have a laundry list of things to look for, that is, training ability, organization development and experience in designing, developing and implementing training programs in the work environment.

Applicants should make it clear in both the cover letter and resume that they not only have training experience, but have the ability to anticipate company needs and plan training programs accordingly. This person should have the ability to work with senior management in suggesting and developing programs that will lead to increased productivity. A summary should read:

Summary: Ten years experience in the design, development and training of employees in programs for organizational development, increase of management effectiveness, and worker productivity.

Applicants for this position would do well to call NEC and find out to whom the Corporate Training and Development Manager reports. The resume—with a good cover letter covering all avenues in the ad—should go the hiring manager.

In the advertisement in Figure 26, the title is somewhat misleading. Although the ad calls for an "area customer engineering manager," the prime requisite is for someone who is a good communicator, manager and organizer of a field service force. The applicant's technical ability (that is, his or her skills with computers) is important, but the technical ability alone will not land this position. The company wants someone who communicates, can handle customer service problems, understands how to run the service end of the business. Personality as well as proficiency is what the company desires.

Figure 25   The Company in This Ad Is Easily Identified

TRAINING

Our Best Begins With You

Almost doesn't count. Not when it comes to quality. Our wholehearted commitment to being the best in the semiconductor industry is one that we back with tangible resources and an open door to new ideas. In essence, our commitment to quality begins with the individual. A lot of personal pride and effort have made us a world leader in microprocessor, ASIC, memory, laser, consumer ICs and other technologies.

Corporate Training and Development Manager

You will be responsible for the design, development and implementation of all Corporate management, employee and organizational development programs, as well as for organizational effectiveness and employee relations consulting for specified internal groups.

This will involve developing, coordinating/implementing Corporate training and development programs to meet future business requirements. You will also refine and manage the Corporate HR three year planning and development strategy and consult with management at all levels regarding training programs/processes which will increase organizational effectiveness.

This position requires a minimum of 5–8 years experience in Training and Organizational Development. Experience should include a minimum of 3 years' "hands-on" experience in designing, developing, and implementing employee/management training programs and 2 years' management experience in Training and/or Organizational Development. Excellent presentation and facilitative skills a must. BA degree in Business, HR Management or Organizational Development is required. An MBA or MSHR is preferred.

We offer competitive salaries and comprehensive benefits. Please send your resume with salary requirements to: NEC Electronics, 401 Ellis Street, Mountain View, CA 94043. We are an equal opportunity employer. Principals only please.

NEC
NEC Electronics Inc.

Figure 26 A Misleading Title

Technical

AREA CUSTOMER ENGINEERING MANAGER

Highly challenging. Highly responsible. Highly visible. Businessland has the career you've been searching for. And now we're searching for you!

We seek an excellent communicator with a BS degree/equivalent and a minimum of 6 years management experience in field service or a technical retail environment. Good operational management skills, people and organizational development skills and a solid understanding of all financial aspects related to service organization including P&L are essential. The successful candidate will manage the service function of an area in accordance with the Corporate Service department goals. Specifically, you will: recruit, train and review the customer engineering staff; ensure hardware repair and system quality assurance; provide policy and procedure direction to centers, maintaining a consistent company-wide service approach.

Highly rewarding. Highly lucrative. Highly satisfying. A career with Businessland has it all. If you have what we're searching for, forward your confidential resume with salary history to: **Randy Maddox, Regional Service Manager, BUSINESSLAND, INC., 1600 S.W. Fourth Avenue, Portland, OR 97201.** No Phone Calls. Principals Only. An Equal Opportunity Employer.

BUSINESSLAND.

A Different Kind of Computer Company

For the right person, the position is going to pay well. The lines "highly rewarding, highly lucrative, highly satisfying" are clues that the position pays a commission in addition to a salary. In other words, the manager is going to earn a bonus on work.

The most important elements in the ad for an applicant to note in replying are (1) field service experience and ability and (2) dealing in a technical, retail environment. The company would love to have an applicant who has both technical and service experience, and knows how to build and handle a field service group. If the applicant does some research, they will find that Businessland franchised a number of units (stores), and may view someone with franchise experience, in addition to the other requirements, as a plus. The summary:

> Summary: Eight years experience as a field manager and service representative for franchised, high-tech company that dealt extensively with retail outlets and consumers. Responsible for profit/loss and budgeting of unit, as well as setting and maintaining service standards.

The next ad (Figure 27) has a number of interesting clues as to the duties and responsibilities of the position. "Shirt sleeve," for example, means the controller does it "himself." This is a private, vocational school, and many educational institutions in this category (private) do not have the funds for large staffs. Hence the "shirt sleeve" suggestion.

Figure 27   Read the "Clues" in the Ad

CONTROLLER

Our client, a Los Angeles-based private vocational school seeks a highly motivated, shirt-sleeved individual to assume responsibility for the financial management and controllership functions. The ideal candidate should possess an accounting degree and a minimum of 5 years recent controllership experience preferably in the private school industry. Please send confidential resume and salary history to:
Personnel Director
L.A. Times Box HH-285
Los Angeles, CA 90053

"Highly motivated" is often a synonym for starting your own department and running it . . . (or cleaning up the mess). The applicant who gets this position will most likely be someone who has had experience in the school sector. He or she will have general as well as specific skills. In other words, someone who can do everything when it comes to accounting. Undoubtedly, there is not much in the way of staff help available. Thus, the school is looking for the self-starter, the energetic individual who can handle a difficult situation with a multitude of responsibilities and duties.

This ad, like many others, has the catch-22 salary history request—which should, of course, be left out. This type position will usually not get an abundance of applicants because of the pay scale (usually lower than what an accountant can make in the private sector) and diverse responsibilities. The blind ad could mean that there is someone already occupying the position. In order, the ad is looking for:

1. Controller experience
2. Fiscal ability
3. Diverse financial skills
4. Private school experience

Summary: Eight years as a hands-on controller/accountant in the public and private sector, including with experience in designing, organizing and running financial and accounting departments in private schools as well as other entrepreneurial settings.

Regardless of what an advertisement says, every position has its limitations and every company its foibles and prejudices. For example, it is difficult for many middle-management executives to cross industry lines, though it should not be. An accountant who displayed skills in manufacturing is equally as capable in a service industry. A marketing director who engineered campaigns in the entertainment field can bring the same creative skills to the real estate industry. Yet, companies hesitate. In almost every ad, they ask or imply that they prefer industry experience.

Job seekers should realize this and prepare their resumes and cover letters accordingly. Transferring skills from one industry to another should not be a problem. Interestingly, when companies seek a CEO, they are perfectly willing to accept a candidate from another industry. They understand that if a CEO has demonstrated leadership skills in one industry, he is perfectly capable of doing it in another.

In Chapter 5, we will explore how an applicant can sell experience in one industry to a firm in another.

5

THE RESUME-BASED

SALES LETTER

I t began with a simple, innocuous line. Ted Fitzpatrick had been using it for as long as he could remember and he never thought there was anything wrong with it. He would have continued to use it if not for a human resource director who finally took pity on him.

Marjorie Dobson had seen Fitzpatrick's resume on numerous occasions. Almost every time the company ran an ad for a management consultant, Fitzpatrick answered. Unfortunately, his qualifications were lacking, but the deficiencies failed to stop Fitzpatrick. Whenever he saw the ad, he sent his resume with the same cover letter.

The first time he sent his resume and cover letter, Dobson stopped after reading the first line. That is all it took. She threw the letter and resume in the wastebasket. The second time he applied, Dobson decided to disregard the cover letter and look at his resume. After one brief glance, she once again discarded Fitzpatrick's resume and letter.

Undaunted, Fitzpatrick continued mailing the same two documents to Dobson every time an ad for a management consultant ran. After the fourth resume, Dobson decided to break her unwritten rule. She was going to call Fitzpatrick, tell him his qualifications did not meet the job, and suggest that he save postage and get additional experience. She was angry at Fitzpatrick's stupidity and decided she would explain exactly why he would never get a job at her firm or, for that matter, at numerous other companies. It had nothing to do with his resume. His unforgivable mistake, insofar as Dobson was concerned, was the cover letter.

That evening she called Fitzpatrick at his home. Her anger had subsided and she mellowed when she heard the friendly voice at the other end of the line. Instead of shouting, she quietly explained why his qualifications lacked. He listened attentively, thanking her for the time she took to call him. The conversation was about to end when Dobson told him there was one more thing she had to tell him; one more aspect of his resume and cover letter that not only hurt him in a quest for a job at her company, but could cost him an interview (and job) in 50 percent of the companies to which he applied.

Fitzpatrick was puzzled but he listened as Dobson slowly explained: "You made one critical mistake in your cover letter. A mistake that caused me to discard your resume the first time and one that almost made me throw it away the second time. You addressed your cover letter to 'Dear Sir.'"

It is the same mistake many applicants still make despite the fact they do not know whether it is a man or woman who will read it.

THE AUTOMATIC TURNOFF

"I get bugged," says Bernadette Senn, "when someone addresses a cover letter to 'Dear Sir.' With half the workforce women, there is a good chance you are writing to one."

Many female human resource professionals regard the "Dear Sir" as a turnoff. "So don't take the chance," cautions Senn, "letters can safely be addressed as 'Dear Sir/Madam' or 'Dear Human Resource Director,' but avoid a specific gender."

There has always been controversy over cover letters. Some question their value while others say they are a waste of time. In today's marketplace, however, the cover letter is indispensable. Rudolph Dew echoes the consensus of opinion in the field when he says "A resume should never go without a cover letter. It shows little thought. A resume without a cover letter is like an incomplete sentence."

Dew is not referring to canned or generic cover letters. "Every one of them," he says, "should be customized for the specific opening."

"Look at a cover letter," explains Al Adamo, "as being split into three parts. In the first, there should be an explanation of the purpose of the letter. For example, 'This letter is in response to your ad in last Sunday's paper.' The second part should highlight your accomplishments and match them against the needs that are stated in the ad. The final portion should close with the applicant asking for an interview. If it is not a blind ad, the applicant should indicate he will be calling to see if he can set up a mutually convenient time for an interview."

SEVEN KEY LETTER RULES

Aside from keeping gender out of the salutation, there are other rules that should be followed:

1. Keep it short
2. Do not mention salary
3. Date your letter
4. Check for spelling errors or typos
5. Avoid the overuse of "I"
6. Customize the letter for the company
7. Make sure the letter indicates a resume is enclosed

Short means no more than one page. Remember, human resource directors may go through 200 to 300 resumes per position. A portion will not have cover letters but at least 50 percent will. They do not have all day to read so the letter should be short, punchy, and contain *sizzle*.

It is the sizzle that most cover letters lack. "The applicant," says Dew, "has to be a salesperson. Imagine he is an insurance salesman. The insurance man never sells insurance, he sells protection for the family. That is the sizzle—the protection. No one is going to buy a policy . . . they buy protection. The same is true of an automobile salesman. He does not sell a car, he sells style, comfort, and status. Hey, that is what people buy."

SELLING THE SIZZLE

An applicant should never sell degrees, duties, or responsibilities in a cover letter. Neither has any sizzle to it. They do not intrigue or rouse the interest of the human resource director or the manager who will do the hiring. Job titles, duties, and responsibilities are the steak. Accomplishments are the sizzle. No human resource director or hiring manager buys steak.

If a position asks for a sales manager who can handle a new product line, the applicant has the perfect clue as to how the cover letter should be structured. To merely say that "I have 10 years experience as a sales manager" is wrong. Everyone who answers the ad is going to say something similar. The sales manager qualification is the steak, there is nothing appetizing about it. The applicant must entice the reader with something like, "With 10-years experience as a sales manager, my specialty was handling the launching of new products. In my tenure at (X company), I designed the sales and promotion plans for six new products and supervised the entire program. Four of those became successful. They are (names). With my program our market share grew from X percent to X percent."

That response has *sizzle*. It whets the appetite of the reader. Sizzle appeals to human needs. Psychologist Abraham Maslow once constructed a hierarchy of needs. He divided needs into two categories, lower and advanced. Lower, or basic, needs had to be fulfilled before a person sought the higher needs. On the basic level were things like the need to be loved, to love someone, the need for food, air, shelter, and sex. On the higher level were needs relating to education, learning, and self-fulfillment.

Advertisers understand this hierarchy. They know the most effective way to reach and appeal to the masses is to concentrate and build commercials around basic needs. That is why some commercials appear to be selling sex rather than shirts. Ads of this type sell the sizzle and it is the sizzle that appeals to the person's basic needs.

The same is true when hunting for a position. When sizzle is put in a cover letter, it is designed to appeal to the needs of the human resource director. A major mistake in cover letters is forgetting the sizzle and concentrating on the steak.

"You want to put *value added* in the cover letter," says Dew. Value-added selling is Dew's definition of what every potential employer is looking for. "They want to know what you can contribute to the bottom line. For example, if you are an engineer and your innovations helped save your previous company X percent in time and costs, say so. Let the prospective employer know what you did (exactly) for your last company and that you can do the same for his."

Hiring is not a philanthropic endeavor. Employers hire on the basis of which applicant can do the most for their company, which applicant can help increase profits or cut costs the most, and which applicant has proven his bottom line value.

VALUE-ADDED SELLING

Value-added selling is no more than the employer asking, "What value can you add to our bottom line? What contribution can you make?" That is the way industry is today and will continue to be. Employers want to know what you can do for them. Cover letters, as well as power resumes, address these issues. That is what makes them effective.

To address bottom line issues, an applicant has to know something about the company. "Cover letters," says Dew, "should not be the kind of documents that you bat out in two minutes. Make sure you research the company and interpret the ad. Determine what they want before you answer."

FINDING AN INSIDE REFERENCE

A reference in a letter ranks alongside value-added selling for importance. That is especially true if the reference comes from a hiring company's current employee. Companies believe their employees are the best in the world. If a cover letter comes in saying that an employee suggested the applicant respond, it has ten times the weight of one without a reference.

The reference need not be someone in a position of authority within the company. It can be a clerk, secretary, almost anyone—as long as it is an employee. Some companies think so much of their employees (and their judgment) that they reward them financially if they recommend an applicant.

Reliance on employee references has increased during the past few years and for good reason. With strong employment and antidiscrimination laws, it has become difficult for human resource people to check an applicant's previous employment history. They can no longer get candid opinions from previous employers and there is a greater chance for error when hiring.

Human resource departments need help and they regard an employee's reference highly. The theory is that no one in the employ of the company would knowingly recommend someone who was undesirable because it could come back to haunt them. After all, both would be working under the same roof. Although all company employees do not know each other, there is a "social relationship" says Dew. "We are all part of the same group" and their opinion is respected.

Finding a reference within the firm can be accomplished. If an applicant does not know anyone within the company, he or she usually has access to people who do. They may belong to a church, civic group, gym, or some other facility where an employee is involved in extracurricular activities; or they may know a banker, accountant, or attorney.

In an applicant's networking circle, there is an excellent chance that someone is acquainted with an employee from the company. It takes effort, but the tracking is worth the time. Cover letters with references definitely take precedence over those without.

If an employee can be found, there are ways to approach them. For example, suppose an applicant's banker knows a customer who works at X company. If the applicant has a good relationship with the banker, he could ask the banker to make a call to the customer who works for the firm. The banker would be introducing one customer to another. He could also mention that the second customer (the applicant) had an interest in the first customer's firm because he was thinking of going to work for them, and he could ask if the customer would mind if the applicant called to get some input?

Generally, a request of that type from a banker would not be turned down. People have faith in bankers. They do not believe bankers would ever have an undesirable character call. The introduction and request from the banker should be enough to get the job seeker into a telephone conversation with the employee. The banker has not been asked to do anything out of the ordinary, either. A customer of his merely wants information on another customer's company. There is nothing of any confidential nature that is going to be revealed. No one is asking the banker for a job nor are they asking the employee. All the applicant wants is information and advice.

In the ensuing conversation with the employee, the applicant should ask some general questions about the company. How do you like it? What are some of the best points? How long have you been there? The conversation should be positive and enable the employee to speak freely. There may be something detrimental said about the company by the employee. If this happens the applicant should not dwell upon it. Recognize and acknowledge it, and go on to another topic. The applicant should keep the interview upbeat.

Towards the close, the applicant should tell the employee that he is going to apply for X position and he will be sending a resume the next week. He should ask if the employee minds if he mentions the employee's name as someone who has told him about the firm. The answer will usually be, "No, I do not mind." Remember, the applicant is not asking the employee to recommend him. He does not have to. All he needs is the employee's name; a name that can be dropped in the cover letter. The mere utilization of it implies endorsement to the human resource director or the hiring manager.

The cover letter is not a document that should be written and mailed in a matter of minutes. It should be carefully thought out. It has to say certain things. "Remember," says Dew, "what you say in a cover letter is always there for someone to reference. Make sure your statements are accurate. They can come back and haunt you."

AVOIDING THE MISTAKE

Cover letters can be harmful. They may cost the applicant an interview opportunity if they contain spelling or typographical errors. These mistakes are unforgivable whether they are in a cover letter or resume. Imagine sending a letter to a prospective client and misspelling his name. The client looks at the letter and immediately believes that "if this person does not care enough to spell it right, how good is his product or service? How much care does he take in preparing it?"

Cover letters, likewise, give the prospective employer his first impression. If it contains a typo, that impression is negative. The typo also gives the human resource department a reason to discard your resume. Anyone careless enough to have typos in a cover letter, may be extremely careless on the job.

Cover letters containing salary requirements are another death knell. If the ad does not state the salary, the applicant takes a tremendous chance by inserting one. If he is too high, his letter and resume will be discarded. Nobody wants to hire someone at a lower salary than the applicant requested since they are certain that kind of employee will leave at the first chance. Employers do not want to hire someone who asks for less than the job pays, either. The prospective employer reasons that the applicant may lack the qualifications.

Directing the cover letter to the correct person can make the difference between getting an interview or having your resume discarded. For example, an ad may say, "Reply to the human resource director." Step one should be to call the company and get the name of the human resource director. Address the cover letter and resume to that person by name.

THE NAME'S THE GAME

We all attach importance to our names. Studies have shown that the impact of direct mail increases dramatically as the name of the person is utilized versus "occupant" or "homeowner." Letters addressed to someone by name get opened first and have a higher priority. "Typically," says Adamo, "I will be drawn to the letter that has my name on it rather than the envelope that just says 'human resource director'."

Finding the correct name also keeps the applicant from making the mistake Fitzpatrick did. There is no confusion as to whether a man or woman is going to receive it.

The search for the best person to send a cover letter/resume to should not end with the human resource director. If an ad is for a salesperson, it is easy to pick up the telephone and find out from the operator who the sales manager happens to be. Send one resume directly to the sales manager and another to the human resource director. If the hiring manager likes what he reads, he may start the interview process by contacting the human resource department. Going directly to the hiring manager has another advantage in that the manager is not going to be receiving the flood of resumes that will hit the human resource department. They may take the time to read it and, in doing so, the applicant may be a step ahead of everyone else if his qualifications are adequate. Although some human resource directors insist they be the ones to screen resumes, they admit the applicant will be a step ahead if he can bypass their department.

If the position is for an accountant, call the accounting department and determine who they report to and send that person the cover letter/resume. If the opening is in production, make a similar call. In almost every instance, it is possible to find out who the hiring manager is going to be.

Fred Peters' search firm often "sends double." That is, a cover letter (with resume) goes to the human resource director and one goes to the hiring manager. "There is no question the human resource department is in the loop so you cannot avoid them, but go for the hiring manager whenever possible."

TWO-TIER OBSTACLES

When applying for a position with a midsize or larger company, applicants face a two-tier obstacle. The first tier is the human resource director. The director is given hiring parameters by the department supervisor, vice president, or manager.

These hiring parameters are going to closely match the classified or display ad. As the cover letters and resumes come in, the human resource department is going to check cover letters/resumes against the job's requirements. There may be three or four conditions the hiring manager asked the human resource director to check. If those conditions are outlined in the cover letter, the applicant is ahead of the game.

In this first tier, judgment is objective (that is, a secretary or human resource person scanning resumes to see if the applicants fulfill the conditions). The second tier involves the hiring manager and will be covered in Chapters 6 and 7.

Not all cover letters and resumes go to the human resource director or the hiring manager. Companies utilize search firms as well. There are *contingency* and *retainer* firms. In the contingency case, the firm is paid a fee if they place an applicant. As a rule, these firms do not handle placement beyond middle managers. If an applicant can bypass the contingency firm, he should do so. The contingency firm is simply gathering applicants and sending them to the company, while at the same time, the company could be generating applicants from other areas.

Bypassing a contingency firm is possible but it takes research. Employment firms do not want to give out the name of the employer. However, an applicant may be able to determine the company through the description of the position that is in an ad placed by the contingency firm.

In the case of retainer firms, the situation changes. The retainer firm is being paid by the company to find and screen applicants. They are dealing with middle management (and above) applicants. They were given the job of finding applicants because the firm itself did not have the time or capabilities. The retainer firm is acting the part of the human resource department and as long as they are on retainer, the hiring company would prefer them to do the screening.

Cover letters to search firms should be for specific positions they have advertised. Usually a search firm will not retain a resume unless they feel the individual is of particular value and has unique skills. Calling search firms to determine the status of a resume is usually a waste of time. The search firm generates as many, if not more, resumes than human resource departments, and they tend to respond only to those candidates they feel should be interviewed.

Search firms, however, can be of value to the person who may be thinking of leaving his company. On the average, the successful recruiter fills about ten key positions a year. If a person has a position, is well thought of, and is developing a reputation, he should keep recruiters informed of his progress by sending them notes and updated resume information. There may come a time when the recruiter finds a position that is ideal.

WINNING COPY

Whether the cover letter is sent to a recruiter, human resource department, or hiring manager, there are elements that it should contain. Think of a cover letter as no more than a short, one-page story. It has an opening, body, and conclusion which should fit the following format:

1. *Opening:* Attention getter that explains the purpose of the letter
2. *Body:* Highlights skills and matches accomplishments against the company's needs
3. *Conclusion:* Ask for the interview and position. Suggest you call to set the time for the interview.

In the opening, the applicant must grab the reader's attention. That means active, dynamic terms instead of passive language. For example, compare the following opening paragraphs of two letters sent by applicants who were exploring the possibilities of future openings at a firm.

1. "It is possible that you may be engaged in a search, now or in the future, which might be satisfied by my qualifications as set forth in the enclosed resume."
2. "I am impressed by your company's reputation, management, and products, and would like to explore the possibilities of joining your staff."

The former is flat, unemotional, and boring. It does not convey the applicant's enthusiasm because it has clauses and conditions. The tone is almost apologetic. The second letter is direct, does not contain qualifying clauses or exceptions, and speaks directly to the reader in language he can understand, and has a sense of urgency and drive to it.

Many employed (but looking) managers send the so-called *broadcast* cover letter. The reasoning for sending the letter may range from an impending layoff to dissatisfaction with a supervisor, or the job seeker may just be curious as to what is out there and how much is being paid. Whatever the reason, these letters should have "life" to them as well. For example:

I am an attorney with broad tax experience. My background includes substantial experience with inventory and taxation. I am seeking a corporate position with emphasis on taxation. I would be happy to provide additional information. Thank you for your consideration.

This broadcast cover letter is low key at best. It says nothing about the company the applicant is addressing. Although it is not possible to gain insight into every possible employer, applicants should generate at least one fact about the firm and tie it into the letter. This letter, which went to a manufacturer, could have been reworded in the following manner:

> I am an experienced tax attorney with considerable manufacturing background, and I have closely followed your company and its sales for the past few years.
>
> I am anxious to join a young, aggressive corporation such as X company, and believe with my background I could be a definite asset with your taxation and other related legal concerns.
>
> I would be happy to meet with you at your convenience and provide greater insight into my capabilities. I will call you to see if we might get together. In the meantime, many thanks for your time and consideration.

This letter has life. The person reading it is not left with the impression that our tax attorney is sending letters to every corporation in town. It appears to be customized.

Notice, too, the writer did not leave it up to the company to call. Why would they call? For the most part, broadcast cover letters will land on deaf ears unless the company that receives the letter has a need—at that moment—for someone with the exact same qualifications as the author of the letter.

Here is an example of a good broadcast cover letter opening that was put together by an engineer.

> I have followed your company closely and am aware of its outstanding reputation in the field of electronic components. I am extremely interested in pursuing the possibilities of employment with your firm.

The next paragraph went into a specific accomplishment of the company that the engineer had followed. It showed that the engineer was aware of the firm and what it was doing.

Broadcast cover letters should mention several of the applicant's accomplishments that would appeal to the prospective employer. The details do not have to be described—these will be in the resume —but every firm wants to know the capabilities of a prospective employee.

Broadcast cover letters are best utilized if the applicant puts out three or four at a time instead of going with a mass mailing. He should follow each with a telephone call to see if there is interest (or an opening) at the company. These letters should bypass the human resource department and end up in the hands of the person who will do the hiring. It is usually the hiring manager who knows, before anyone, whether or not he is going to be seeking someone for a new or old position.

Broadcast cover letters contain other elements aside from a punchy, intriguing opening. They should give rationale for the applicant's interest in another company, but they should not mention anything about a person's desire to leave his present company, nor anything negative in the letter.

For the applicant's protection, broadcast cover letters should have a line that says something like, "At this time, my firm is not aware of my decision to leave." Without that caution, a prospective employer could end up calling the applicant's place of employment and putting everyone in an embarrassing position.

ONE-ON-ONE APPROACH

Broadcast and other cover letters should be written as if the applicant were talking, one-on-one, across a desk to the hiring manager. Too many read like legal documents. For example, the following was sent to a search agency:

> In reviewing your current search assignments, you may possibly have need for a seasoned management consultant with more than 20 years of increasingly complex experience, ranging from . . . to . . .

With slight editing, the opening was revised to give it more life:

> In reviewing your search assignments, you may have need for a seasoned management consultant with more than 20 years of experience, ranging from . . . to . . .

Applicants often have trouble with the opening of cover letters that are in response to an ad:

> Enclosed please find my resume in response to the Jones & Jones ad for a sales manager in last Sunday's newspaper.

Contrast this with:

> I was fascinated by your ad in last Sunday's paper for a sales manager and have enclosed my resume for your consideration.

The second opening connotes enthusiasm, which is an ingredient every sales manager must have. By eliminating the "please" and such words as "find" and substituting active words and verbs, cover letter openings can be dramatically improved.

With positions that generate hundreds of applications, the distinctive, unusual opening may be the applicant's best approach:

> Your advertisement in the *Chicago Daily News* described your product in one word: Distinctive. I can sum up my experience, skills, and qualifications for the Regional Manager's position you have open in one word as well: Qualified.

Daring? Yes, but it could stand out from the pack and that is one of the goals of a cover letter.

Broadcast cover letters should contain active words as well:

> I am writing this in view of the fact I have followed your company for some time and have been impressed by its reputation, management, and products. I would like to explore the feasibility of my possibly joining your firm.

Now, take out the extra words and insert active terms:

> For some time, I have been impressed by your company's reputation, management, and products and would like to explore the possibilities of joining your staff.

Broadcast cover letters require editing and just as much thought as a letter that is sent to the human resource director. The following opening paragraph of a broadcast letter is an example of how some applicants fail to hit home with correspondence.

> I am an experienced sales manager seeking an opportunity for advancement and challenge in sales management.

The opening does not exhibit any knowledge on the writer's part of the company's present situation. Suppose it said this: I am an experienced sales manager who has watched your company's growth, and I have some fascinating ideas as to how you might increase your market share.

A hiring manager reading the latter opening is going to be more intrigued by it than the former.

THE GREAT MOTIVATOR

That is the idea of every cover letter—spark interest and curiosity. Curiosity is one of the greatest motivators in society. If an applicant can generate those feelings in a human resource director or hiring manager, he has an excellent chance of obtaining an interview.

The following opening to a broadcast cover letter went to a firm from an engineer:

> Your company has had an outstanding reputation as a leader in the field of electronic components, and I am interested in exploring the chances of joining your firm in a senior manufacturing capacity.

The opening tells the company what the job seeker wants but it says nothing about what the seeker may be able to do for the company. That could come in the following paragraphs, but the executive reading the letter may never get beyond the first paragraph if there is nothing to entice him. The letter must address the company's needs. This letter could have been reworded in the following manner:

> Your company has had an outstanding reputation in the field of electronic components, and I believe I can add to that renown through the innovative designs and creative approach that I have brought to the industry during the past decade.

Cover letters can also get directly to the subject:

> Can you use a data processing manager who:
>
> 1. Increased productivity 12 percent by revising computer work schedules?
> 2. Cut costs of the computer system by 21 percent during a three-year period by developing and utilizing a "link" system?
> 3. Provided daily instead of weekly sales updates by alternating payroll and production runs and running sales on a 24-hour basis?
> 4. Did all three of the previous items without spending any additional monies for data processing?

Words that can be used in the opening paragraph range from *excited* to *fascinated* and *intrigued*. Use descriptive verbs that have enthusiastic connotations.

MATCHING REQUIREMENTS AND QUALIFICATIONS

The body of the letter should be devoted to comparing the applicants accomplishments with the needs expressed in the ad. For example, examine the Regional Sales Manager ad in Figure 28.

Figure 28   Regional Sales Manager Ad

Regional Sales Manager

Looking for sales manager who is experienced in field management and has had dealings with consumer packaged goods. Must have ability to develop independent sales distributors and train distributor sales personnel. Prefer business degree. Travel 50 percent of time. Write.

What does the ad say? Primarily, the employer is looking for the following:

1. Experience in field sales management
2. Experience with consumer packaged goods
3. Experience in developing independent sales distributors
4. Experience in training sales personnel
5. Business degree
6. Travel oriented

The applicant's cover letter for this position should address these points. It can be done as shown in the cover letter in Figure 29. The applicant has addressed each of the key issues in the ad. At the same time, he has not gone into specific accomplishments—that is an issue for the resume to address. The cover letter, however, gives any human resource person the ability to determine whether this applicant may be a candidate.

The applicant mentions the will call if he does not hear from the prospective company. In some cases, this spurs the human resource person to read the resume and reach a decision as to whether to call the applicant in for an interview.

The letter is enthusiastic and states the candidates qualifications —and it does it in less than one page. It does one other thing: It helps overcome any prejudice that the human resource department (or hiring manager) may have against someone that does not have industry experience. Many employers prefer to hire people from their industry. It is safer. Cover letters that compare qualifications to requirements without ever mentioning the industry are excellent vehicles. They help get the applicant by the human resource department.

In many cases, the cover letter may sell the hiring manager. It shows the relationship of one industry to another without mentioning the two are different. It gives human resource people, or hiring managers with little imagination, a chance to see the viability of

**Figure 29   Cover Letter for
Regional Sales Manager Position**

Dear _____

   I was fascinated by your ad in Sunday's Times as I am a perfect fit
for your Regional Sales Manager position. Below you will find my
qualifications matched with your requirements.

1. Experienced in field sales management. I have ten plus years in
territory sales and three of those have been in sales management as a
district and zone manager.

2. Experience in consumer package goods. For six years I have been
responsible for (X) line, which is sold exclusively to consumers.

3. Experienced in developing independent sales distributors. Our entire product line is handled by independents and my responsibility
includes that area.

4. Experienced in training sales personnel. I have been training for
the past nine years. To date, more than 325 personnel have been
personally trained by me.

5. Business degree. I have a BS in Sales Management from Duquesne
and have a year of advanced business management from LaSalle.

6. Travel 50 percent. In my ten plus years, I have averaged 65 percent
travel each year and I enjoy it.

   I have attached a resume which details my specific accomplishments. I look forward to hearing from you and will give you a call in
two weeks to see if I can answer any other questions.

Many thanks.

                                                         Sincerely,

bringing in someone from X to Y industry. This approach works
best in the cover letter when neither industry's name is mentioned.
   Now, examine the Civil/Environmental Associate Engineer ad in
Figure 30. The cover letter for this position in Figure 31, should
match the following requirements:

1. Experience in water treatment process and research
2. Degree
3. Experience in working with outside consultants
4. Management of plant
5. Experience in laboratory with water chemistry

Figure 30   Match the Requirements to the Ad

Civil/Environmental Associate Engineer

Duties include operating/supervising water treatment pilot plant for ozone-peroxide process; performing water chemistry analyses; coordinating lab work and schedules; liaison to other groups and outside consultants and managing and evaluating pilot plant data. Must have four years experience in water treatment process and research and operations, and demonstrate strong oral and written skills. Requires BS in civil, environmental, or chemical engineering with a MS degree preferred.

Figure 31   Cover Letter for
Civil/Environmental Associate Engineer Position

Dear _____

I read your ad in last Sunday's Tribune with great interest as I have those exact requirements and have been searching for a challenging position in the engineering field.

Experience in water treatment process and research. For the past three years I have been responsible for the city of (x) and its water treatment plant.

Degree. I have both a BS and MS in civil engineering.

Experience in working with outside consultants. Due to the small city staff in our city, we worked extensively with outside consultants on all phases of water and water treatment.

Management of Plant. I have managed the city of (x) water treatment plant for the past three years and prior to that I was assistant manager in the city of (xx) for its water treatment facility.

Experience in laboratory with water chemistry. I have more than a decade of laboratory work with water chemistry, including four years with the city of (xx) where I was supervising chemist and another two years with the Department of Water and Power where I handled the same function.

I have enclosed a copy of my resume which gives you more specific information as to my background and accomplishments. I look forward to meeting with you and sharing ideas.

I will give you a call in a few weeks to see if there is any other question I can possibly answer.

Many thanks for your time and consideration.

Sincerely,

QUALIFYING IN THE LETTER

The idea is to qualify the applicant in the cover letter. Cover letters of this type ensure that the human resource person is not going to miss this candidate or his qualifications. Whether the response is going to the human resource department, the hiring supervisor, or a search company, it is a good idea to use a requirement and qualification format or something similar. Take, for instance, the ad for Chief Executive Officer (Figure 32).

This ad ran in *The Wall Street Journal* in the early part of 1991. It was placed by a search firm and before the position was awarded, there were more than a dozen applicants who went through an intensive interviewing process. The cover letter sent by the candidate who was selected is shown in Figure 33. With a CEO position (Figure 33), the language of the opening paragraph should be modified to reflect refinement and restraint rather than enthusiasm. Most companies picture a CEO as dignified and constrained. Search firms are no different.

Not every cover letter has to be structured in the requirement/ qualification format. It is possible to write them and answer the requirements in paragraph form as well. For instance, an ad in one East Coast newspaper was for a Senior Project Engineer. The cover letter that was sent to the human resource department is shown in Figure 34.

It is possible to state qualifications without reiterating requirements of the firm. It can be assumed the company with the opening knows the requirements and there is no need to restate them. There is a pitfall, however, in this approach. If an untrained human resource person gets the cover letter and resume and the comparisons are not made, that person may not be capable of pairing requirements to qualifications. The idea of restating the requirements is to keep the screener from tossing the cover letter and resume aside.

Figure 32   Ad Needing a Requirement and Qualification Format

---

Chief Executive Officer

Leading retail bakery chain is seeking an experienced individual with a BA or BS Degree. Experience is the key to this position. Nationally known company ($35 million in sales) seeks dynamic professional with proven record in top level corporate management in order to bring sales to $100 million in five years. Experience must include background in financial administration, sales management, consumer goods, product development, production, advertising and promotion, and market planning. East Coast location. Generous compensation. Send resume or brief letter to:

**Figure 33   Cover Letter for
Chief Executive Officer Position**

Dear _____

In response to your advertisement in The Wall Street Journal of (date), I have listed some of my qualifications to parallel your stated requirements.

Requirements	Qualifications
1. dynamic professional with top level management experience	1. former president of $100 million corporation, board chairman of two subsidiaries
2. proven track record	2. built sales from $15 million to $100 million by internal growth
3. financial administration	3. P&L responsibilities for this division
4. sales management	4. former vice-president of sales for $50 million a year company
5. consumer goods	5. entire line was marketed to consumers
6. product development	6. developed three new successful products in three years, each accounted for an added 9 percent in sales
7. degree	7. MBA, Stanford

There are several other areas of accomplishment which I have detailed in the enclosed resume. I would be happy to answer any additional questions at your convenience.

Look forward to hearing from you.

Sincerely,

**Figure 34   Cover Letter for
Senior Project Engineer Position**

Dear _____

I read your ad for a Project Engineer in last Sunday's Herald with great interest. My professional qualifications and career interests are exactly in line with your requirements.

In your ad you are looking for an engineer with seven plus years of experience in design and installation of high speed duplicating machines. You also asked for someone who had supervised more than a half-dozen professionals.

I have had ten years experience with X company as a design engineer and have specialized in the installation of high speed duplicating machinery. Throughout that span, I have supervised ten other professionals.

Thank you for your consideration and I look forward to the opportunity of discussing this with you further.

Sincerely,

For example, a recent ad in the *New York Times* was for a Senior Cost Accountant. One of those responding had a resume that matched the qualifications perfectly. His cover letter in Figure 35 did not match requirements to qualifications.

This cover letter and resume never made it through the initial screening. The first obvious error was that it failed to mention the position that the applicant was after. The screener, who had more than 300 resumes to examine that day, quickly tossed this one aside when it failed to identify the position.

The qualifications portion fell short, too. Although it matched the requirements, the order in which the job seeker listed his experience was not in the order of importance. With this job, cost accounting experience in the field or industry is going to be the most important match. Employers assume that anyone they hire is going to be "high energy" and will have "excellent communication skills." The applicant failed to illustrate any of these attributes with an example.

Cover letters are needed, but properly structured letters are the key to getting in the door for the interview. A cover letter that is not focused will almost always be a waste of time because it will fail to hit the mark.

**Figure 35   Cover Letter for
Senior Cost Accountant Position**

Dear _____

In response to your ad in Sunday's Times, I have enclosed a resume for your perusal. The position is one that I have been hoping to find for the past year and would appreciate the opportunity to discuss it with you first-hand.

The following will give you an idea of my background and how the experience in it fits your requirements:

high energy level and producer
excellent communication skills
seven years of cost accounting experience in the field
degree in accounting from New York University

I appreciate your time and consideration, and I look forward to hearing from you.

Sincerely,

TEN KEY LETTER RULES

Some rules to keep in mind about cover letters are:

1. They should arouse interest. There should be a strong opening and the body should carry through. Think of the cover letter as a sales letter.

2. They should reiterate accomplishments listed in your resume that match the job qualifications.

3. They should not be longer than one page. Ideal length is no more than three or four paragraphs.

4. They should appeal to the prospective employer's self-interest. There should be something in it about your ability to increase sales, production, or whatever. Cover letters enable you to transmit information about yourself that can impact the employer's bottom line.

5. They should be individually typed (or run off on a word processor). Do not use mimeographed copies of the same cover letter for each job application.

6. They should be addressed to an individual whenever possible. If you know it is going to the human resource director, call and find out his or her name.

7. They should reference something the applicant has learned about the prospective employer's company. By doing so, the applicant shows the company he has been doing homework and is truly interested in the position.

8. They should never be negative. You lose when talking poorly about any company (or the prospective employer's firm) or individual. If the prospective firm has been doing poorly and the applicant (as well as everyone else) knows, terms such as "improving performance" are preferable to anything that might be negative.

9. If the applicant has discovered something interesting about the firm while doing research, he should mention it in the letter. Once again, make sure it is not negative.

10. Do not include salary requirements.

6

POWER RESUMES—

WHAT THEY SAY

Walter Parson will never forget that day. It was his 18th anniversary with the firm. He was sitting in his 14th floor office overlooking the crowded expressway and thinking the current prosperity might never end. There were many in Houston, Texas, who felt the same way. The Texas economy was booming, oil was in demand, land prices were soaring, and unemployment was at an all-time low.

The weekend before, Parson and his wife celebrated by putting a down payment on a small, acre-and-a-half farm on the outskirts of the city. It was the first step in their plan. They intended to eventually sell their Houston home, remodel the old, 700-square-foot farmhouse, and use it for their retirement home. The money they received from their Houston home would more than pay for the farmhouse.

Like many in the accounting profession, Parson was conservative. He did not owe much nor did he intend to. He saved and invested his money. Aside from several investments, all designed to pay dividends when he reached age 65, Parson had enough in the bank to live a year without working.

He smiled as he thought of his financial situation and how fortunate he was. Parson would not have felt as secure if he had known what was happening in a brokerage house a few floors below. The price of oil had dropped once more. The aberration was now a trend.

The collapse of oil prices and the Texas (and oil belt) demise in the early 1980s is old news, but to Parson, it will never be forgotten. A few days after his 18th anniversary with the large oil company, Parson was called into the chief financial officer's (CFO) office and became a casualty of the economy. Parson got one break, however. His boss told him the firm would carry him on the payroll for another 60 days. He could, in fact, utilize the services of the office for anything during that period. His boss would also be available for any references to future employers.

One look at the headlines in the Houston paper made Parson realize that he was not the only executive without a job. It also made him aware that there would be countless job seekers on the market and if he wanted to stay in his hometown, he was going to have to be a step ahead of the competition in his approach to getting a new position.

That evening, Parson and his wife discussed their predicament and made several decisions. They both came from Houston and wanted to remain in the area. The oil industry was in trouble and the chances of obtaining a position that had any longevity in it were not good. Parson knew the oil industry well, however, and there might be many independent accounting firms willing to hire someone with his experience and expertise. These firms had been impacted by the economy as well, but Parson knew they did not have an abundance of men with his skills. There was a chance he could find a job in his industry, but a number of things would have to change—including his resume.

From his experience with the oil company, Parson knew that human resource departments took in hundreds of resumes for every management position. He remembered how his firm's human resource department worked. The department was busy and flooded with applications. To alleviate the rush, the human resource director took one of the secretaries and gave her a list of three or four requirements for each job. Then he told her to go through the resumes and throw out any that did not have the correct parameters.

Parson and John Scully, the human resource director, had even joked about the procedure one day over lunch. The conversation came back to Parson and he realized that if his resume was going to get beyond the human resource department, it would have to be special. That afternoon he called Scully. Scully knew the situation and Parson did not hide it: "I need some help with a resume. Could you spare me 15 to 20 minutes for some advice?"

When they met, Scully suggested several things such as networking. He also mentioned that perhaps Parson should slow down, think things over, and not send resumes out in mass without targeting specific companies.

Parson explained his plan and Scully was impressed. It was well thought out and targeted an industry where there might be positions available. Parson did not forget about networking, either. He had already made a list and divided it into three categories. The next day he would start making calls but first he needed a resume.

TEN POWER INGREDIENTS

The direction that Scully provided was critically important to Parson as well as any job seeker. He gave Parson a format to follow. It was the formula for a *power* resume:

1. Stay away from functional resumes.
2. Stay away from objectives.
3. Do not give your age, marital status, or graduation dates, unless you know it will be to your advantage.
4. Make sure your resume gives specific accomplishments, not duties and responsibilities.
5. Write in clear, concise terms. Use active words.
6. Tailor-make the resume to the company.
7. Be sure to use a summary at the beginning of the resume.
8. Limit the resume to two pages.
9. Do not put in salary requirements or references.
10. If you have space, insert extracurricular activities.

Scully explained the reasoning for each. Functional resumes are difficult for human resource directors to follow. They concentrate on describing specific functions but they lack dates and the name of the company involved. Too often they appear to be hiding something about the applicant because the dates and company names are missing.

OBJECTIVES OUTDATED

Stating objectives is outdated, and they are usually vague, at best. An employer assumes if you are applying for a position, you want that specific job. The employer is interested in what the applicant can do for his company, and not what the applicant's goals are. Employers want to look at a summary which outlines the type of experience someone has had. For example, in Parson's case, his summary read:

> Summary: Twenty-one years of increasingly responsible positions in accounting and auditing for the oil industry. A specialist in depletion and tax allowances.

To avoid any discrimination, avoid mentioning age. The resume should also stay away from any dates that might indicate the age of the applicant. The year that a degree was granted enables human resource directors or hiring managers to do some arithmetic and come up with an applicant's approximate age. Mentioning the age of a son or daughter is another giveaway.

For some positions, it is wise to leave marital status out. This is true when it comes to jobs that require much travel. Human resource directors may look at the status and surmise that the extent of travel is going to harm the marriage. Marital status can be harmful in a woman's resume, as well. The human resource person (or hiring manager) may begin to wonder, "What happens if she gets pregnant and has to take a leave of absence?"

Too many applicants list previous jobs and stress their duties and responsibilities instead of accomplishments. In Parson's case, he wrote it this way:

> Responsible for tax depreciation and filings. Have *saved* the firm nearly $15 million in taxes during the past six years by *applying* little known tax breaks to operation. With the new tax law, *revised* our reporting procedures and inventory accountability to *save* the firm $1.5 million in additional taxes.

Those are accomplishments and they display the skills and abilities that a prospective employer is interested in seeing. They say, "I can add value to your bottom line."

USE ACTIVE TERMS

Clear concise terms with the proper verbiage is important. Active verbs should be used. Cut out pronouns (i.e., I, we, they). Several of the terms in Parson's description of his accomplishments fit this category and are highlighted. Others are:

acquired	fabricated	processed
accomplished	implemented	purchased
approved	initiated	rectified

calculated	instituted	revamped
conceived	launched	selected
computed	labeled	specified
controlled	maintained	suggested
created	managed	tested
cut	marketed	trained
delivered	minimized	translated
designed	modified	unified
edited	negotiated	upgraded
eliminated	originated	visualized
enhanced	presented	verified

Avoid acronyms. A hiring manager may (or may not) understand them, but the human resource people may draw a complete blank. Do not take the chance.

Power resumes are not generic. Each is tailor made for the position and company. Qualifications in the resume should match requirements in the ad. Cover letters should be targeted as well. The applicant should pretend that this is the only resume and cover letter he intends to send out and the company he is trying to interest is the only one with whom he intends to talk. Mass mailings may make an applicant feel as if he is doing something, but they can be a waste of time.

Resumes should be limited to two pages. Studies show that a reader absorbs about 60 percent of what is on page one of a resume and that absorption drops to about 40 percent by the time they get to page two. Page three becomes a total waste. Human resource directors believe anything over two pages is too long and applicants who go on for three and four pages are not astute. Often a three-page resume can lead to the loss of an interview. Power resumes are limited to a two-page format.

SALARY—THE CATCH-22 PITFALL

Salary requirements in a resume enable a screener to eliminate resumes. Any salary that is not exactly on the mark works against the applicant. It is either too high or too low. You cannot win.

There are many cases when extracurricular activities should be included. Someone applying for a sales position should include memberships in civic organizations, clubs, and so on. This shows the hiring manager that the applicant is personable and likes to associate with people—one of the requirements for a salesperson.

The inclusion of extracurricular activities (if they fit) is not a bad idea for other occupations, either. Think of it from the hiring manager's perspective. If he has two or three leading candidates for an accounting or engineering position and all three are equal, how does he judge? One way may be to look at the person's sociability. Perhaps the accountant may one day have to supervise people. If he shows an ability to get along with them in his resume, that may weigh in his favor.

Parson followed these guidelines. He was not, he admits, a writer but he found that power resumes are anything but creative pieces of literature. They involve structural rules and utilize specific verbiage.

Parson also followed the cover letter pattern outlined in Chapter 5. He sent resumes to four different accounting firms in the area. A week later, he followed with a telephone call. One of the firms had no openings, but the other three wanted to talk to him. As a result of the interviews, he found himself with two job offers, each starting at almost $8000 more than he was presently making.

Parson landed a position because he was mindful of the old saying, "You never get a second chance to make a first impression." That first impression, when searching for a job, is often the resume.

A resume is not intended to land a job—only to obtain an interview for a position. It is an advertisement for the individual who is selling his services. Remember, however, that effective ads do not sell products, they sell benefits to the users of those products. Power resumes do the same.

THREE RESUME ROADS

In putting a resume together, a job seeker can take one of three roads. He can utilize a chronological, functional, or combination-of-both resume. Power resumes are chronological; whichever format is selected, these additional rules should be kept in mind:

1. Never send a picture. It allows a screener or hiring manager to exercise his prejudice.
2. Never give a reason for leaving your previous firm. That is best left to the interview stage when it can be explained face-to-face.
3. Make sure the resume is neat, on plain white paper, and without typographical errors.

4. Under no circumstances should you use your present company's stationery or postage meter. It says to the screener that you are taking advantage of the firm and you may do the same to his if you obtain the position.

5. Be careful of where you put educational accomplishments. Many positions ask for certain requirements, however, the only time educational experience goes in front of work experience is if the applicant is seeking a teaching or similar job. In that case, the hiring manager is going to be equally interested in educational experience.

Be mindful of the competition and the resumes they are submitting. In order to stand above the pack, as Parson did, the resume, cover letter, and interview have to be carefully thought out. Examples of resumes are shown in Figures 36–68. Some are excellent while others need a phrase, paragraph, or slight rewording to make them *power* resumes. Every one of these resumes—with the revisions described—landed a new position for the person who wrote them. Each could be classified a power resume with the revisions. Some of the positions, as in the case of the CEOs, were high paying, well into the high six figures. Others were in industries that were extremely competitive and the applicants were up against 200 to 300 resumes in some cases. In the end, each of these resumes won an interview for the applicants and a position. In some cases, the name of the employer (or company) has been deleted. In others, the name of the firm has been changed.

THIRTY POWER RESUMES

Resume 1 (Figure 36) needed a few revisions before it could be classified a power resume. It violates one of the key rules—it has an objective. Objectives, if they are stated, should be followed by a summary. Human resource directors tend to disregard objectives. A human resource director reading this objective may not understand the person's background or what type of position he is seeking. Applicants should remember that human resource people may not understand terms such as *key country operations of major international manufacturing firm*. The objective should be explicit: To manage either regional or corporate operations of a major international manufacturing firm. The objective was removed from this resume and in its place was put the following summary:

Summary: More than 18 years of increasingly responsible health industry experience in domestic and international manufacturing

Figure 36   Resume 1: Resume with an Objective

JOHN M. B.
17 East _____ Street
_____ New Jersey 08805
(212) 421 _____ (Business)

OBJECTIVE   To manage and direct regional or key country operations of a major
                 international manufacturing firm.

1978 to   Management Consultant to President, _____ Inc., New York
Present:

                 Responsibilities: To structure and manage affiliated firm which will
                 market unique dental equipment, developed and manufactured by
                 parent company, to major U.S. health care firm(s).

                 Results: Completed regional marketing research and product exposure
                 of Dental Lock System. Have advanced clinical research to point now
                 permitting licensing negotiations with prospective partners.

1977 to 1978:   General Manager and Managing Director, _____ Inc., Philippines

                 Responsibilities: To organize and make operational this personally
                 conceived joint-venture, health care company in accordance with
                 approved business plan.

                 Results: Completed incorporation, registration, key staffing and start-up
                 of venture in nine months and within operating budget.

1976 to 1977:   Deputy Managing Director, _____ Hong Kong

                 Responsibilities: To redirect corporate resources toward organizational
                 and product areas of visible strength and to reduce areas of high
                 exposure and/or unsatisfactory productivity.

                 Results: Negotiated joint-venture in the Philippines; eliminated marginal
                 company division and unprofitable branch in Hong Kong and Thailand,
                 respectively; deleted outdated, high cost speciality products and
                 successfully introduced competitive generic line in three markets.

1973 to 1976:   Director of Operations - Asia, _____ Philippines and Japan

                 Responsibilities: To direct three regional managers toward attaining
                 growth and profitability commitments in nine subsidiary and/or
                 distributorship markets under their supervision.

                 Results: Approximated or exceeded budgeted targets for three years in
                 all major markets; achieved most successful new product introductions
                 in history of both Philippine and Japan branches. As first regional
                 director, established uniform area-wide planning, budgeting and
                 reporting programs.

1970 to 1973:   Executive Vice President for _____ Far East and resident Vice President in joint-venture companies, _____ and Shimadzu Searle, Japan.

Responsibilities: To develop and expand going and new product line activities in Japan, Taiwan and Korea. To represent all elements of joint-venture companies to and from American and Japanese partners on a continuing basis.

Results: At end of three years, pharmaceutical joint-venture sales more than doubled; headcount expanded by one-third to one hundred fifty persons; shared profits consistently exceeded budget. Turned around instrumentation operation into sound, profitable licensing arrangement. Established corporate entries into both Korea and Taiwan.

1956 to 1970:   From Area Manager to Assistant Regional Director for _____ , (or its international subsidiaries) for ten (10) Far Eastern countries.

Responsibilities: To develop and be accountable for long and short-term operating plans; to manage and direct activities of country and area operations to which assigned. Sales and marketing responsibilities present in all assignments throughout fourteen year term.

Results: Successful start-up operations in Thailand, Taiwan and Korea permitted establishment of viable subsidiaries in all markets. Attained still unbeaten record of successful new product introductions for ethical company. Recruited and developed record number of first class marketing executive throughout the area.

EDUCATION: AB Rutgers University, Biological Sciences and Latin American Affairs, 1948–1952.

Postgraduate credits: Georgetown University; University of Maryland; New York University Graduate School of Business Administration; Carnegie Mellon University; 1952–1979.

MILITARY: U.S. Army, Public Information, 1952–1954.

LANGUAGES: Spanish, French, Thai, Japanese.

PERSONAL: _____ 200 pounds; health excellent; three children.

120

and marketing of drug, health care, and other medical related products.

The narrative in the body of the resume needed improvement as well. It had too much narrative and not sufficient bulleted items. The resume body was restructured with an average of two bulleted accomplishments under each position. The first entry, for example, had the applicant's responsibilities. It was followed by these two bulleted accomplishments:

- Supervised and completed marketing research and development of new dental system called the Dental Lock System.
- Conducted clinical research of system which allowed for licensing of the system which could account for $5 million in fees during the first year.

In addition, the graduation dates as well as the military dates were removed.

The summary in Resume 2 (Figure 37) is lengthy. The bulleted items under "major strengths" are effective as are the bulleted items under each "major accomplishments" section. Notice under the major accomplishments there are specific numbers. This was an excellent resume that needed little revision. In this case, the education dates were left in because they would not "age" the candidate to any great extent. It is up to the applicant to use his or her judgment as to the impact of a graduation date. In this case, there was none.

Resume 3 (Figure 38) is a power resume for this CEO. The summary is brief and succinct but still has room for improvement. A slight change was made in the first sentence to reflect the executive's CEO and general manager experience:

Summary: Senior results-oriented executive with 18 years experience in upper management as Chief Executive Officer in both public and private sectors. Major experience, strengths, and skills are:

The achievements are specific and to the point. His medical background and capabilities are exhibited. There is no guesswork involved. Any human resource person or hiring manager will immediately be able to see his qualifications.

Resume 4 (Figure 39) is a power resume that required no alterations. This executive wound up with a new job after only three weeks with a 25 percent increase in salary and fringe benefits. The extracurricular activities are a plus which are usually not found in the resume for an engineering position.

Figure 37   Resume 2: Summary Too Lengthy

Residence: (213) XXX-XXXX
Business: (213) XXX-XXXX

Yorba Linda, California 92686

SUMMARY OF QUALIFICATIONS

Chief Financial Officer with experience in financial management, financial reporting, and taxation. Expertise in supervision and development of accounting staff and the ability to communicate effectively with top management. Experienced in the Health Care, Real Estate, Engineering, Consumer Products Electronics, and Aircraft Industries. Major strengths:

- Financial Analysis
- Systems/Procedures
- Data Processing

- Financial Reporting/Presentation
- Analysis/Problem Solving
- Supervision and Administration

EXPERIENCE

1985–Present

VICE-PRESIDENT, FINANCE

Reports to the Chief Operating Officer with responsibility for all financial functions of the corporation including consolidations, general accounting, billing and collections, taxes, data processing, and monthly reports to the Board of Directors. Worked with lenders and investors involving numerous partnerships and joint venture projects. Total staff of 50.

Major accomplishments include:

- Reduced numbers of days of accounts receivable days by 11.
- Secured $6.8 million of real estate and equipment financing for two syndications.
- Reduced capital expenditures by $300,000 for one subsidiary, while maintaining operational capabilities.
- Performed a profitability analysis on the various lines of business, within the corporation, providing the basis for a corporate reorganization.

1984–1985

AUDIT MANAGER

Responsible for all aspects of engagement administration including client relations, billing, practice development, and staff development. Clients have included real estate and engineering companies.

Major accomplishments include:

- Trained staff in use of the firm's audit software for Micro Computers.
- Maintained client relations during transition from Mihaylo and Company to Coopers & Lybrand.
- Selected as a liaison to local University faculty to update them on the use of micro computers in accounting and auditing.

1981–1984

GENERAL PRACTICE MANAGER

Developed client relations and managed all aspects of tax and audit engagements. Major responsibilities included staff training and development. Client base included real estate, consumer products, electronics, and aircraft companies.

Major accomplishments include:
- Development of business plans for several clients, including financial projections and extensive narrative on product development, design and marketing.

1977–1981

As an Audit Senior, responsible for supervision of audit engagements and staff development. Clients included a mining/manufacturing concern, a local airline, several hospitals, and a real estate investment/management company.

As an Audit Staff, applied audit procedures to all financial statement accounts. Included experience in cost accounting.

EDUCATION

BA, California State University, Fullerton—1977

PROFESSIONAL AFFILIATIONS

California CPA Certificate—1979
American Institute of CPA's—Member—1981–Present
California Institute of CPA's—Member—1980–Present

Figure 38   Resume 3: Resume Needing a Change to the Summary

Residence: (XXX) XXX-XXXX
Business: (XXX) XXX-XXXX

SUMMARY

Senior results-oriented Executive with 18 years experience in both public and private sectors. Major experience, strengths and skills are:

- Development of Human Resources
- Financial Controls
- Community Relations

- Professional Staff Relations
- Quality Assurance/Risk Management
- Communications

EMPLOYMENT

1983–Present

CHIEF EXECUTIVE OFFICER

Responsibilities:

- Management of the inpatient and outpatient services of a non-profit corporation consisting of a 97-bed acute care hospital and a 96-bed psychiatric hospital (recently sold).

Achievements:

- Created programs and systems in patient care areas that permitted the hospitals to reach agreement with the California State Attorney General for probation rather than removal of the hospital license, because of 150 major medical deficiencies.
- Negotiated sale of the psychiatric hospital which provided one million dollars in excess funds and retired a debt carrying a 20% interest rate.
- Improved financial condition within two years from an annual two million dollar loss to one-half million profit from operations while retiring accumulated debt of over six million. Accounts receivable reduced from 120 days to 60 days and accounts payable from 180 days to 45 days.
- Negotiated the purchase of the radiology and laboratory departments which resulted in additional revenues of over two million dollars.
- Created an independent practice association which assisted in resolving a devastating medical staff rift; negotiated 36 contracts with preferred provider and health maintenance organizations.
- Negotiated settlement of three union contracts and the decertification of the fourth union which provided annual savings in excess of $300,000. Implemented cost efficiency programs that reduced expenses by over seven million annually.

1977–1983   Company Name

SPECIAL PROJECTS MANAGER

Responsibilities:

- Overall management of the inpatient and outpatient services of a non-profit 68-bed hospital. Corporate responsibilities included sale of facility and completion of Certificate of Need, for American River Hospital.

124

Achievements:

- Developed programs in physician recruitment, out-patient services, community development and marketing which enhanced the hospital's image, and increased revenues by over one million dollars.
- Created long-range plan and management by objectives program resulting in improvement of hospital services, employee morale and productivity.
- Corrected major problems associated with accreditation and received maximum accreditation status within one year.

1976–1977

GENERAL MANAGER

Responsibilities:

- Retained to develop and implement new management and financial systems.

Achievements:

- Programs implemented corrected budget overruns resulting in cost savings of over $250,000 per year, grant funds were increased by over one million dollars per year, and financial systems reflected accurate and complete reports.

1971–1976

ASSOCIATE ADMINISTRATOR

Responsibilities:

- Primary responsibilities for professional services, personnel and education departments for 3,200 personnel and professional staff of a regional medical center comprised of 14 facilities including a 750-bed graduate training hospital.

Achievements:

- Centralized personnel, supply, and other support services; created management systems for conversion to a regional medical center resulting in savings of over $750,000 per year.
- Designed programs which reduced professional and hourly employee turnover by over 200%.
- Served management as chief labor contract negotiator with seven unions.
- Developed successful programs by creating educational programs in MBA, MHA, B.S. in Nursing, B.S. in Laboratory Technology, and technical programs in EMT, Paramedics, LVN, and nursing aid. Created new physician residencies in pediatrics and urology, affiliated with Stanford University.

Figure 39　Resume 4:　A Power Resume

Name
Address
Hawthorne, CA 90250

Residence:　(XXX) XXX-XXXX
Business:　(XXX) XXX-XXXX

SUMMARY

A Professional Manager with over twenty-two years in increasingly responsible position in Program Management, Business Development, Consulting and Project Engineering. Positions held include Director of Centaur Business Segment and Director of Space Programs. Major strengths include:

- Planning/Organizing
- Negotiations
- Problem Solving
- Cost Analysis/Control

PROFESSIONAL EXPERIENCE

1986–Present

DIRECTOR BUSINESS SEGMENT/SPACE PROGRAM

Responsible for developing new business as well as managing existing programs valued in excess of $30 MM. Provided market forecasts, assisted in strategic planning and established revenue goals of $20 MM per year for all space programs.
Accomplishments

- Established a strategically critical project team to support product improvements and generate in excess of $12 MM of new sales.
- Resolved customer concern on program costs and meeting delivery schedules identified $500,000 of administrative costs alone attributable to excessive contract changes by customer. Identification and resolution of problem improved customer relations and provided schedule relief.

1982–1986

PROGRAM MANAGER

Responsible for quality, cost and schedule of an estimated $8 MM in revenue per annum. Hired engineering and administrative staff to support the Missile Ordinance Arming Switch expanding product line.

Accomplishments

- Developed and implemented improved cost control methods and exception reporting thus improving program visibility on the Air Launch Cruise Missile (ALCM) Program. Increased efficiency of operations and reduced costs by over $250,000 within first year.
- The ALCM Program was approximately five months behind schedule with cost overrun when initially assigned. ALCM was completed on schedule and was extremely profitable.
- Managed numerous successful proposals and was effective in negotiating major contracts in excess of $2 MM.

126

1976–1982

SENIOR PROJECT ENGINEER

Assigned to the ATF3-6 Engine Program as project engineer with full budget responsibility for developing and implementing programs designed to correct engine performance problems.

1973–1976   CONSULTANT

On assignment with the following major corporations:
specializing in the field of Heat Transfer, Stress and Fluid Flow Analyses.

1969–1973

STAFF SCIENTIST II

Responsible for the successful thermal design and analysis of OSO-7 Spacecraft. All in flight temperatures were predicted within 5°C. Initiated and authored successful unsolicited proposals, generating revenues in excess of $250,000.

1967–1969   CONSULTANT

On assignment to the following major corporations:
Heat Transfer, Fluid Flow and Engine Performance Analyses.

1964–1967

ANALYTICAL DESIGN ENGINEER

Performed heat transfer, thermodynamics and fluid flow analyses on the RL-10, RL-20, 250K and 350K rocket engines taking into account the effects of aerodynamic heating.

EDUCATION

Bachelor of Science, Aerospace Engineering—University of Florida
Post Graduate courses in:
Propulsion, Heat Transfer, Mathematics and Public Speaking.
Numerous Professional Seminars.

PROFESSIONAL AFFILIATIONS

Toastmasters International, CTM
Technical Marketing Society of America
American Society of Mechanical Engineers

OTHER

Volleyball, snow skiing, scuba diving, music and sailing

Resume 5 (Figure 40) misses in several areas. It is too long (three pages) and the executive also gives away his age by stating "40 years of business experience." Certainly, his resume classifies him as a senior executive but with a little math, a firm is going to guess that this man is in his sixties, which may be too old for many firms that need a treasurer.

There are too many other dates, as well. The dates for his degrees and the dates of his professional affiliations. The professional affiliations can be cut considerably. Another item to be cut are those positions which are so old they have no bearing on the person's ability. The first two employment ventures could be deleted.

The resume was revised and did not reflect employment farther back than 1967. Educational dates were removed as were dates on other activities. Deceptive? Not really. Applicants should not give away everything in a resume nor should they reveal anything they feel may be harmful. Qualifications that date back 40 years are going to make firms think before they invite the candidate in for an interview.

Resume 6 (Figure 41) is close to being a power resume. The summary can be improved by indicating the candidate's production experience along with his management experience—management is a broad term. The summary was revised and worded to read "more than 20 years of successful experience in all phases of management and production including Operations."

The bulleted accomplishments are well done. The dates under education should be deleted. The reference to 1964 may not bother many prospective employers (insofar as age) but it could be a stumbling block. There is no need to have it—or the typos that were corrected.

Resume 7 (Figure 42) is a power resume with well-placed bullets and highlights. The date of graduation was deleted. The breakdown of positions in his latest job is an aid and shows the progress he has made. The summary is short and contains all pertinent information. Summary and accomplishments are structured perfectly. The accomplishments are bulleted and well-done. The candidate has also found space to include his extracurricular activities which many engineers may neglect to include. They can, however, make a difference.

In Resume 8 (Figure 43), a summary indicating more than a dozen years of hospital administration experience was added. The objective was too general and was deleted. The dates of degrees, although not too "old," were deleted. The question mark on the resume is the area where the candidate talks about the firm he established. The questions that could arise range from "how did he start a business while working for someone else" to "how much

Figure 40   Resume 5: A Resume That Misses in Several Areas

Residence: (XXX) XXX-XXXX
(Ans. Mach.)

A bilingual Financial Executive with 40 years of business experience in banking, public accounting, ocean transportation, electric and gas utilities. Major strengths include:

- Investment Analysis
- Banking Relations
- Negotiations
- Employee Benefit Plans
- Accounting and Taxes
- Planning

EXPERIENCE

1975–1987   Company Name

TREASURER

Responsible for cash management for all affiliated companies in the Industries family, banking relations, stockholder records and transfers, taxes, insurance, employee benefit plans, assisting long-term financings, and legislative activities. Major accomplishments include:

- Evaluated, recommended and purchased a $50 million preferred stock portfolio with leverage, yielding an after tax return of over 20% per year. Realized capital gains of over $3.5 million in two years.
- Planned, implemented and administered ESOP and 401(K) plans with investments over $20 million.
- Prepared and testified against a flow-through witness hired by the Federal government and won the continued use of normalization accounting in rate-making, preserving over $20 million in annual revenue.
- Achieved up grading of company's commercial paper rating from A2 to A1 by Standard and Poors.

19XX   Company Name

TREASURER AND ASSISTANT SECRETARY   1971–1975

Responsible for financing, cash management, taxes, budgets and forecasts, financial analysis and financial reporting. Major accomplishments include:

- Negotiated and secured seven-year term loans with major banks for $50 million, with interest caps, resulting in savings over half a million dollars.
- Developed, presented and obtained approval from Public Utilities Commission to increase depreciation rates, paving the way for rate increases of $3.2 million per year.

ASSISTANT TREASURER, MANAGER OF FINANCE
SERVICES AND TAX SERVICES   1969–1971

Responsible for financing, taxes, financial reporting, and credit and collections. Major accomplishments include:

- Arranged short-term borrowing's of $90 million using master trust notes.
- Worked with two major utilities and successfully implemented financial forecasting utilizing time sharing computer systems.

- Negotiated with government agencies in property tax valuation, resulting in substantial savings.
- Arranged lines of credit totaling $125 million.

MANAGER, TAX SERVICES   1967–1969

Responsible for taxes and pension fund matters involving actuarial valuations and IRS approvals. Major accomplishment includes:

- Negotiated and settled with IRS on investment tax credits and other issues, to the company's satisfaction and benefit.

SUPERVISOR, TAX ACCOUNTING   1959–1967
STAFF CONSULTANT   1958–1959

Responsible for tax administration.

1955–1958   Company Name

SENIOR IN-CHARGE ACCOUNTANT

Within 3 years promoted from Junior Accountant to Senior In-Charge Accountant. Responsible for audits and the preparation of tax returns. In charge of audits of UCLA, GM Chevrolet Div. (Van Nuys), finance companies, building materials, manufacturing companies, etc.

1952–1955

Completed MBA work at UCLA. Served as Teaching Assistant in accounting and statistics.

1949–1952   Company Name

SPECIAL FINANCIAL OFFICER & EXECUTIVE ASSISTANT

Reported to Manager of Finance with responsibilities for cost accounting, foreign exchange and budgets.

- Joined company as junior accountant, in two months became full accountant, and executive assistant one month later.
- Presentation of budgets to Ministry of Transportation.
- Accomplished foreign exchange transfers between sterling and dollar blocs.

1943–1949   Company Name

ASSISTANT MANAGER   1945–1949
CHIEF ACCOUNTANT   1943–1945

Reported to the President with responsibilities in loan administration and accounting. Major accomplishments include:

- Prepared and presented the banks review to the Comptroller Of Currency which passed.
- Set up and managed a small department to handle clearing for all member brokerage firms of the Shanghai Stock Exchange.

EDUCATION

B.S. in Civil Engineering, St. Johns University, Shanghai, China, 1943
MBA, UCLA, Westwood, California, 1955
Attended over 40 seminars and workshops in various financial and management areas, from 1974–1987 to stay current with financial knowledge and management skills.

PROFESSIONAL AFFILIATIONS

CPA, California, 1958 to present, Arizona, 1958–1975, Hawaii, 1976 to present.
Past member, California and Arizona Society of CPA's.
Member, American Institute of CPA's, 1958 to present.
Member, Hawaii Society of CPA's, 1976 to present.
AGA-EEI Taxation Committee, 1962 to 1975. (AGA Chairman 1969–1970)
EEI Finance Committee, 1978–1987
Financial Executives Institute, 1980 to present (Board member, Hawaii Chapter 1987)
Tax Foundation of Hawaii, Trustee, 1976–1987 (President 1984–1985)

OTHER AFFILIATIONS

Board Member and Treasurer—Salvation Army, American Cancer Society, Maricopa County of Retarded Children.
Board Member—Better Business Bureau, Friends of East West Center.
Member, Chamber of Commerce Taxation Committee.
Member, Rotary Club of Waikiki (past Board Member and Chairman of International Services).

OUTSIDE INTERESTS

Tennis, Swimming and Hiking

LANGUAGES

Chinese (Mandarin and Shanghai), English.

Figure 41   Resume 6: Summary Needs Some Improvement

Name   Private: (602) XXX-XXXX
Scottsdale, Arizona 85260   Business: (602) XXX-XXXX

SUMMARY OF QUALIFICATIONS

Executive with more than 20 years successful experience in all phases of management
including Operations, Engineering, Product Development, Sales, Marketing, and Service
with major companies manufacturing electronic and electro-mechanical products.

EXPERIENCE

Company Name   1975 to Present

Leading worldwide manufacturer of micro-processor based electronics weighing products
for industrial and commercial applications.

Vice President & General Manager—Scale Division—Arizona   1983 to Present

Responsibilities including Manufacturing, Sales, Marketing, Product Development, Quality
Assurance, Purchasing, Manufacturing Engineering, Human Resources, and Accounting.
Division was in a transition from R&D to marketing-driven emphasis.

- Increased sales by 30%. Instrumental in obtaining the largest OEM contract ever
  awarded the Division.
- Improved the product reliability by 25%.
- Reduced division financial loss.
- Reorganized departments to gain greater efficiencies.
- Established New Product Release Procedure and Engineering Docket Review for
  improved financial, schedule, and information control.

Vice President of Operations—_____—Arizona   1981 to 1983

Requested by President to take charge of new plant and product line. Hired and developed
new management team. Department responsibility included Manufacturing, Production
Control, Quality Assurance, Purchasing, Manufacturing Engineering, Human Resources and
Accounting.

- Adapted automation and robotics to the production process.
- Implemented numerous manufacturing computerized systems for control and
  measurement.
- Improved output by 50% while reducing staff by 12%.
- Reduced cost of numerous products by 25%; implemented cost accounting system.
- Implemented MBO program for all management positions.
- Increased overall plant quality level by approximately 30%.

Vice President of Operations—Process Control Division—New Jersey   1975 to 1981

Progressively promoted from Manufacturing Manager & Operations Manager. The
Department responsibilities included Manufacturing, Project Engineering and Design, Quality
Assurance, Production Control, Purchasing, Human Resources and Plant Accounting.

- Increased output by 375% with 54% increase in employees.
- Increased Project Engineering output by 60% through use of standards and better
  scheduling techniques.

132

- Profits increased from a loss to a 19% pre-tax profit. Return on assets 40%.
- Inventory turns reached 9 times based on selling price.
- Established an effective Quality Assurance Organization.
- Reduced project order turn around time by 50%.
- Developed and implemented computerized inventory, production, and cost systems.

Company Name—New Jersey   1974 to 1975

Manufactured and service computer peripheral devices

Manager, Logistics and Production Control

Responsible for setting up main logistics and refurbishment depot for nationwide service company. Had total budget responsibility for facility.

- Administered installation of real-time computerized control & ordering system.
- Reduced total spares inventory investment by 25% while improving service response time.
- Hired nine remote inventory depot coordinators who reported to the main logistics facility.
- Set-up three refurbishment facilities which reduced cost by 30% over previous expense incurred from production plants.

Company Name—New Jersey   1967 to 1974

Satellite Systems and Subsystems

Manager of Production Services

Progressively promoted to this position responsible for Production, Material Planning and Control utilizing an MRP System.

- Implemented a computerized fabrication scheduling and manloading system.
- Set-up Manufacturing Test Department by transferring work formerly done by Design Engineering. Group grew from 12 to 86 technical employees.
- Improved schedule performance by 50% and reduced cost by 30% on a major classified project.
- Assigned to three major projects as Manager of Manufacturing Projects.

Company Name—New Jersey   1964 to 1967

District Engineer, New Brunswick Gas Distribution District

Supervised staff of 59 employees consisting of various levels of field customer service personnel. Performed engineering design for large commercial and industrial metering stations.

EDUCATION

MBA—Drexel University, Philadelphia, Pennsylvania, 1971. 3.7 GPA.
BS—Commerce and Engineering, Drexel University, 1964. Top 20% of class.
Participated in Cooperative Program.

AFFILIATIONS

Vice Chairman of Management Institute—Glassboro State College
Member of South Jersey and Scottsdale Chambers of Commerce
Member of Kiwanis International
Member of American Electronics Association

Figure 42   Resume 7: Power Resume with
Well-Placed Bullets and Highlights

Name   Office: (XXX) XXX-XXXX
Address   Home: (XXX) XXX-XXXX
Simi Valley, CA 93065

Summary

Over 17 years experience in outside sales and zone sales management. Expert in establishing and developing a dealer sales network by using strategic zone planning, sales projecting, financial consulting, sales training, promotional and advertising assistance. Sales transactions ranged from $500 to $500,000 per transaction, with total zone sales of $5 million per year.

Experience

1973–1988   Company Name

Dealer Development Manager—Los Angeles Zone   1988

Responsible for sales of two lines of outboard products and accessories, working exclusively with existing dealers within six counties including Los Angeles.

- Initiated new market policy which resulted in both lines complementing each other in the market place, resulting in stronger and more strategically placed dealers.

Zone Sales Manager—Los Angeles Zone   1986–1988

Responsible for sales of outboard products and accessories to all dealers in zone along with expanding dealer network.

- Through strategic zone planning and financial consulting, increased dealership network by 20% over a one year period.
- Achieved 116% of yearly sales quota, along with winning the top monthly national sales award for the country.

Zone Sales Manager—Dakotas and Surrounding Area   1974–1986

Responsible for sales of outboard products and accessories in North Dakota/South Dakota and portions of Montana, Wyoming and Minnesota, along with expanding dealer network.

- Strengthened dealer network by adding new dealers where needed.
- By sales presentations, training, and promotional and advertising assistance, increased dealer's unit sales by an average of 21% per year.
- Identified and implemented plans which increased sales from 750 units to 2,000, a 267% increase.
- Developed seven major trade areas into the highest market penetrations in the country, from approximately 20% to 34%.
- Awarded "top" national honors for outstanding sales.
- Winner of six monthly national sales awards.
- Awarded trip to world series games by Mercury Marine and Sports Illustrated for winning sales product presentation contest.

Entry Level Sales Training Position—Los Angeles   **1973–1974**

- Completed training to be a zone sales manager.
- Assisted dealers in conducting sales promotions.
- Won branch contest for designing and building an accessory display which doubled sales for a local dealer.

1971–1973   Company Name

Outside Salesman   **1971–1973**

Responsible for outside sales of industrial air filters in Los Angeles area.

- Increased clientele base from an existing 20 businesses to 150, ranging from body shops to high rise buildings and hospitals.

Education

B.S. Business (Marketing) 1971, California State University Northridge

Personal

Married. Active in tennis, swimming, boating and chess.

Figure 43   Resume 8: Resume That Needs Material Taken Out

Name

Objective: Executive position in a mid- to large-sized progressive healthcare
                    organization located in a highly competitive market.

PROFESSIONAL EXPERIENCE—HOSPITAL:

1977   Hospital Name
to
Present   SENIOR VICE PRESIDENT—OPERATIONS, 1984 to Present

- Directed operations of hospital centers: 3 separate facilities, 530 beds.
  Operating budget $82MM, 1500 FTEs.
- Implemented productivity standards, performance measures, financial
  objectives and control systems; reduced operating costs 7%.
- Developed physician recruitment program and negotiated contracts
  for all hospital-based physicians.
- Planned and implemented new programs that generated $6.3MM in
  additional annual revenue.
- Developed strategic plans for 5 "Centers of Excellence."

SENIOR VICE PRESIDENT—ADMINISTRATIVE SERVICES, 1981–1984

- Directed 25 support and clinical departments; operating budget
  $29.5MM, 650 FTEs.
- Directed the Prospective Payment System (PPS) Task Force, identified
  financial impact of PPS and developed utilization management
  functions.
- Developed Quality Management and Legal Affairs Departments.
  Reduced IBNR incidents by 50%, lowered malpractice premiums by
  $1MM and decreased the settlement to reserve ratio by 50%.
- Reduced incomplete medical records to 400, implemented master
  patient index and unit record system.
- Directed $11MM renovation program.

ASSISTANT ADMINISTRATOR, 1979–1981

- Directed 10 support departments; operating budget $6.5MM, 303
  FTEs.
- Reorganized material management function, decreased staffing,
  centralized stores, increased inventory turnover, improved access to
  supplies and eliminated lost charges.
- Replaced all major financial information systems and implemented a
  clinical information system covering 8 separate sites with a
  300-terminal network.

ADMINISTRATIVE ASSISTANT, 1978–1979

- Directed 6 support departments; operating budget $3.8MM, 173 FTEs.
- Prepared cost/benefit analysis, directed site selection, negotiated contracts and directed construction of 4 primary care satellites; increased market penetration by 35%.

ADMINISTRATIVE RESIDENT, 1977–1978

Directed hospital planning function.

1975
to
1976

Hospital Name

SURGEON'S ASSISTANT/INSTRUCTOR

Assisted on surgical cases and instructed residents.

1972
to
1975

Hospital Name

OPERATING ROOM TECHNICIAN

Served as second assistant, scrub or circulator.

PROFESSIONAL EXPERIENCE—OTHER:

1983
to
1986

Company Name

PRESIDENT

Established data processing consultation and software firm and secured 3 contracts to develop new products.

EDUCATION: MHA, 1970, Hospital Administration, Xavier University, Cincinnati, OH
MA, 1972, History, University of Cincinnati, Cincinnati, OH
BA, 1968, History, University of Cincinnati, Cincinnati, OH

PROFESSIONAL American College of Healthcare Executives, Member
AFFILIATIONS: Healthcare Financial Management Association
Hospital Management Systems Society
American Society of Law and Medicine
Michigan Society of Gerontology

PROFESSIONAL Comprehensive Health Planning Council of Southeast Michigan
SERVICE: Greater Detroit Area Health Council, Research Committee
Michigan Hospital Association, Data Management Committee
Hospital Material Management Quarterly, Editorial Board

time will he take off to start his own business if he is working for us?" That area did little to enhance the applicant's employment opportunities and was deleted.

In Resume 9 (Figure 44), the objective terminology is not specific. Senior executive position can mean a multitude of different things. A summary was needed and the objective was deleted. The summary read:

> Summary: Nearly 30 years experience as senior consultant and partner with expertise in areas ranging from administration of 300 plus member firm to handling all marketing and training activities for nationally-known consulting firm.

The schooling and military dates were deleted. Honorably discharged is sufficient.

A summary was needed in Resume 10 (Figure 45). It read:

> Summary: More than 20 years experience in managing, directing, and promoting medical related associations.

Although many of the bulleted items are well-done, several needed to be clarified. For example, there is a section where the candidate "redesigned financial Chart of Accounts." What kind of positive effect did this have? Did it improve cash flow? If so, how much?

The related experience is not necessary and one of them (1952–1962) certainly dates the candidate as someone who might be in his sixties. If so, there will be many companies that will shy away from interviews. These dates (as well as those pertaining to education) were removed.

Resume 11 (Figure 46) is an excellent engineering resume that needs a summary. The objective does little to enhance the candidate and was removed. The way it was worded would pinpoint the industry and limit the applicant's options. The summary read:

> Summary: More than 20 years of increasingly responsible positions as superintendent, project engineer, and general manager.

The bulleted items are all specific and to the point.

Resume 12 (Figure 47) became a power resume with the help of a few additions. Use of acronyms (i.e., IPO candidates) could confuse those in the human resource department and were spelled out.

In Resume 13 (Figure 48), the objective—as many are—is too broad. It was replaced by a summary:

> Summary: More than 20 years experience as financial analyst, financial manager, and in information systems for small and medium-sized organizations.

Figure 44   Resume 9: Resume with an Objective That Is Not Specific

Name

OBJECTIVE: Senior Executive position or consulting partner.

EXPERIENCE:

1981 to   Company Name
Present

CHIEF ADMINISTRATIVE OFFICER
- Directed all administrative activities of 300 attorneys and 350 support personnel in five offices during a period when the firm doubled in size.
- Implemented a system to recover the costs of certain services for clients; system now contributes more than 25% of the firm's profits annually.
- Implemented a comprehensive, but affordable, management information system incorporating all five offices on one computer network.
- Developed and implemented a profit planning program which has materially improved the firm's cash flow and profitability.
- Analyzed the firm's cash flow and annually negotiated a line of credit of up to $12MM.
- Recruited, trained and developed a strong 15-person management team.

1963–1981   Company Name

PARTNER IN CHARGE OF CONSULTING, 1977–1981

- Responsible for managing the practice, marketing, training consultants and quality control of all projects.
- Increased profits by more than 200% and revived a troubled consulting practice.
- Implemented a multi-million dollar Profit Improvement Program for a consumer product company.
- Implemented a Profit Management Program for a heavy machinery manufacturing company; reduced costs by 10%.
- Developed a program in Cyprus to return three major businesses to profitability after years of loss.
- Analyzed the managerial efficiency of a major public utility controlled by the City of Cleveland.
- Directed numerous computer system implementations.

PARTNER IN CHARGE OF CONSULTING, 1969–1976

- Developed a profitable consulting practice and an effective consulting staff. Responsible for marketing services, recruiting personnel, training consultants and managing projects.
- Installed a sophisticated computerized production and inventory system for a Fortune 500 company.

139

- Directed a twenty-consultant project funded for two years by the World Bank to improve the business climate of a province in South Korea.
- Directed several strategic planning programs for profit improvement and long-term growth.
- Directed numerous data processing and financial projects for hospitals.
- Negotiated several mergers and acquisitions for clients.
- Implemented accounting and profit planning systems.

DIRECTOR OF FINANCIAL CONSULTING, 1963–1969

- Managed a multi-plant company and a multi-product manufacturing plant for clients; made them both profitable.
- Implemented an extensive profit planning system for a large company; increased profitability.
- Implemented comprehensive financial systems.

1958–1963	Company Name

SENIOR FINANCIAL ANALYST

Responsible for strategic planning, profit management and pricing strategy for the headquarters of the largest automotive division.

EDUCATION:	MBA, 1958, Finance, University of Wisconsin, Madison, Wisconsin BBA, 1957, Finance, University of Wisconsin, Madison, Wisconsin With honors. Cotterman Fellowship Grant.
MILITARY:	United States Marine Corps, 1st Marine Division, Captain, 1955
PERSONAL:	Married, three children. Excellent health.

Figure 45   Resume 10: Resume That Needed a Summary

Name

OBJECTIVE: Staff leadership/management position in an association or research-oriented company.

EXPERIENCE   Company Name

1984 to   SCIENTIST/MEDICAL COMMUNICATIONS
Present   Developed science policy for Board of Trustees and House of Delegates.
- Introduced teleconferencing to reduce expert panel costs by factor of 10.
- Researched and wrote major policy document on drunk driving.
- Streamlined selection process for expert panels.
- Staffed panel and wrote report on medical applications of lasers.
- Instituted quality control for all medical communications.

1981–1984   Company Name

EXECUTIVE DIRECTOR

Chief Operating Officer of 50,000-member professional association with $6.5MM annual budget and $1.5MM annual trade show, public and professional education programs.

- Reorganized and reduced staff from 108 to 88.
- Reorganized wage/salary and benefits schedules.
- Introduced and implemented zero-base budgeting.
- Redesigned financial Chart of Accounts.
- Organized legislative/public policy program.
- Reorganized House of Delegates procedures.
- Instituted Marketing Division to generate non-dues revenue.

1964–1981   Company Name

DIRECTOR, DIVISION OF CONTINUING MEDICAL STUDIES, 1973–1981

Created 2,500-hour annual continuing education program, administered $3MM budget, staff of 15, and committees of volunteers.

- Conceptualized and directed hotel and resort-based seminars.
- Conceptualized and produced live courses via communications satellite and Video Clinic Courses on videocassettes.
- Experimented with interactive courses on computer-interfaced laser disc.

DIRECTOR, SECTION ON FOOD SCIENCE, 1968–1973

Identified research with promising applications, analyzed impending federal legislation and regulation, developed teaching programs.

- Initiated and implemented new research society in total parenteral nutrition; society grew from zero to 3000 members in 3 years.

- Worked in South America with USAID on programs to combat malnutrition.
- Staffed Advisory Committee representing U.S. food industry on health matters.
- Conceptualized and produced television programming for 3 international nutrition conferences.

PUBLIC AND PRESS RELATIONS, 1964–1968

Maintained relations with national press, ran press room for large scientific conventions, worked with U.S. State Department in Viet Nam.

- Recruited U.S. physicians for volunteer duty in Viet Nam.
- Wrote report to White House on civilian medical needs in Viet Nam.

RELATED EXPERIENCE:

1962–1964   MODERN MEDICINE PUBLICATIONS, Minneapolis, Minnesota

EDITOR of "Surgery and Immunology."

1952–1962   OMAHA WORLD-HERALD, Omaha, Nebraska

MANAGING EDITOR, Sunday Editions
350,000 circulation metropolitan newspaper with staff of 85. Rose to managerial position from reporter/photographer.

EDUCATION: BSC, 1952, Writing, University of Omaha, Omaha, Nebraska
Diploma, 1963, Medical Writing, University of Minnesota, Minneapolis

BOOKS: Resuscitation After Myocardial Infarction, 1965
Treatment of Multiple Personality Disorder, 1986

TELEVISION PROGRAMS:

"Malnutrition in the United States," 1969
"South American Poetry for North Americans," 1971

MEMBERSHIPS: Chicago Society of Association Executives
Case-Study Writing Group, CSAE—DePaul University
Professional Convention Management Association
American Medical Writers Association
American Association for Advancement of Science

142

Figure 46   Resume 11: Resume That Needed a Summary

Name

OBJECTIVE: Management position within electric power generation or process industry.

EXPERIENCE:

1964 to
Present

Company Name

DIRECTOR OF TECHNICAL SERVICES, 1986 to Present

- Instituted annual problem-solving goals and rigorous technical analysis techniques; annual savings greater than $250K.
- Chairman, Karn 4 Task Force. Solved 10-year operating problems and increased turbine availability by 15%.
- Instituted departmental training plan based upon service requirements thereby optimizing training efficiency.
- Established annual goals to reduce costs through the displacement of contracted activities with company employees; estimated total 1986 savings $900K.

DIRECTOR OF FIELD MAINTENANCE SERVICES, 1984–1986

- Supervised department of 225 employees performing major maintenance work at all Consumer's fossil and nuclear plants; annual department budget of $10MM.
- Modified structure and accountability of department. Management consultant audit reported significant increases in productivity, accountability and work continuity.
- Assembled, justified and implemented a plan to accept approximately 60 employees into the department at the construction halt of the Midland Nuclear Plant. This activity provided lower cost services for the corporation and preserved jobs for employees.

GENERATING PLANT SUPERINTENDENT, 1977–1984

- Supervised 787 MW electric generating plant during design, startup and commercial operation phases. Plant employed 175 people with $10MM annual budget and rated 4th nationally in thermal efficiency; high availability was recognized for merit by General Electric.
- Selected as Chairman of the "Cost of Quality Task Force" within the Energy Supply Department. The quality improvement measurement and corrective action system developed involved approximately 55 separate departments and 4,500 employees.
- Instituted corrective action system and rigorous technical analysis to resolve root causes of plant problems.
- Assigned to lead "Campbell Complex Energy Issues Team." Provided public utility issue information to general public. Task included training employees in public speaking and organizing a voter information team. Effort resulted in highest percentage of employee participation within Consumers Power Company.

- Organized department startup team employing several innovative activities to insure design, spare parts, and problem-free startup and operations; resulted in most successful plant startup in 22 years.
- Selected as Consumers Power Company's representative to EPRI Project CS-3745, Human Factors Design Guidelines for Fossil Plants. Guidelines are presently in use throughout United States.
- Appointed Chairman of staffing project to develop and implement coordinated staffing plan for 2 new and 7 operating plants in conjunction with the retirement of 2 plants.

MAINTENANCE SUPERINTENDENT, 1972–1977

- Supervised a maintenance department of 55 people with $4MM budget.
- Organized and controlled first large scale fossil unit outage within the company to employ detail planning, estimating, network diagrams and real time cost accounting control mechanisms. The system is presently in use in same general format in all plants.
- Working with consultant, developed and implemented the first short interval maintenance scheduling system within Energy Supply Department. This system would also be adopted by all major generating plants within company. System increased maintenance productivity a minimum of 30%.
- Organized and implemented first full-scheduled maintenance program within company. The task included staffing and training new employees and their supervisors within a period of 90 days.

ENGINEER (VARIOUS GRADES), 1967–1972

- Working as a Project Engineer with design engineers and contractors, implemented major projects for the plant: boiler and economizer element replacement, Service Water Recovery System (environmental) and plant makeup air system.

ENGINEERING TRAINEE, 1964–1967

EDUCATION: BS, 1964, Mechanical Engineering, University of Illinois
               Champaign, Illinois

Figure 47   Resume 12: Avoid Use of Acronyms

T. _____

SUMMARY: Over 8 years experience encompassing financial analysis, strategic planning, mergers and acquisitions, financial consulting, transaction structuring, equipment leasing, and marketing of financial products and services. Transactions ranged from $100 thousand to $150 million, primarily for Fortune 500 companies and financial institutions.

EXPERIENCE:

6/85 to Present   _____ SECURITIES INC., Chicago, Illinois

Senior Associate

- Supervise an associate and two analysts, administer office and increased revenues through P/L management.
- Structured a joint-venture opportunity between the leasing group and a merchant bank, created a $20 million private placement opportunity and uncovered several IPO candidates.

2/84–5/85   _____ CORP., Schaumburg, Illinois

General Manager and Vice President

- Directed the newly formed unit with a staff of 15, generating income of $600,000 + in 1984, primarily through lease brokering.
- Structured transactions for leasing subsidiaries so their tax benefits, generated through normal operations, could be sold.
- Developed client relationships with major regional banks and Fortune 500 companies, which resulted in $380 million of committed transactions for 1985.
- Persuaded Borg-Warner units to use our services; resulted in a $14 million volume in 1984, and a $20 million backlog for 1985.
- Directed a major real estate client in entering into a $400 million joint venture with a national development company.
- Developed short-term, collateralized, tax-exempt notes for investment by pension funds and bank trust departments.

7/83–2/84   _____ Schaumburg, Illinois

Director of Finance

- Developed and organized an in-house investment banking group.
- Worked with the Commercial Finance group developing a three-year, strategic plan to double volume and achieve a 30% ROE.
- Formed relationships between the Commercial Finance group and the banking community to induce loan participations.

11/80–7/83   _____ ACCEPTANCE CORPORATION, Chicago, Illinois

Assistant to the Treasurer

- Supervised staff in managing worldwide debt programs.
- Negotiated or assisted in the negotiations of more than $300 million of medium and long-term debt issues.
- Aggressively managed $1.2 billion commercial paper portfolio by setting rates and maturity, thereby lowering the effective cost.
- Set-up a Eurodollar arbitrage program generating $100 thousand annually.
- Was responsible for capital budgeting, forecasting, fixed asset acquisition, lease vs. buy, and competitor analyses, consulting and financial product development for line units.

6/78–11/80   _____ INTERNATIONAL, INC., Prospect Heights, Illinois

Financial Analyst

- Assisted in financial investigations and analyses preliminary to mergers or acquisitions, performed various other financial analyses.
- Helped in the development of financial time-sharing and automated subsidiary financials.

11/72–6/78   _____ COMPANY, Deerfield, Illinois

Store Analyst, 6/76–6/78

- Performed site location and gross profit analyses on proposed units return on investment and market penetration reports.

Distribution Coordinator/P.D.Q. Supervisor, 11/72–6/76

- Positions held while attending school.

EDUCATION: M.B.A., 1981, Accounting, DePaul University, Chicago, IL
B.S., 1976, Finance & Marketing, University of Illinois, Chicago, IL

PROFESSIONAL ORGANIZATIONS:

International Association of Business and Financial Consultants
National Association of Securities Dealers - Registered Representative

PERSONAL: Single, excellent health
Junior Governing Board of the Chicago Symphony, Member

Name

OBJECTIVE: A senior-level management position in a financial or general management
capacity with an established medium or large organization.

EXPERIENCE:

1981 to   <u>Company Name</u>
Present
<u>DIRECTOR, ECONOMIC ANALYSIS</u>, 1985 to present

- Developed, as part of a rate agreement, an effective reporting
  mechanism agreeable to the company's largest customer, the
  northwest Indiana steel industry, regarding utility operating
  performance.
- Analyzed and recommended courses of action to the Chief Financial
  Officer relative to possible under-valued assets and how to improve
  their performance.
- Analyzed and monitored those factors of the steel industry impacting
  NIPSCO operations.

<u>DIRECTOR, INFORMATION SERVICES</u>, 1981–1985

- Reporting to Chief Operating Officer, led 140-person computer
  operations and application department with $23MM annual budget.
- Obtained the commitment to increased devotion of resources and
  instituted prioritization process to demonstrate progress on existing
  large backlog of outstanding projects.
- Saved $3–$4MM annually in computer hardware expenditures.
- Instituted long- and short-range planning into computer environment.
- Installed professional management structure and philosophy into
  technocracy.

1965–1981   <u>Company Name</u>

<u>FINANCIAL CONSULTANT, CONTROLLER'S STAFF</u>, 1972–1981

Directed staff of analysts who performed studies and developed
recommendations to marketing and manufacturing management in the
areas of:

—pricing
—manufacturing practices and cost
—product profitability
—selling costs
—customer profitability

ASSISTANT MANAGER, INDUSTRIAL DEVELOPMENT (INRYCO),
1970–1971

Project responsibility for 2 industrial real estate developments including construction and project financing at the Milwaukee subsidiary of Inland Steel.

FINANCIAL ANALYST, STAFF OF FINANCIAL VICE PRESIDENT,
1965–1970

- Capital expenditure analysis (primarily raw material) and acquisition studies.
- Cost and simulation analysis of steel industry collective bargaining.
- Steel industry comparative financial analysis of performance.
- Preparation of corporate profit plan and administration of General Office Budget.

EDUCATION: MBA, 1962, Finance, Columbia University, New York, New York
AB, 1960, Economics, Cornell University, Ithaca, New York

MILITARY: Lieutenant, United States Naval Reserve, 1962–1965

AFFILIATIONS: Rotary Clubs International
"Who's Who in the Midwest"
Cornell and Columbia Clubs of Chicago

PERSONAL: Married, three children. Excellent health.

Several of the bulleted items were also made more specific. Notice that some (Instituted long- and short-range planning into computer environment) do not give any specific results. These were all revised. Education and military dates were deleted.

Resume 14 (Figure 49) is an excellent resume but a summary is missing. This candidate was going after a CEO position—and he landed one. His summary was written and read:

Summary: More than 25 years line and staff management experience including 16 years as CEO of $56 million subsidiary of major corporation.

Resume 15 (Figure 50) belonged to a talented, marketing oriented CEO with more than 20 years experience in his industry. A summary was called for (and inserted) and the education was placed at the end of the resume. As a rule, education should never lead off a resume unless the position being applied for is in the educational field.

The applicant who sent out Resume 16 (Figure 51) has extensive legal background but there was no summary to let prospective employers know. The resume was revised with a summary that indicated the applicant had more than a decade of legal experience in the medical field and with medical associations:

Summary: Fourteen years of experience as attorney and legal advisor/counsel for medical associations

Although the bulleted accomplishments related to the legal and medical field, they are written in everyday English so that anyone (human resource director, assistant, etc.) can understand the qualifications of this candidate.

In Resume 17 (Figure 52), the objective did nothing to enhance this candidate's resume. Once again, a summary had to be written to reflect the applicant's experience, not his objectives.

Summary: Fifteen years experience in market research and brand management for leading consumer product companies in country.

The educational dates, although not that old, did nothing to enhance the candidate's resume and were removed.

A sales management candidate put together Resume 18 (Figure 53), a perfect power resume with a concise summary and specific, bulleted accomplishments. Although he had several solid leads, he answered a half-dozen blind ads with this resume and a cover letter, and ended up with two job offers.

Figure 49 Resume 14: Excellent Resume Needing a Summary

Name

OBJECTIVE: Senior general management position with P&L responsibilities.

EXPERIENCE:

1987 to
Present

Company Name (Division of _____ Group Inc.)

EXECUTIVE VICE PRESIDENT

- Selected by corporate management to be successor for president of this $60MM, 4-facility division.
- Identified sales and marketing strategies for growth.
- Developed strategy to improve productivity and reduce inventory and manufacturing lead times.

1971–1987

Company Name

PRESIDENT, METAL PRODUCTS GROUP, 1979–1987

- Led organization from marginal profitability to most profitable in corporation (52% ROI) in 5 years.
- Directed growth from $12MM sales in 1979 to $56MM in 1984.
- Quadrupled plant output without substantially changing facilities or personnel; from $1MM/month to $1MM/week.
- Converted operations of 4 plants from "Job Shop" to "Just in Time."
- Implemented Manufacturing Requirements Planning Systems (MRPII).
- Implemented Total Quality Systems (Phil Crosby Program, SPC, Quality Circles).
- Introduced robotic manufacturing operations.
- Implemented computer-aided design and engineering systems.
- Reduced plant turnover from 320% to 24% in 2 years.
- Nullified 2 union campaigns.
- Replaced seniority system with employee rating system.
- Negotiated and directed acquisition of metal fabricating company.
- Negotiated and directed acquisition of store fixture product line and marketing rights.

TREASURER AND ASSISTANT TO PRESIDENT, 1976–1979

- Advised on capital investments and acquisitions.
- Conducted collection and disbursement studies to improve float and collections.
- Converted group medical insurance to self-insurance.
- Consulted on technical and operational problems.
- Conducted marketing studies for new products.

150

GENERAL MANAGER, 1972–1976

- Directed 2-plant, US/Mexico border operation manufacturing electronic components.
- Expanded both Mexico and US operations by 64%; moving from loss to profit.

DIRECTOR OF CORPORATE PLANNING, 1971–1972

- Performed investment and acquisition studies.
- Served as internal consultant.
- Handled public relations with security analysts.

1968–1970   Company Name, Division of Management Corporation

CONSULTANT

Consulted for a variety of companies and projects including indirect employee productivity, production scheduling, and inventory and production control.

1961–1968   Company Name

SALES ENGINEER, 1965–1968

Responsible for industrial sales of semiconductor products.

FIELD SERVICE ENGINEER, 1963–1965

Served as technical representative for radio products to customers, assembly plants and dealers.

EDUCATION: MS, 1971, Industrial Administration, Purdue University
    West Lafayette, Indiana
BS, 1961, Industrial Engineering, Purdue University
    West Lafayette, Indiana

Figure 50   Resume 15: Resume with Education Moved to the End

Name

PROFESSIONAL EXPERIENCE:

1983 to
March, 1985

Company Name

Company Name is a $650 million corporation with 2,600 employees.
Primary product is orange juice, although a broad line of citrus products
are sourced, processed and marketed. Marketing budget exceeds $100
million. Vertical integration includes packaging (glass and plastic plants
and a corrugation facility) and distribution (trucks and railcars).

PRESIDENT, 1984–1985

- Direct responsibility over purchasing, manufacturing, processing,
  distribution, finance, R&D, MIS, marketing and sales.
- Developed a three-year strategic plan to focus direction for growth
  and profitability in a highly competitive citrus industry. Primary
  industry issues related to _____ new category entry,
  _____ coupled with supply and pricing/margin issues as
  a result of freezes.
- Restructured organization commensurate with newly developed
  strategic goals and objectives. Recruited key personnel in marketing,
  sales and R&D. Reformulated product line and redesigned package
  graphics to overcome inferior competitive position.
- Managed balance sheet to enhance return. Revised salary/bonus
  program. Initiated productivity improvements generating $3.1 million in
  annual savings. Achieved volume and profit goals while accomplishing
  national share gain.

SENIOR VICE PRESIDENT, MARKETING/SALES, 1983–1984

- Upgraded sales force and broker network to improve quality/
  productivity. Developed tactical marketing programs to achieve
  stated goals. Initiated and completed selection process of a new
  advertising agency and introduced a new creative campaign.

1970 to
1983

Company Name

SENIOR VICE PRESIDENT, MARKETING, 1982–1983

The Company Name, a $250 million division, ranked second to Gallo in
industry sales, was composed of wineries in New York and California,
and had trademarks which included Taylor, Great Western, Taylor
California Cellers, Monterey and Sterling.

- Modified strategic plan based on redefined goals. Marketing orientation
  redefined to maximize profit and share in a rapidly changing industry.
  Introduced Vivante, a new, economy-priced wine. Developed an import
  strategy and plan.

SENIOR VICE PRESIDENT, MARKETING OPERATIONS, 1980–1982

VICE PRESIDENT, CARBONATED MARKETING, 1976–1980

Company Name Japan is one of the largest international operations for the company. Market share exceeded 40% with a marketing budget in excess of $100 million. Total _____ system exceeded 25,000 people.

- Developed strategic plans to maximize growth and profitability; process resulted in strategic repositioning of _____ and _____ . Developed and modified annual business plans in a fast-paced, competitive environment.
- Developed, market-tested and expanded several new products/ packages: _____ potato chips; 5-Alive carbonated fruit drink; Real Goal, a high energy drink; and 300 and 500 milliliter one-way glass containers, the first to be mass-marketed in Japan. Of major importance and impact was the development and expansion of liter-size returnable bottles; additionally, developed and marketed a liter vending machine (50,000 units).

MANAGER, CORPORATE BUSINESS DEVELOPMENT, 1973–1975

- Coordinated worldwide plastic bottle activities.

PROGRAM MANAGER, 1972–1973

- Coordinated all activities for commercializing plastic bottles in U.S.: R&D, manufacturing procurement/coordination, contract negotiations, financial and sales forecast planning, and creative development. Program implemented into 25% of U.S. while being managed; volume and share goals attained.

MANAGER, NEW PRODUCTS DEPARTMENT, 1970–1972

- Developed and tested concept of a 10% carbonated fruit drink product.

1964 to 1969

Company Name

BRAND MANAGER, INSTANT PRODUCTS, 1968–1969

FIELD SALES, Baltimore, Raleigh, Atlanta, 1964–1968

EDUCATION:

M.B.A., University of North Carolina, _____
B.A., Duke University, _____

PERSONAL:

College Honors: Student Body Court of Appeals, "Who's Who in American Colleges and Universities," President of Junior Class, Football Scholarship, Dean's List

Age: 43   DOB: 1/18/42   Height: 6′   Weight: 180#
Married, two children. Excellent health.

Name

OBJECTIVE: Managing counsel responsible for planning and implementing litigation services or regulatory affairs in a corporate or association environment.

EXPERIENCE:

1981–1987   Company Name OFFICE OF Location

DIRECTOR OF MEDICOLEGAL AFFAIRS/ASSISTANT TO THE GENERAL COUNSEL

- Managed and conducted trial and appellate litigation of several nationally prominent, multi-million dollar damage suits.
  —Resolved six complex, class-based antitrust, civil rights and healthlaw suits without payment of damage awards or monetary settlements and without modification of challenged Association policies; concluded four such actions through litigated dismissals and summary judgments.
  —Recovered $250,000 settlement in insurance contract dispute following successful partial summary judgment action on key trial issues.
  —Worked closely with outside counsel to conduct all aspects of litigation, to control strategic planning and management of joint defenses in multi-defendant antitrust actions, to organize and administer joint defense funds and coordinated preparation of expert witnesses, and to draft *Amicus Curiae* briefs in healthcare/antitrust cases before the United States Supreme Court.
- Served as Staff Secretary and Counsel to AMA Council on Ethical and Judicial Affairs and Board of Trustees' Committee on Medicolegal Problems.
  —Planned, organized and managed National Conference on Medical Ethics in 1986 co-sponsored by AMA and Hastings Center for Biomedical Ethics.
  —Developed numerous published reports, studies, monographs and position statements on medical ethics and medicolegal/healthlaw issues establishing AMA policies relied on by courts and legislative or regulatory bodies.
- Managed division responsible for providing corporate staff support and legal counsel to senior management and AMA policymaking units on medicolegal, regulatory and constitutional issues affecting the medical profession.

1977–1981	Company Name

ASSOCIATE ATTORNEY

- Conducted litigation of complex, multi-party lawsuits and class actions encompassing all phases of discovery and depositions, motion practice, trials and appeals.
- Responsible for advising diverse group of corporate clients with respect to a broad range of antitrust, regulatory and corporate problems.

1975–1977	Company Name

STAFF ATTORNEY

Responsible for investigation, settlement and administrative litigation of antitrust and trade regulation matters.

PROFESSIONAL LICENSURE AND AFFILIATIONS:

Bar Admissions: Admitted to Indiana Bar, 1975, and Illinois Bar, 1977.
Admitted to practice before several United States Courts of Appeals and District Courts.

Organizations: American Bar Association: Sections on Litigation and Antitrust Law Past Member, Sherman Act Committee and Economics Committee, Monograph Project on Use of Economic Experts in Antitrust Litigation Chicago Bar Association

EDUCATION: Indiana University Law School   J.D., 1975
Bloomington, Indiana

Honors: Graduated Cum Laude
Officer, Phi Delta Phi; Phi Delta Phi Scholarship, 1974–75

Indiana State University   M.S., Economics, 1972
Terre Haute, Indiana

Honors: Graduated with High Honors
Graduate Teaching Assistant, Department of Economics, 1972

Purdue University   B.S., Economics, 1971
West Lafayette, Indiana

Honors: Graduated Cum Laude
Honors Program in Business and Managerial Economics, 1969–71
President's Academic Awards, 1969–71

PUBLICATIONS: Authored and edited contributions to "Law and Medicine" section of Journal of the American Medical Association; authored published reports, policy statements, studies and monographs. Reprints available on request.

Name

OBJECTIVE: Senior level position in a marketing organization.

EXPERIENCE:

1984 to   Company Name
Present
               DIRECTOR OF MARKETING RESEARCH

- Directed newly-formed department with a staff of 3 professionals and $2 MM budget; recruited department manager.
- Established testing standards/philosophy which led to identification of significant improvement in Tropicana orange juice.
- Designed multi-staged packaging research study which convinced Beatrice management to adapt new graphics.
- Identified and established in-house employee panel to screen product/package prototypes; annual savings of $100 thousand.
- Developed new product concept screen which identified several high potential candidates for R&D to develop.
- Initiated analysis of trade promotion spending.

1978–1984   Company Name

               MARKETING RESEARCH MANAGER, 1980–1984

- Managed 6 professionals and $3 MM budget in Personal Care area.
- Developed research programs that identified three successful new products for division (Soft Sense Hand & Body Lotion, Curel Hand & Body Lotion and Halsa Shampoo/Conditioner).
- Identified and formulated research components of new product development process to reduce risk of new product failures.
- Examined the validity of Assessor laboratory test market and recommended management-endorsed policy on use of technique.
- Identified need and acquired funds for diary panel data as means to gain strategic insights into hair care category.
- Developed advertising research policy for US consumer products; gained management approval of policy.
- Developed technique to effectively and efficiently differentiate new product winners and losers at the concept stage.
- Organized and administered audit of department productivity/research study accountability.

PROJECT MANAGER, 1978–1980

- Conducted advertising weight test on Johnson's most profitable brand. Identified significant risk in reducing spending levels.
- Identified reasons for failure of new scouring pad product which resulted in the company selling it to another firm.
- Assessed risk of competitive entry on the Pledge franchise which correctly identified no competitive response was necessary.

1976–1978   Company Name

BRAND RESEARCH MANAGER, 1977–1978

- Conducted strategic segmentation study utilizing conjoint analysis to determine needs and gaps in full-flavor cigarette market.
- Developed research programs that led to the successful introduction of Winston Long Lights.

ASSISTANT BRAND RESEARCH MANAGER, 1976–1977

- Analyzed image tracking of Winston vs. Marlboro which led to the development of a new advertising campaign.
- Conducted tests to improve Winston's flavor vis-a-vis Marlboro.

1974–1976   Company Name

ASSISTANT RESEARCH MANAGER, 1975–1976

- Identified improved Snackin' Cake formulation vs. Procter & Gamble's new entry through product testing.

MARKETING RESEARCH ASSISTANT, 1974–1975

- Conducted research which led to the introduction of Stir 'N Frost cake mix.

EDUCATION: MBA, 1974, Marketing, Michigan State University, East Lansing, MI
BS, 1972, Business Administration, University of Evansville, IN

PROFESSIONAL ACTIVITIES:

American Marketing Association, Member
  Speaker, Marketing Conference, 1983
  Chairperson, Strategic Planning Conference, 1985
Harvard Business School and DePaul University, Guest Lecturer

Figure 53   Resume 18: Excellent Power Resume

<u>RESUME</u>

Name:
Address:
Telephone:

<u>Summary of Qualifications:</u>   More than 14 years sales/sales management, finance and insurance experience in automotive and mobile home field.

Work Experience

Long Beach, July, 1982 to Present

*New Car Sales Manager. One of top 20 Buick dealers in U.S. for overall sales. Ranked #1 in sales in L.A. Zone in 1988. 96% rating in NVID (New Car Vehicle Delivery & Inspection). Direct set-up and display at Long Beach Auto Show each year. Trained all new sales personnel. Responsible for inventory control and sales of new car sales department. Appraised all trade-ins.
*Finance & Insurance Manager. Trained in F&I in a Ryan School. Developed and maintained dealer/lender relationships.
*Closer. Managed team of 5. Out of 4 teams, always #1 or #2.
*Salesman. New and used car. Always ranked in top 5 out of 20.

Homes, Lomita, June, 1980 to July, 1982

*Salesman for firm that sold 25–30 units, each valued at $30,000–$50,000, per month. Managed company's yearly display at Dodger Stadium's Annual Mobile Home Show.

Homes, Lomita, June, 1979 to June, 1980

*Sales Manager for firm that specialized in mobile home resales. Supervised staff of 5. Responsible for in-park purchases of existing mobile homes for resale. Created all print advertising. Responsible for opening/closing escrows.

Homes, Lomita, Feb., 1978, June, 1979

*Salesman for one of major developers of mobile home parks in South Bay. Sold homes within specified parks in addition to add-on accessories such as air conditioning. Assisted buyers in choosing colors, carpeting, awnings and other add-ons. Liaison with manufacturers, set-up and transportation companies.

Brokers, Lomita, Feb., 1976 to Feb., 1978

*Salesman for resale of mobile homes. Did appraisals of homes for banks and other lending institutions. Opened and closed escrows. Negotiated offers between buyers and sellers.

Oldsmobile, Torrance, Nov., 1975 to Feb., 1976

*Salesman. Number 1, 2, or 3 out of 20 during tenure. Sold new and used cars for one of high volume South Bay dealers. Volume more than 200 cars per month.

Market Basket Food Company, Torrance, June, 1969 to Oct., 1975
*Assistant grocery manager. Responsible for ordering, displays, gross sales in grocery dept. Opened, set-up new store (in Palmdale) for chain. Designed uniform displays and schematics which became format for all stores. Started as part-time box boy while in high school.

Education

El Camino College, majored in business _____
Torrance High School, graduate, _____.

Power resumes should never go over two pages and they can be as little as one. Take, for instance, Resume 19 (Figure 54). By reformulating, adding a summary, and bulleting the appropriate specific accomplishments, a mundane, two-page resume is turned into a potent power resume—Resume 20 (Figure 55).

Power resumes depend more upon language than length; substance over superfluousness; qualifications over generalizations. When these elements are combined, an everyday resume can suddenly become a potent sales tool and door opener.

THE FAB WORKSHEET

Management Recruiters International (MRI), one of the largest executive recruiting firms in the country, has put together a special "FAB" worksheet. FAB (Features/Accomplishments and Benefits) is what every company and hiring manager looks for when they examine a resume. MRI utilizes the worksheet in Figure 56 with applicants who are trying to put together a resume. It is divided into three sections.

The worksheet can be used by anyone trying to put together a resume. It eliminates much of the writing requirement and enables the applicant/resume creator to simply "fill in the blanks." Beneath "Features," the applicant fills in factual characteristics, attributes, or skills. Next to that is the "Benefits" column which lists the "value to the (previous) or present employer. The last column, "accomplishments," is a supportive statement based upon past performance.

For example, Joseph Brown was the sales manager for the XYZ Widget company, a Fortune 500 firm that had been making widgets for more than 40 years. During his time with the company, Mr. Brown was responsible for all sales and sales promotion activities. In thinking back to his achievements, he remembered an occasion just a few weeks after he had been given the position of sales manager. That was when he designed the company's first quarterly sales program; a program that was so successful it resulted in an increase of 10 percent in sales of the firm's red widgets.

How do those facts translate into the FAB Worksheet? Take the first—what was the factual characteristic, attribute, or skill that Joe had. In other words, what position did he occupy? He was sales and promotion manager, responsible for the company's sales. Those are the facts that belong in the first column.

The first column always contains the title of the position, whether it is sales manager, controller, marketing manager, and so on. Just the facts.

Figure 54   Resume 19: Mundane, Lengthy Resume

Resume

Name:
Address:
City:
Marital Status:
Children:
Birthdate:

Objective: To obtain a challenging position with a growing, contemporary, communications company.

Work Experience

March, 1987 to Present   Communications,

Outside sales manager for local communications company that specializes in marketing, selling and servicing state-of-the-art two-way radio equipment and paging systems throughout the Los Angeles area to the business and professional community. Responsible for all outside sales and service activities.

Salary: $2,000 month + 8% commission from gross sales. $200 month car allowance.

August, 1982 to March, 1987   Communications,

Started as Radio Communications Representative (RCR) 2, promoted to RCR 1, and elevated to Account Executive in January, 1985. Responsible for all closed circuit TV, two-way radio/paging, and communication equipment sales in West L.A., Beverly Hills, Hollywood. Acted as interim Zone Manager for first quarter of 1984. Supervised personnel, handled paperwork, receivables, product presentations, etc. during this period. Created special telemarketing program which was adopted by entire region, and created special "cold call" program.

Salary: $1500 week guarantee, plus 7½% commission of gross sales.

January, 1979 to August, 1982   Men's Wear,   CA

Started as salesman and advanced to store manager. Duties and responsibilities included overall management of the store including inventory control, billing, merchandise selection, buying from various reps and fashion marts, and hiring and firing.

Salary: $200 week guarantee plus 5% commission of any sales over $1,000.

November, 1978 to January, 1979   CA

Started as part-time stockman. Promoted to full-time retail sales. Duties included direct sales and inventory control analysis. Received four "Top Sales" awards.

Salary: Started $5.25 hour. Full-time, $175 per week plus 5% commission.

Education

Sacramento City College, 1980–1981

Attended College and majored in Business Administration. Chairman, Freshman class activity committee.

High School, 1973–1977

Graduated with Academic, college prep major. Member, Varsity Football team. Member, Varsity baseball team.

Activities

Member, Tarzana Rotary. Program chairman, 1982–83. Member, Tarzana Rotary Board of Directors, 1984.

Figure 55   Resume 20: Resume 19 Transformed into a Power Resume

Name:
Address:
City/State:
Telephone:

Summary: 11 years experience of sales/sales management experience in products sold to both business and consumers.

March, 1987 to present,   Communications, Los Angeles

Responsibility: Outside sales manager for Los Angeles based communications company selling and servicing state-of-the-art radio equipment and paging systems.

*Opened 35 new accounts first three months with firm.
*Increased area business by 64% during first year with firm.
*Attained 135% of quota every year for first two years.

August, 1982 to March, 1987,   Communications, El Segundo

Responsible for sales/rental of all closed circuit TV, two-way radio/paging, and communication equipment sales in West L.A., Beverly Hills, Hollywood.

*Created special telemarketing program which was adopted by entire region in 1983. Led to an 84% average sales increase throughout region.
*Created special "cold call" program that enabled company to increase new accounts by 41% during first 9 months of 1984.
*Handled all product presentations and devised new strategy that led to 12% more presentations (and 22% more closes) for region.

January, 1979 to August, 1982,   Men's Wear, Sacramento

Store manager. Responsible for sales, inventory, management of $1.5 million a year facility.

*Developed follow-up procedure for in-store sales personnel that increased sales 22%.
*Developed "thank you" note procedure that increased repeat sales by more than 61% and led to increase of $210,000 in sales during one year.

November, 1978 to January, 1979   Men's Store, Los Angeles

Retail sales. Started part-time, promoted to full-time salesperson in temporary position.

*Received four "top sales" awards for being one of top two salespeople for month.

<u>Education</u>

Sacramento City College. Attended and majored in business administration.

Figure 56 FAB Worksheet

FEATURES:
Factual Characteristic, attribute, or skill. (FACT)

BENEFITS:
Resultant satisfier. Value to employer. (BOTTOM LINE AND PERSONAL)

ACCOMPLISHMENTS:
Supportive statement based on past performance. (PROOF)

The second column shows what Joe did for the employer insofar as developing products or programs. What he created. In Joe's case, he created and designed the company's first quarterly sales program. What an employee gives to an employer; that is, the creative ideas, programs, and so on always belong in column number two, Benefits.

The third column always contains the accomplishments or results. In Joe's case, the result was a 12-week program that resulted in a 10 percent increase in the sales of red widgets. This is the quantifiable portion of the resume—the bulleted accomplishments that you will see outlined in each of the power resumes.

To sum up Joe's FAB sheet (at least the first entry), it would look like the following:

> Sales and promotion manager, responsible for company's sales and promotion efforts throughout the country.
> • Designed first quarterly sales program that resulted in a 10 percent increase in the sale of red widgets during a 12-week period.

Everything is quantifiable. The FAB Worksheet can work for every occupation and every job applicant. If you're stumped as to where you should begin a resume, simply start filling in the FAB Worksheet. Go through each position (Facts/Features), remember the programs you developed or the ideas contributed (Benefits) and then list the results (Accomplishments/Proof). Do this for each position, and it will not take long before you have the ingredients for a power resume.

For a closer look at a resume that has a number of features, benefits, and accomplishments, read Resume 21 (Figure 57). Resume 21 was sent to a retained search firm. Normally, these firms are not interested in unsolicited resumes; however, the president of the company said he was intrigued by the format. This six-page document cannot actually be classified as a resume. It is a summary of the job seeker's work history and abilities. If it were sent to a human resource department in this format, it would have been thrown aside without a second glance. It does, however, have something that makes it interesting—the chronological portion of the resume has accomplishments listed alongside each position. Note, for example, the last position (Manager, Sales Support), and the two major accomplishments listed alongside. Note that most of the accomplishments are not quantified; they are generalizations. But, with a little work (by the headhunting firm), this resume was reconstructed and turned into a power resume (Figure 58). Note the difference between the initial version and the power resume, and how much more succinct and informative the power resume turns out.

Figure 57 Resume 21: Intriguing, but Lengthy Resume

KEY STRENGTHS

Exceptional communication skills
Market planning and analytical abilities
Creative problem solving
Technical understanding; learning ability; intelligence
Enthusiasm, drive

EXPERIENCE RESPONSIBILITIES

Manager, Sales Support
_____ International, 11/90–Present

Plan, develop and facilitate execution of training programs for worldwide subsidiaries. Coordinate development of global sales support materials to complement strategic marketing direction. Create support materials for product launches and other major marketing projects, to communicate strategic direction to sales, ensuring proper tactical execution. Conduct technical training for key management personnel.

Manager, Sales Training
_____ 11/89–11/90

Developmental assignment encompassing planning, implementation, and ongoing evaluation of training for field sales and selected in-house personnel. Responsible for developing sales representatives' selling skills. Planned and executed sales seminars and sales management meetings. Responsible for communications to the field sales force.

Product Manager
_____ 5/87–11/89

Developed, coordinated and implemented strategies and programs aimed at eye care professionals, consumers and the retail trade. Bottom-line responsibility for sales of $45 million and expense budgets ranging from $2MM to $3MM. Analyzed sales and market data to develop plans, programs, pricing, forecasts and user models. Managed agencies in development of professional and retail sales/support materials. Extensive coordination with manufacturing, finance, legal, regulatory, R&D and sales departments as well as key optical and retail accounts.

ACCOMPLISHMENTS

- Manage development of training program for use worldwide. Responsible for content, structure, and management of external consultants to complete the program within expense guidelines.
- Created and conducted 2-day technical and product training program for support staff throughout the International organization.

- Conducted training for new and experienced sales representatives including selling skills, product knowledge and technical education to address professional and retail customers.
- Developed comprehensive field training materials that increased representatives' product and technical knowledge, improving their sales effectiveness prior to the administration of in-house training.

- Successfully launched new rigid gas permeable contact lens care products.
- Managed first all-encompassing consumer/trade programs, resulting in two of the three largest month's sales volumes on record.
- Achieved market share gain on a mature brand, the first growth in 2 + years.
- Developed and managed multi-pronged program to quickly and successfully reduce massive trade inventories.
- Devised plan to creatively utilize excess inventories, avoiding over $80K in spoilage expenses.

165

Manager, Pharmaceuticals, 9/84–5/87

Managed $1.5–$2.0 million territory selling ocular prescription and contact lens care products to eye care professionals, optical chains and distributors, retailers and wholesalers. Addressed professional associations on issues related to contact lens care. Devised and implemented planograms for retailers. Assisted in training new sales representatives, interviewing and in-field assessment of potential hires.

- Achieved 99%, 110% and 122% of quota in 1985, '86, and first half of '87 respectively.
- Increased distribution of lens care products by more than 70 SKUs.
- Selected as Management Development attendee, Leadership Council Member, and Salesperson of the Year nominee, 1986.

Vice President/Marketing Director, Bank of _____ 7/83–9/84

Developed and implemented marketing plans and budgets to achieve growth and profit objectives. Heavily involved in planning, promotion, pricing, product development, advertising and PR. Designed, administered and participated in sales development program. Member of Executive Management Committee, participating in strategic planning and key decisions.

- Conducted comprehensive sales program to increase cross-selling effectiveness, contributing over $65K in earnings.
- Developed process for agency evaluation, resulting in the selection of the first advertising agency whose skills, talent, and philosophy suited the bank's needs.

Research Analyst/Marketing Consultant, _____ Associates, 7/79–7/83

Second-in-command, participating in management of daily business and major decisions. Extensively involved in creation of sales programs for banks, including design, creation of training support and sales materials. Responsible for installation of in-house computer. Sold sophisticated management system and marketing services to financial institutions of all sizes. Consulted regularly with clients in areas of sales, pricing, product development, improving marketing effectiveness and training.

- Contributed to 300% + increase in gross revenues between 1979–82.
- Directly contributed to the growth of client base exceeded 500%.
- Wrote articles for publication in national and regional banking journals.
- Selected to address _____ Banker's Association on NOW account development and pricing.

Marketing Assistant/Marketing Officer, _____ Bank & Trust, 6/78–7/79

EDUCATION
Bachelor of Arts, with Distinction, Communications
University of Colorado, Boulder -
G.P.A. 3.8 overall; 3.9 in Major (4.0 Scale)

HONORS
Phi Beta Kappa, Initiation,
Phi Beta Kappa, Ten Outstanding Juniors Award,
Gates Foundation Scholarship,
Regent's Scholar

REFERENCES
Available upon request.

BENEFITS AND FEATURES

I can offer an employer:	As evidenced by:
Analytical abilities	• Developed user models to aid in forecasting sales and market trends. • Utilized inventory models to forecast sales and gauge impact of promotions. • Created computer matrices to evaluate pricing alternatives and their impact on sales volume and revenues. • Routinely used SAMI, IMS, HPR and other data sources in developing and evaluating plans and programs.
Achievement oriented performance	• Academic excellence. • Recognized as Salesperson of the Year nominee, Peak Performer, Leadership Council member and Management Development attendee. • History of ongoing promotions and career advancement. • Initiated and managed promotions function during its infancy.
Flexibility	• Wide-ranging skills. • Moved from marketing-based career in finance industry to medical field. • Adapted to continuous changes in management, organizational structure, and responsibility for variety of functions. • Ability to work with individuals at all levels, from all areas of the organization.
Broad-based marketing experience that has contributed to my flexibility and ability to creatively solve problems involving complex issues.	A background that includes: • Medical marketing • Consumer marketing • Trade promotion • FDA-regulated industry • Service and product marketing
Depth of marketing experience that has supported outstanding skill development in the areas of strategic and tactical planning, analysis, forecasting, and communication.	• Over 20 products managed. • Experience ranging from new product launches to mature items. • Extensive coordination with manufacturing, sales, finance, regulatory, R&D, medical, legal, senior management, and key accounts.

I can offer an employer:	As evidenced by:
Experience in marketing-related positions that has provided me with expanded vision and broader strategic thinking as well as a systems approach to management and communication.	Successful experience in: • Sales • Training and development • Sales support • Market research • Supervision • Team building • Project management
Exceptional communication skills with the ability to cogently and authoritatively express ideas in writing or orally, in group presentations or one-on-one.	• Wrote marketing plans submitted executive management. • Responsible for all communications to the field sales force. • Authored article for regional banking publications. • Made presentations at all national and regional sales meetings. • Presented plans and product performance updates to senior management. • Developed presentations for senior management delivery to executive committee.
Intelligence and quick learning abilities	• Phi Beta Kappa graduate; B.A. with distinction. • High school valedictorian. • Successful career change from financial industry to medical field; placed first in all phases of Rx training. • Selected to develop technical training program for use by employees worldwide.
Creative problem solving	• Developed unique programs and initiated use of tools to reduce trade inventories from 8.2 to 2.1 months' supply in one quarter. • Devised functional approaches to incorporate consumer promotion into numerous products with a variety of packaging forms. • Addressed market need by developing and implementing packaging change to increase consumer safety.

I can offer an employer:	As evidenced by:
Leadership	• Selected to assist District Manager in hiring, training, and evaluating employees. • Provided direction and motivation to obtain salesforce support and involvement in the tactical execution of marketing programs. • Created and implemented employee development programs. • Numerous professional awards and academic honors.
Organizational skills	• Routinely manage 4–6 projects simultaneously. • Coordinated all aspects of successful product launch. • Orchestrated all elements involved in executing promotional programs across entire product line.
Team player	• Participated in assessment and reallocation of budget funds to support attainment of corporate goals and department objectives balanced against personal MBOs. • Coordinated implementation of promotional programs involving all products and product managers within the division.
Energy, drive	• Routinely manage 4–6 projects simultaneously • Maintained schedule of 70 to 80 hours per week while implementing training programs. • 50% overnight travel in sales territory.

Figure 58   Resume 22: Revised Power Resume with Altered Format

RESUME

Name:
Address:
City/State:
Telephone:

Summary: More than 10 years of increasingly responsible positions in sales, sales management, and sales training for two of the country's leading pharmaceutical and optical companies.

May, 1987 to present, _____ International, San Jose

Served as product manager, promoted to sales training manager, and finally manager, sales support for Fortune 500 optical company. Responsible for design and development of sales training programs for worldwide sales force.

* Managed and budgeted development of worldwide sales training program that resulted in 8% increase in sales performance first year it was introduced.
* Developed collateral training materials to increase product and technical knowledge. Materials accounted for a reduction of 5% the first year in amount of time representatives had to devote to learning new products.
* Managed team that launched new optical lens product that accounted for $24 million in additional sales during first six months.
* Managed introduction of improved new optical product that gained market share on mature, leading brand for the first time in two years.
* Devised plan to utilize excess inventories that resulted in savings of $80,000 in spoilage expenses.
* Developed and managed company's first trade program that resulted in sales increases of 20% and 22% during first two months of the program.
* During four years with company, attained at least 99% of yearly sales goals during the first six months.

July, 1983 to Sept., 1984, _____ Bank

Marketing director of midwest bank with responsibilities for all phases of marketing including advertising, promotion, pricing, and product development.

* Developed cross-selling program that led to increase in earnings the first year of $65,000.
* Developed selection criteria for bank's first advertising agency.
* Member of executive management committee, and participated in strategic planning and key decisions.
* Designed, administered in sales development program for all of bank's officers.

July, 1979 to July, 1983, _____ & Associates

Analyst, consultant and assistant to the president for firm that specialized in selling management and marketing services to financial institutions. Responsible for designing and creating sales programs, training support, sales materials, assisting in pricing and product development for client companies.

170

* During tenure with company, gross revenues grew 300% from increased business.
* Number of clients increased 500%, with my sales team accounting for nearly one-half of the total.
* Wrote seven articles that were published in national and regional banking journals on behalf of our company.
* Selected as delegate from company to address statewide banking convention on subject of sales training and support.

Education

Bachelor of Arts with Distinction, Communications, University of Colorado.

Honors

Phi Beta Kappa, named one of "Ten Outstanding Juniors" Award. Phi Beta Kappa, Initiation.
Winner, Gates Foundation Scholarship
Regent's Scholar
Named sales development trainer of the year, 1989, by the Sales Management Association.

How does a CEO (Chief Executive Officer) search for a position? Usually, they never do. For the most part, companies hire search firms to uncover CEO candidates. Still, a CEO needs a resume. A company that is searching for a CEO may have a number of executives on the search committee who may not be familiar with the candidates. In many cases, the company that needs a new president may be a subsidiary of a larger firm in another industry. The parent company may have executives on a search committee who may not be familiar with the subsidiary's industry. Thus, even presidential candidates need resumes. Resume 23 (Figure 59) is an example of a good CEO resume. It is not, however, good enough to be considered a power resume. Even CEO resumes should have summaries, and this one does not. A summary might read something like the following:

> Summary: More than 14 years experience in the computer hardware/software industry, with extensive experience in the marketing and financing of equipment and companies within the industry. For the past three years, CEO of the country's leading computer consulting firm with more than 225 employees.

Unquestionably, the outstanding feature of Resume 23—whether it be for a CEO or manager—is the specific accomplishments that the applicant has listed under each position. Note how quantifiable each one is, and how they made this candidate's performance stand out. This resume, incidentally, was utilized by a headhunting firm to fill a position.

Notice, too, the dates in this resume—they are given and there is no attempt to conceal age. The candidate goes back more than a quarter of a century to give his college graduation date. Any executive committee or board studying this resume would know immediately that the candidate is somewhere around fifty years old. While that age may be "old" for some positions (such as managers), it is considered young for a CEO. In fact, some on the board even questioned whether the candidate was experienced enough because of his relatively young age.

Resume 24 (Figure 60) is close to a power resume, but it needs two changes in order to make it one. First, the objective should be removed. The fact the candidate is looking for "challenge . . . responsibility . . . advancement opportunities" will be no surprise to any employer. The lines are a waste of space. The second change involves the candidate's most recent position, MIS Manager. Note that under the bulleted accomplishments, there are no specifics or quantifiable items. All four items are generalizations. The applicant's remaining positions do, however, list

Figure 59   Resume 23: CEO's Resume

PROFESSIONAL EXPERIENCE

_____ & Associates   1989–
President

The Firm is an action-oriented consulting and support organization that takes great pride
in the ability to implement plans as well as dig, analyze, organize and structure programs
in support of clients. We focus totally on the computer, communication, imaging and
peripherals marketplace. Within imaging, I have particular expertise in both document and
professional graphics environments.

To date, I support ten American and Japanese companies in these business areas:

- Strategy Assistance   • Quality/Customer Surveys
- Interim Management   • Policy Development
- Product Planning   • Distribution Channel Optlmization

I have acted as President of a communications company in securing first round financing;
personally made the first sales and then staffed a Sales and Marketing function for a
startup scanner manufacturer; developed numerous strategy/channel/product plans and
conducted due-diligence investigations.

_____ Corporation   1985–89
Director, _____ Marketing   and 1970–75

Major products offered through this $120 million, highly profitable world-wide sales and
marketing organization include electronic printers, scanners, workstations, copiers and
publishing software.

- Developed and implemented business plans which brought three major hardware
  products and the corporation's first application software product to market, resulting
  in a 50 percent increase in new-business profit opportunity.
- Arrested OEM sales decline by opportunity identification, organization development,
  and aggressive entry into the VAR channel of distribution. Implemented first
  private-label copier sales arrangement in _____ history.
- Reduced operating overhead in Europe by $4 million by transitioning from direct
  account coverage to third parties.
- Planned and led formation of the first joint marketing arrangement between the
  _____ 4,000-man direct sales organization and resellers. This resulted in a 60
  percent increase in sales productivity and dramatically decreased channel conflict.

In the earlier period, with _____ mainframe computers I rose from individual
contributor to Midwest "Fortune 100" Sales Team Manager. The Midwest was unIquely
successful in new-account penetrations under my leadership.

_____ Systems Division   1980–1984
Vice President and General Manager

Fifty five million dollar subsidiary specializing in the development of performance
enhancement products, subsystems and systems compatible with _____
Corporation computers. Forty five percent of sales were through international channels.

173

- Conceived and conducted a manpower reduction of 45 percent to restore profitability while new products were developed.
- Directed creation of products which replaced 60 percent of the firm's revenue with higher margin, state-of-the-art systems.
- Conducted both company and product acquisitions as alternatives to in-house developed technology.
- Managed vendor selection, installation and implementation of an integrated MRP system resulting in a 15 percent WIP reduction and reduced flow times in response to customer demand.
- Selected and installed a large VAX-based multi-user CAD and engineering database utility system for PCB design, reducing cycle time for new designs by 30 percent.

_____ Corporation   1977–1980
Director of Marketing

Manufacturer of rigid disc storage devices and private-branded reseller of a full line of magnetic media. _____ was acquired by _____ in 1977.

- Integrated stand-alone company's world-wide sales and marketing force into _____ with zero unplanned personnel turnover.
- Re-positioned existing product line and developed new products resulting in 10 percent improvement in gross margin.
- Initiated major OEM relationships resulting in 20 percent annual revenue growth.
- Structured and negotiated business arrangement with a Japanese trading company adding 10 percent to total sales by 1980.

OTHER EXPERIENCE   1966–1977

General
National Sales Manager

_____ Inc.
Product Marketing Manager, International
    (Lived and worked in Europe three years)

EDUCATION

M.S.   Massachusetts Institute of Technology; Sloan School of Management   1966
B.S.   Yale University; Industrial Administration and Engineering   1964

174

Figure 60   Resume 24: "Near-Power" Resume.

NAME:

ADDRESS:

OBJECTIVE:

Project management position offering immediate challenge, major
account responsibility with career advancement opportunities.

PROFESSIONAL
SUMMARY:

Over 12 years of domestic/international experience with demonstrated
success in planning and directing projects/operations for large
entrepreneurial businesses. Technically oriented to state-of-the-art
computers/information systems. Qualified in service-oriented
businesses including management and consulting. Expertise in all
phases of marketing/sales strategies.

EXPERIENCE
SYNOPSIS:

MIS Manager–   Company, Los Angeles; 04/90–Present

Responsible for the development of a new practice to expand the
nation's leading real estate management consulting company into
design, construction, and asset management information systems
technology solutions and services.

- Develop and implement Executive Information System with decision
  support tools such as sales leads database for target marketing
  practices.
- Create a new Technology Forum Seminar Program, promote
  membership sign-ups, and conduct executive seminars to create
  "client-glue."
- Assist clients with diagnostic review, selection, and implementation of
  the innovative integration of construction and property management
  systems.
- Build practice infrastructure methodologies and product communication
  tools for client presentation and promotional campaigns.

V.P./Co-Founder–   Corporation, Los Angeles; 09/87–04/90

Responsible for the operations of Management Information Systems (MIS)
Consulting services for analysis, evaluation, pre- and post-implementation
support of real estate-oriented information technologies.

- Successfully launched start-up company with a $19 million business
  operations plan for a five-year forecast.
- Built and managed nationally recognized consulting resources for
  complex projects of $1 million to $5 million budget and maintained
  annual sales growth of approximately 120%.

- Established project management programs, pricing, and contract administration policies resulting in 35% net profit on contracts while maintaining a repeat business ratio of over 65%.
- Created national business relationships through sales staff to represent major computer manufacturers via OEM, VAR, MAP, and VAD cooperative marketing and direct sales programs.

Operations Manager–   , San Jose; 10/84–09/87

Responsible for managing and marketing a service bureau branch specializing in real estate and manufacturing systems database design, development, training, and personnel/systems time-sharing services.

- Completely organized the West Coast operation of a $450 million company, the largest computer resources service bureau in the nation.
- Profitably managed at 220% gross sales rate, various levels of business development, contract negotiations, tracking, reporting, and monitoring projects in excess of $7 million.
- Employed and directly worked with over 30 industry technicians, and sales/marketing experts offering integrated services using IBM, VAX, UNIX, PCs, and numerous graphics and utility programs.

MIS Consultant–   , San Jose; 10/83–10/84

Responsible for assisting in implementation and management of a $5 million computer graphic data center at _____ Division and supervising nine (9) other senior technical computer specialists.

- Designed, built, and managed 6.5 million-sq.-ft. of mix-use real estate facility and drawing information with over 13,000 employee records.
- Developed user training, production standards, and database generation and maintenance procedures for over 350 employees.

Project Engineer–   Corporation, San Francisco; 04/81–05/83
Assist. Project Engineer–   , Milano/San Jose; 04/79–03/81

Responsible for various levels of commercial, residential, and public utility design, engineering, and management in excess of several billion dollar construction costs.

- Produced design and documentation of various disciplines such as: site plan, architectural, structural, mechanical, piping, and electrical information.
- Analyzed design models for multidisciplinary interference checking and communication with shop/field crew for manufacturing and installation.

EDUCATION:

Bachelor of Science	Business Administration; University of _____/CA; 1987 Emphasis on Management and Marketing
University/College Program Credits	Construction Technologies; 1976–1978 Emphasis on Design, Engineering, and Building Construction Practices

LECTURES/
SEMINARS:

                _____ Company Technology Forum Seminar; 1990
"Integrated Construction & Facilities Management Systems"

                _____ Company Technology Forum Seminar; 1990
"Computer-Aided Design & Graphic Systems for Property Management"

                _____ Conference in Chicago; 1988
"Strategic Value of Image Technologies"

PUBLICATIONS:

                Co-Authored _____ Handbook; 1983

specific accomplishments so that any potential employer can evaluate the candidate's worth and the size project/company with which the candidate has experience.

Resume 25 (Figure 61) is an example of a candidate understating accomplishments in the summary. Notice the candidate is seeking a Chief Executive Officer, Chief Operating Officer, or Executive Vice President position; however, he never states—in his summary—that he has CEO background and experience. The summary is an applicant's opportunity to impress human resource people and hiring managers; and they can do it in just a sentence or two. Resume 25 fails to show the broad range of experience and knowledge this candidate has garnered over the years. It was rewritten by a headhunting firm and sent with the letter shown in Figure 62.

Summary: More than 20 years of increasingly responsible positions in the high technology/computer industry, including three years as president of a $225 million company. Extensive background in market research, product development, sales management, and strategic planning with multinational experience.

The firm made a second revision with this resume. Under the applicant's experience there were accomplishments; however, they were difficult to read because they were in a narrative format. The search firm rewrote the positions the candidate had from 1974 to 1982. The bulleted items for the most recent position read:

- Managed product development efforts of 280 people, and had complete responsibility for 2,200 employees in $225 million company in the United States and United Kingdom.
- Increased profitability of company by an average of 12% the first two years, and 8% the third.
- Launched two new product lines during three years, with the first obtaining a 5% market share after 24 months, and the second accounting for 4% of the market after just nine months.

The second set of accomplishments for the years 1974 to 1982 were written as follows:

- In two years of handling large accounts for Honolulu district, increased sales 22% and profits 14% for area.
- Added three major accounts in Hawaii area, that increased company's market share from 9% to 15%.
- Highest performer in Southern California district (1978 to 1979) with sales of $12 million, an increase of 18% over the previous year.

Figure 61   Resume 25: Power Resume

Name: _____   Home: (714) XXX-XXXX
Address: _____   Message: (714) XXX-XXXX

OBJECTIVE: CEO, COO, or Executive Vice President of a growing technology
                company.

SUMMARY: Successful computer industry executive with over 20 years of
                multinational experience in a wide range of activities including software
                development, sales management, marketing, research and
                development, and general management. Proven leader and problem
                solver with analytical, organizational, development, and strategic
                planning skills. Experienced at identifying market opportunities and
                implementing appropriate business strategies.

                Major Accomplishments:

                • In two years improved the performance of a $225M division of
                  _____ Information Systems Group from a loss of
                  $11.2M to an EBIT of $7.0M.
                • Led the refocusing of a $20M R&D activity, in Europe and the USA,
                  into a set of interlocked development plans to eliminate duplication
                  and accelerate the delivery of a new product line.
                • Established the market requirements and worldwide launch strategy
                  for a new high-performance minicomputer range with an emphasis on
                  networking and distributed relational database management.
                • Through acquisition and investment, established subsidiary
                  companies in Spain, France, and South Africa.

EXPERIENCE:
1982 to present   _____ COMPANY, CA

                President
                Began with _____ International, U.K., in 1982 and moved
                through increasingly responsible positions including Director of Marketing
                _____ Information Systems International U.K. and Vice
                President Research and Development _____ CA. In the
                Director of Marketing position, established the market requirements and
                product plans of a new, yet revolutionary, _____ product
                family based on the integration of _____ networking
                technology. In the R&D position coordinated the product development
                efforts of 280 people in the U.K. and U.S. to achieve coherent worldwide
                development of a single set of products. In January of 1988, assumed full
                P&L responsibility for _____ a $225M organization
                comprised of 2200 employees in the U.S. and the U.K.

1974 to 1982   _____ CORPORATION, _____

                Branch Manager, London, U.K.
                Initially hired as Senior Account Manager, Honolulu, HI, responsible for
                new sales and management of large accounts in Hawaii. Highest

179

performer in the Southern California district in 1978/1979. Became the Branch Manager, London, U.K., and led the _____ effort to penetrate large central government business with a focus on the National Health Service.

1971 to 1974   _____ HOSPITAL, Honolulu, HI

Manager of Systems Programming
Designed and developed the system software infrastructure for an on-line patient information system on a Burroughs mainframe.

1966 to 1971   _____ INDUSTRIES, CALIFORNIA

Performed varying engineering and systems programming tasks in programs relating to NASA and U.S. Air Force.

EDUCATION: BSEE, _____ University, 1965
                  MEE, _____ University, 1966

PERSONAL: Married for 20 years with two teenage sons. Grew up in Hawaii. Spent nine years in the U.K. as a family.

Figure 62   Cover Letter to Accompany Rewritten Resume

Name
Address

November 29, 199X

Mr. Herbert M. Smith
XXX Corporation
XXX South Coast Dr., Suite XXX
Costa Mesa, CA 92626

Dear Herb:

It was a pleasure discussing _____ situation with you, and I look forward to continuing our conversations. As I explained, since May I have been trying to raise sufficient capital to form a software company based upon technology developed whilst I was President of _____ Computer Systems Company.

Due to the current uncertainty, the venture capital community is very risk adverse and I am now focusing on a search for a new situation. I would be grateful, therefore, if you would advise me of any opportunities you may encounter in your activities over the next few months.

Attached please find a brief resume. To give you a different perspective, I would like to make some specific observations regarding my background and style:

- Although my primary emphasis for 20 years has been the Sales and Marketing of computers and associated products, I have a highly technical education and significant R&D management experience. This combination tends to make me a generalist.
- Because of my origins in Hawaii and 10 years of experience in Europe, I am comfortable in a multi-national and multi-cultural environment. I believe this empathy for the other's point-of-view translates into a unique level of effectiveness when presented with leadership challenges.
- Although I have limited myself to three large companies in the last 20 years, I have always been involved with smaller operations in them. I am somewhat of a risk taker and have tended to confront the status-quo rather than succumb to it.

I hope things are well with you and that despite the current uncertainty your business prospects are bright. I will keep in touch periodically by phone to advise your of my progress.

Sincerely

Name

Enclosure
WJFX34/ss

- In two years of managing U.K. government sales efforts, our team added three major contracts worth in excess of $50 million.

Resumes do not have to be long in order to get the point across. This Resume 26 (Figure 63) is a superb example of a power resume with an excellent summary and a clearly defined list of accomplishments. Notice how quantifiable every entry (bulleted item) is in the resume. A prospective employer can easily see the accomplishments of this manager.

The resume is ideal for a product and/or sales manager looking for a similar (or advanced) position. Note, too, that the candidate has experience in both the medical and novelty field; a qualification that will make it easier for him to switch industries should he decide to do so.

Resume 27 (Figure 64) lacks only one thing to qualify as a power resume—a good summary. The summary never says what specific skills the applicant has built through the years. When reading it, it is hard to tell if the applicant is in marketing or whether he is a strategic planner. The headhunting firm that had this resume rewrote the summary to read as follows:

Summary: A versatile, experienced marketing and product manager with more than a decade of experience in both the trade and consumer optical and pharmaceutical industry.

Resume 28 (Figure 65) is a perfect power resume that has a clear summary and specific accomplishments under each position. Note how quantifiable each the bulleted item is.

Resume 29 (Figure 66) is another power resume with an excellent summary and clearly defined list of accomplishments.

Resume 30 needs a more definitive summary. It also lacks dates on the most recent position, and not all of the accomplishments are specific. Note the old version (Figure 67) and revised version (Figure 68).

Figure 63   Resume 26: Ideal Power Resume

Summary: Product manager with more than nine years of progressively responsible experience in the introduction, management and sales of new products in the medical field.

Work Experience

Division, of, Chicago, Feb., 1988 to present

Associate Product Manager, responsible for development and introduction of new products to medical technology field.

* Introduced new product, designed and implemented marketing plan that led to 8% share of market in first year.
* Product manager for firm's three leading medical products with each accounting for approximately 15% of company's total sales.
* Developed strategic plan for medical product division for long term (five year) growth.
* Attained at least 110% of sales goals for each of years with company's medical line.

Inc., St. Louis, October, 1984 to Jan., 1988

Territory Manager (midwest) for largest manufacturer of surgical equipment in country.

* 40% increase in dollar sales; 45% in unit sales during first year with company.
* Developed sales training course that was adopted and used with all incoming sales representatives.
* Selected as specialty products representative for company's annual convention.
* Designed sales strategy to overcome distribution problems with discount distributors. Plan led to new channel opening, and increase in units of more than 50% and increase of dollars generated of more than 38% during first two years.

Associates, Forest Hills, NY, Jan., 1982 to Sept., 1984

Sales Representative for wholesale novelty division of one of country's three largest toy manufacturers.

* Developed new product introduction campaign for complete line of novelty products. Went from no sales to more than $22 million in first year.
* Organized regional distribution network that led to the opening and development of more than 200 accounts.
* Conducted market research and created packaging with product mix to improve sales in slower moving lines. First year results showed 13% (unit) improvement in lines.

Education

Graduate, Business Administration, Syracuse University
MBA, Marketing, Chicago University
Graduate, Dale Carnegie Course
Graduate, Professional Selling Skills II

Figure 64   Resume 27: Power Resume

Summary of Qualifications

A versatile, action-oriented executive who has delivered significant results in key marketing management positions. Has demonstrated sound business judgement, decisiveness, and well-developed planning, analytical, and communication skills at a consistently high level of performance in a variety of progressively responsible and challenging assignments.

Career Highlights

Sunnyvale, California   1984–1991

_____ Manager, Corporate and Trade Marketing   (1990–1991)

A new position created to exploit strong growth in sales and profits in the key Corporate Optical and Retail Trade market segments. Responsible for development and implementation of marketing and sales strategies for Contact Lenses and Contact Lens Care Products to Corporate Optical and Retail Trade Accounts. Key achievements:

* Developed and executed Signature evaluation program with _____, Inc. which resulted in their commitment to use the product in over 1000 stores.
* Increased usage of the Concept and Gas Permeable Lens Solutions to over 1800 Corporate Optical outlets, representing a growth rate of over 300% from prior year.
* Developed a comprehensive, competitive Retail Promotional Calendar for Consumer Products Sales Force responsible for $37 million in sales.
* Restructured co-operative advertising reporting and payment procedure so claims were processed in a more timely manner. Estimate first year savings in excess of $200,000.
* Led a taskforce that evaluated our contact lens care product sampling methods and sales force compensation. Recommendations now being implemented will reduce sampling cost, improve sales force focus on product objectives, and reduce the opportunity for product diversion.

_____ Product Manager   (1985–1990)

First transferee from international affiliate to headquarters in the history of Barnes-Hind. Responsible for the development and implementation of strategies and tactics required to attain product sales goals. Key achievements:

* Successfully introduced Concept. This product achieved profitability in Year 2 and is now ranked third in its category. Sales will exceed $7.1 million in Year 3.
* Pioneered development and execution of direct-to-consumer marketing programs for soft contact lens care products. Included activities in broadcast and print media as well as point-of-sale promotion.
* Developed and implemented Saline marketing programs that resulted in full year sales of $8.2 million, a 112% increase over prior year.

_____ , Ontario   1984–1985
Product Manager   (1984–1985)

Developed, implemented, and monitored marketing and sales strategies and tactics for contact lenses and contact lens care products. Reported directly to General Manager.

Key achievements:

* Established formalized marketing process for all products.
* Introduced two new lens and one new lens care products.

Prior Experience

_____ Canada Inc. Toronto, Ontario
Marketing Associate (1982–1984)
Marketing Research Analyst (1982–1982)

_____ Inc. Toronto, Ontario
Medical Sales Representative (1980–1981)

Education

M.B.A. Marketing/Finance - _____ University, Toronto, Ontario
M.Sc. Pharmacology - University _____ Toronto, Ontario
B.Sc. Physiology - _____ of Toronto, Toronto, Ontario

Figure 65   Resume 28: Excellent Power Resume

Name: _____
Address: _____
Telephone: _____

Summary: Nearly ten years of increasingly responsible real estate development positions for major corporations in the restaurant/hospitality and retail home improvement field. Handle market research, site selection, lease negotiation, budgeting, design, development and on-going maintenance for selected sites.

WORK EXPERIENCE

Los Angeles, from April 1987 to present

Vice president of real estate development for _____, publicly held major retail home center chain in (number of states). Handle all site development ranging from selection and lease negotiation to monitoring each store's operational budget as it relates to maintenance and expense.

* Organized the company's first real estate development department, and created a company prototype of a "build to suit lease" document that could be used as model for all future new developments.
* Handle company's capital budget of $15–$20 million per year. Supervise staff of 20–25; maintain 65 units and 12 different departments in stores that are approximately 115,000 square feet.
* Developed 10–12 locations per year, each with building budget of $7 to $10 million, and 20 year leases.
* Developed new market growth strategies which resulted in new units generating first year sales of nearly $50 million.
* Have increased company's net worth through leasehold assets by $70–$100 million each year.
* Have opened 37 stores in western part of U.S. Company had total of 30 when I started in 1987.
* Prepare and monitor all rent budgets, insurance and other expenses.

from Sept., 1985 until April, 1987

Assistant vice president, real estate for $3 billion discount department store chain, with complete responsibility for all real estate/site selection and development along eastern seaboard.

* Department added economic net worth of approximately $55 million through leasehold improvements.
* Renegotiated all existing leases, and increased the company's economic worth by nearly $10 million during my tenure at the corporation.
* Developed five–six new units per year. Each lease between $7–$10 million for 250,000–400,000 square foot units located in established shopping centers, with unlimited use to sublet, and all for 20 years.
* Developed on-going risk/benefit analysis for all properties and leases.

June, 1983 to Sept., 1985

Assistant director real estate development, responsible for coordinating and negotiating hotel management contracts which provided present value income to company on the basis of fees to be paid over the contract life.

* Typical contracts negotiated provided a present value of anywhere from $750,000 to $2.2 million. Annualized, these contracts provided the company with an average of $7.5 million in additional economic worth.
* Negotiated and coordinated development of company-owned hotel properties. Total costs ran approximately $35 million.
* Handled all expansion budgets for restaurant/lodge development. Coordinated approximately (number) of restaurant developments at (amount) and (number) of lodge developments at (dollars).

Education

Graduate,
Graduate,

Figure 66   Resume 29: Excellent Power Resume

```
_____ , CPA
_____ , STREET
_____ , CANADA
        V6P 4M9
       PBX & FAX
```

SUMMARY

Results-oriented professional with 15 years experience in management as senior financial/
administration officer in both public and private sectors. Major experience, strengths and
skills include:

- Financial Controls
- Budgeting/Forecasting
- Negotiations

- Personnel Management
- Cost, accounting and tax
- Computer Systems

EXPERIENCE

_____ Horticulture Inc. (Subsidiary of _____)

Leading producer and worldwide distributor of horticulture products for professional
growers and retail consumers with annual revenues of $65 million. Conglomerate parent
company with multibillion dollar revenue located in _____

Financial Manager of North America   1989 to Present

Responsible for creating a reliable financial environment for our companies in North
America. Resolve financial issues directly with parent company. Prepare for acquisitions
in North America and potential relocation of headquarters to the United States.

Accomplishments

- Created a consolidated financial reporting package that reduced monthly
  preparation time by 40%.
- Formulated accurate sales and profit trend report to assist management's
  evaluation of daily progress toward budgeted objectives.
- Implemented new accounts payable computer system. Reduced accounts payable
  from 90 days to 45 days.
- Developed systems and trained staff to complete audit and tax functions which
  reduced external professional fees by $100,000 in one year.
- Facilitated main-frame and personal computer management which resulted in
  integrated systems and doubled the efficiency of the present resources.
- Introduced policies and procedures that resulted in the creation of centralized
  purchasing and reduced operating costs by 10%.

US Administration and Accounting Manager   1987 to 1989

Responsible for start-up of a new business in the US through acquisition. The business
expanded to three production locations within twelve months.

Accomplishments

- Negotiated settlement of the acquisition and integrated the new operation which
  resulted in additional revenues of five million dollars to the parent company.
- Designed accounting system including standard cost based budget to evaluate
  profitability of products.

- Maintained control of a capital expenditure budget in excess of three million dollars.
- Managed the closure of a production facility and recovered $650,000 from the sale of redundant assets.
- Hired, trained and developed a professional staff to assist with management functions. Saved approximately $50,000 in recruiting fees.
- Established written personnel and administrative policies which led to informed employees and minimized turn-over to less than 20% in the first year.

North Iowa Community Action Organization

Non-profit corporate administrator of five million dollars in Federal, State and local grants that provided twelve self-help programs and services to low income families.

Comptroller

Responsible for all aspects of the agency, including grant application and management, management information systems, personnel policies and safeguard of corporate assets.

Accomplishments

- Implemented computer system upgrade to produce financial statements that were understandable to Board members.
- Created applications for funding to Federal, State and local governments. Awarded five million dollars in program funds.
- Established procurement policies that were reviewed and accepted by Federal, State and independent auditors for compliance with grant guidelines.
- Maintained corporate administrative expenses at 4% of total funding.

Bertram Cooper & Co.

Regional certified public accountant firm with seven offices in two states specialized in personal and corporate taxation, small business services, audit and computer installations.

Professional Office Manager   1978 to 1985

Progressively promoted to this position responsible for generating fees while maintaining professional quality.

Accomplishments

- Provided consultation and planning expertise to 300 individual and corporate clients.
- Audited banks, governmental entities and private businesses with revenues ranging from two to 20 million dollars.
- Consulted and installed computer systems including client training of computer applications. Established both main-frame and personal computer systems.

Regatta Inn Corporation   1977 to 1978

Manager and shareholder of a restaurant and lounge with revenue of $600,000. Responsible for accounting, payroll, personnel and food service.

Hinky Dinky Stores   1970 to 1977

Co-manager of a supermarket chain store with revenues of 10 million dollars. Responsible for personnel, scheduling, training, quality of service and profit performance. (The chain was sold to Cullum Companies.)

EDUCATION

Hamilton Business College, Mason City, Iowa, Administrative Accounting
Iowa State University, Ames, Iowa, Industrial Administration

HONORS

Outstanding Young Men of America
Certificate of Merit, Lifesaving Award from President of USA
Governor's Award for Community Volunteer Project.

OTHER

Sailing, water and snow skiing, running, swimming, fishing, reading business topics, civic activities and short courses.

Figure 67   Resume 30: Old Version

Name
Address
City
Phone

PROMOTION MANAGEMENT

Broad based experience developing and implementing fully integrated promotion
plans . . . . consumer . . . . sales . . . . trade. Played pivotal role in major national
promotions: Michael Jackson Victory Tour . . . . NFL & NCAA Final Four
sponsorships . . . . and Frequent Buyer program. Areas of special competence:

Promotion Planning & Analysis	Package Promotions & Consumer Offers
Targeted & Minority Promotions	Trade Shows & Major Event Presentations
Major Media Production	Co-op Advertising Management
P.O.S. Production	Package Design

Consistently developed programs playing key role in significant sales increases.

Director of Promotion, _____ Optical, Consumer Division

Recruited in 1988 to develop start-up department for $500MM contact lens and LENS
PLUS cleaning solution group.

- Produced all consumer, sales and trade promotions and designed development
  program for promotion execution.
- Developed print advertising, free standing inserts, point-of-sale materials, coupons,
  refunds, bonus packs and national sweepstakes.
- Produced full-year promotion plan and conducted semi-annual Regional Sales
  Manager meetings.
- Redesigned total retail package line.
- Brought promotion functions in-house. Saved $1.5MM.

Representative promotion programs:

- Gained highest trade participation in corporate history and 8% sales increase with
  national back-to-school promotion.
- Initiated "Trip to Anywhere" promotion resulting in 6% sales increase.
- Devised retail sampler pack for hotels and convenience stores generating $5MM in
  first year revenue.
- Designed and implemented advertising deduction prevention program resulting in
  deductions being reduced from $400,000 to $10,000 monthly.
- Produced first national television commercials in company's history.

Manager - Promotion _____ Norcliff Division   1986–1988

Developed and executed consumer, sales force and trade promotions for all brands.

- Produced TUMS presentation for retail trade contributing to doubling of TUMS sales
  in three years. Created full-year TUMS promotion program designed to maximize

trade inventories, increase display activity and increase multiple purchases. Program increased sales 30%.

- Implemented sponsorship of Starship Music tour for OXY Acne Preps and produced major TUMS trade incentive program sponsoring NFL events.
- Developed OXY calendar promotions increasing back-to-school sales 12%. Created OXY brand educational module used in high school biology classes.
- Managed and co-produced "Frequent Buyer" program for ORAFIX. Redemption program exceeded 50% vs. normal 5%.

Senior Associate Manager, _____   1984–1986

Played pivotal role in music marketing and major event promotions.

- Coordinated ticket promotions at local level for Michael Jackson Victory Tour . . . largest promotion in Pepsi history . . . increasing sales 22%.
- Developed Hispanic targeted promotions for Menudo tour . . . largest minority event ever . . . produced promotions for Lionel Richie tour . . . coordinated Goodwill Games sponsorship and Iron Man Triathalon . . . and produced media advertising for Pepsi's One Million Dollar Pay Day game.
- Produced most successful Mountain Dew promotion in history . . . sponsorship of NCAA Final Four. Sales increased 14% during promotion.
- Implemented school can collection program resulting in increased 28% vending machine placement. Only event in history endorsed by Association of U.S. Governors.

Sales Development Manager   1982–1984

Conceptualized, designed and produced all sales promotion and P.O.S. materials. Authored divisional and corporate business reviews used by top management.

Established Vaseline Intensive Care Lotion Competitive Defense Presentation. Secured 30% shelf space and features in 92% of chain stores.

Sales Representative   1978–1982

Prepared and presented national distribution study discovering distribution gaps in Almond Joy products and executed test market for Cadbury's "Classic" bar leading to new item introduction.

Exceeded sales quotas each year. In 1980 recognized as top salesman for new distribution.

EDUCATIONAL   -   B.S., Marketing, Babson College

PROFESSIONAL   -   Cited by AdWeek magazine as one of "A Dozen Rising Stars" in field of Promotion, March 1989.
Honored by Advertising Association of California for outstanding contribution in field of promotions.

Figure 68   Resume 30: New Version

Summary: More than a dozen years of consumer and trade sales promotion experience with major consumer manufacturing and marketing companies. Extensive experience in point-of-sale merchandisers as well as promotional tie-ins.

Work Experience

_____ Optical Consumer Division, May, 1988 to present

Director of Promotion. Responsible for all consumer and trade promotions, as well as point-of-sale, advertising, and other marketing programs.

- Started promotion department and saved company $1.5 million by bringing activities in house.
- Developed national "back-to-school" program that resulted in highest trade participation in company history and 8% sales increase.
- Developed "trip to anywhere" promotion that resulted in 6% sales increase.
- Developed and marketed retail sampler pack for hotels and convenience stores that generated $5 million in its first year.
- Saved company up to $400,000 a month with the design and implementation of "advertising deduction prevention program."
- Produced first TV commercials in company's history.
- Developed national sweepstakes that resulted in 12% increase in trade orders, and 7% increase in consumer sales.

_____ Division, Sept., 1986 to May, 1988

Promotion Manager for Fortune 500 pharmaceutical company. Developed and executed consumer, salesforce, and trade promotions for all brands.
[Note: the four bulleted accomplishments remained the same in this revised version.]

_____ Company, May, 1984 to Sept., 1986

Manager for leading soft drink manufacturer, with responsibility to tie-ing in products to major musical events and performers.
[Note: the four bulleted items in the original resume remained the same in this revised version.]

_____ Inc., June, 1982 to May, 1984

Manager for leading pharmaceutical and cosmetic firm with responsibility for all sales promotion and point-of-sale materials.
[Note: the accomplishment listed under this position in the original resume remained the same.]

_____ Inc., February, 1978 to May, 1982

Representative for one of three largest candy manufacturers in country.
[Note: the two bulleted items remain the same in this version as they did in the original.]

7

THE POWER INTERVIEW—

TIED TO THE RESUME

A n interview for a position is no different than a sales call. For the unprepared salesperson, the call is a disaster. The same is true of the applicant who decides he can "wing" it. Ask Steve Bledsoe. For his entire working life, Bledsoe had been a communications or public relations specialist who had little to do with sales. He learned, however, that coming out on top in an employment interview was similar to a successful sales call.

Bledsoe had more than 20 years of corporate experience. The last company he worked with had gone bankrupt, and so after 4 years with a parts manufacturer and another 20 years in the aerospace industry, Bledsoe found himself out of work for the first time in his life.

THE 30-DAY/$10,000 RULE

For months, Bledsoe had been answering advertisements and sending resumes but to no avail. The forecast from the headhunter he had talked to months before came back to him: For every $10,000 in salary, you can expect to be out of work for a month.

Bledsoe was not about to wait six months for a job interview. He had several techniques in mind that would enable him to bypass human resource departments and go directly to the hiring manager. One of them even enabled him to get into a firm and interview with a hiring manager despite the fact the company was not actively looking for anyone.

Bledsoe's technique is one that can be emulated easily. He researched his industry (aerospace) thoroughly and ended up selecting close to 100 firms that he believed could offer him a job. Of the 100, he selected 25 for special treatment. To each of the 75 remaining firms he sent resumes and cover letters to human resource directors. Based upon statistical averages, he figured that one or possibly two of the 75 firms would contact him. The remaining 25 firms he considered to be extremely desirable employers. He was determined to get a third party endorsement for each one.

He started his campaign with the 25 by visiting the library and finding annual reports from as many of the companies as possible. He called a local stockbroker for remaining reports that he was not able to find at the library. With each report, he ran down the list of outside directors and selected one from each company who lived nearby. He then wrote a letter to each of these that said:

> I am interested in finding out more about X company. I know you are a member of the Board and I wondered if you might offer me some counsel. I do not want to waste your time, but I need about 15 to 20 minutes. I will call you next week to see if you might have some time in your schedule.

THE DIRECTOR'S ROLE

Bledsoe called three directors the next week and each scheduled an appointment with him without even questioning his motives.

"What he discovered," says Robert McDonald, "is that directors know they have a responsibility to the corporations they serve. They are more than willing to meet with someone and discuss the company. You may never see the CEO or chairman, but the story with outside directors is entirely different."

Bledsoe's script was straightforward. He told each director he was interested in exploring employment opportunities with the firm. He had done some research into the firm and was excited about the possibilities in it. His area was public relations and he thought the company might be able to use his services.

Invariably, the director would ask him about his experience and Bledsoe, instead of describing his job history, would pull out a resume and give it to the director to read.

"The job seeker," cautions McDonald, "has to remain perfectly silent while the director is reading. Do not interrupt. Give him a chance to finish."

POWER REFERENCES

Once the director finished, Bledsoe asked if there was anyone at the company the director thought he might talk to about opportunities. The director suggested someone and before Bledsoe left, he asked one more key question: "Do you mind if I mention your name?" The director agreed and Bledsoe had an entree few applicants could match. He also opened another door. Many directors have their own firms and are potential employers as well.

There are few references more effective than those that come from a director. Executives are attentive to a request from any officer or director. Within a week after he sent the first letter with the director's reference in it, Bledsoe found himself with an appointment with a hiring manager.

The moment Bledsoe entered the vice president's office for the interview, the advice given him by the outplacement counselor came back to him. Too many applicants try to wing a job interview. If you do, you fail. A job interview should be rehearsed and decisions have to be made. That first decision comes within 30 seconds of the door opening.

TAKING THE POWER POSITION

"When a job seeker walks into an office," explains McDonald, "he has 30 seconds to determine where he is going to sit. Some people may say, 'Well, what's the big deal, who cares where you sit?' but seating is the initial step in the selling process. It also determines who holds the power."

Most applicants enter an office and dutifully follow the interviewer to his desk, where the executive sits on one side and the applicant on the other. In that situation, the executive occupies the *power* position, he is in control and has the authority.

"Ideally," says McDonald, "you do not want that to happen. You do not want the interviewer to be the boss—at least not at this stage of the game. You want to be on equal footing."

Psychologically, many hiring managers regard themselves as superior if they sit behind the desk and the applicant is on the other side. If that happens, the hiring manager may get a subconscious feeling that the applicant is beneath him. Although they are only subconscious impressions, they play a role in how the hiring manager views the applicant. If he does not think highly of the candidate, he will not think much of the candidate's ability to do the job. To avoid these thoughts, it is important for the applicant to steer the

interviewer to the seating location that is going to be most beneficial to him.

The location must be selected within seconds of entering the
office. The applicant may meet the hiring manager at the door,
shake hands, and follow him. The process takes less than 10 to 15
seconds, that is the approximate time the applicant has to scan the
room and pick a location. If, for instance, there is a chair at a
90-degree angle to a couch with nothing between the two, this is
where the applicant should try and be seated. Two chairs, side by
side, away from the desk, are another possibility. The applicant can
turn one and face the interviewer with nothing between them. The
object is to be able to sit across from the interviewer without any
obstruction, a location where the power relationships are equal.

There are ways to steer the interviewer to the correct location. As
soon as the applicant enters the office, he should rapidly scan the
office and decide where they should sit. Bledsoe did exactly that
and he saw a couch and armchair adjacent to each other on one side
of the office. As the hiring manager shook his hand, turned and
headed back behind his desk, Bledsoe realized the manager was
not going to ask him to sit on the couch. Bledsoe said, "Do you
mind if we sit over here?" and he headed for the chair, leaving the
couch for the interviewer.

"Most interviewers," says McDonald, "will acquiesce. You may
have to be somewhat assertive, but it will not hurt. The key is to get
the hiring manager to sit where you want. The interview must be on
equal power terms."

The second key to a successful interview is to establish a relationship or rapport. The applicant must show the interviewer the two
have something in common. Employment counselors and headhunters estimate when an applicant makes it to the interview stage
with a hiring manager, 80 percent of the manager's decision is going
to be based upon trust and the rapport the manager has (or does not
have) with an applicant.

"A hiring manager," says Rudolph Dew, "looks at someone and
thinks, 'This person is going to be working with our group. Can he
get along with them?' In other words, can he get along with me?"

As Al Adamo puts it, "The difference is often a gut feel. How
does the hiring manager feel about the applicant—instinctively."

Those instincts are colored by initial impressions. That means
dress, speech, handshake, and the manager's innate prejudices. For
example, some managers may not like bald or heavyset applicants.
Others may dislike people with accents.

"You have to know the probability of the type of behavior a manager is going to have," says Dew. "For example, New Yorkers talk

fast. That is great if you are going for a job interview in Manhattan but it will not fly in Phoenix or Los Angeles. Slow it down."

PREJUDICE IN THE INTERVIEW

Dress is another factor and human resource director Bernadette Senn thinks it has been overblown, especially where women are concerned. "Obviously, for the man there is the suit and tie. Too many people, however, give women bad advice. They tell them they should come in with the standard white blouse and bow tie. That can be ridiculous. It is fine for a woman to wear a dress and bright colors as long as they look professional."

Prejudice? Probably, but there is not an employment interview that lacks that element. The best preparation for the applicant is to dress conservatively, be enthusiastic, and be prepared. If the applicant knows what to say and do, they will be miles ahead of the hiring manager/interviewer.

Few hiring managers take the time to prepare for the interview. The candidate is not the most pressing thing on their mind and they tend to leave the interview procedure to the last minute. "They may look at the resume a few minutes before hand, but they do not have a plan as to what they should find out," says Dew.

That leaves it wide open for the applicant. Bledsoe had been well-coached and as he and the hiring manager headed for their seats, he quickly scanned the room, looking at the pictures and decor. On the executive's desk was a photograph taken during a fishing trip. On the wall were several pictures of deep sea fishing boats and a bookcase on the far wall had a fishing rod that had been carefully placed on the top shelf. It did not take a genius to see what interests the hiring manager had.

SETTING THE HOOK

As they sat down, Bledsoe made a comment about one of the pictures and asked a question about fishing. This gave the executive and Bledsoe common ground; a topic with which they could break the ice.

McDonald calls this the *hook*. You are selling and like any salesperson you have to grab the customer's attention and interest. This is not done by immediately jumping into a conversation about the "product" (i.e., the applicant). Effective hooks are casual and conversational. They are designed to build rapport.

This can be an awkward period for the applicant and the hiring manager and it is up to the applicant to smooth it out. McDonald suggests one way to *set the hook* is to first spot the thing in the office that relates to the manager's interest and then tell a short story that ties into it.

"I do not mean to tell a 10-minute tale," he explains, "because all that will do is bore the listener. Make it quick and snappy. A minute or two is sufficient. There is nothing like a story to get someone's interest. After all, we have been telling them for thousands of years and people never get tired of hearing a good one."

The rapport established during this phase of the interview is the most important thing the applicant can do during the session. "It is amazing," says Ms. Senn, who has sat through more than 2000 interviews, "how far an applicant will go who can establish communication as opposed to the applicant who cannot." One is virtually assured of the job while the other is assured of not getting it.

SCOPING THE INTERVIEW

While finding the hook and establishing rapport is critical, there is another element equally as important—time. "I call it *scope*," says McDonald. "How much time does the executive have to spend with you? That must be determined. One of the biggest mistakes some job seekers make during an interview is they find a hook, discuss it, and never get into the job interview phase. Suddenly, the door opens and the secretary pokes her head in and says 'Mr. Brown, I do not mean to interrupt, but I wanted to remind you of your 11 A.M. meeting.' You look at your watch and it is 10:55 and the interview has not even started. You are dead. There is no way you are going to be able to sell the executive on your talents in five or less minutes."

Thus, scope—determining the executive's time parameters—is crucial. Once the hook is established (or placed), the applicant should say something such as, "Mr. Jones, I want to be sensitive to your time. I realize you probably have other appointments and I do not want to infringe on them. How much time do you have for our interview?"

With that question, Bledsoe found the vice president had 30 minutes. He also appreciated the fact Bledsoe asked. It put him at ease.

Once scope is determined, the applicant has to listen closely and be aware of transitional phases in the interview. For example, Bledsoe and the vice president spent just over 10 minutes talking about fishing and boating. Suddenly, the vice president said, "It certainly has been interesting talking about fishing. I'm glad we have some common interests. Perhaps one of these days we might even get together for a day-long trip."

This remark, to the astute applicant, means that the executive has had enough of this type of conversation and is ready to get down to business. He wants to talk about the candidate and his qualifications. The transition will not always be that obvious, therefore it is critical that the applicant listen carefully to what is being said. The subtle reference the manager gives the applicant about moving on to another part of the interview can be misread. "The natural reaction," explains McDonald, "when someone hears a phrase like 'perhaps one of these days we should get together' is to take out your calendar and try and schedule a date. It is a sign to most applicants that they are really hitting it off—and they are. Now they have a chance to really get buddy-buddy with the hiring manager. But the executive is not really asking to get together. He is saying he wants to get on with it."

The interviewer may take a more direct transition. He could say, "Well, it has been fun talking about fishing, now tell me about yourself." That is a cue to get on with it, too. The interview is on and your skills should be on display. This is the transition to the middle of the sales call.

A KEY TRANSITION

When a hiring manager asks an applicant to "tell me something about yourself," he is not asking for a life history. He is searching for information and he wants to see if the candidate fits the job description. At this point, the key is for the applicant to address the company's (and position's) needs. If the applicant has been able to research the firm, he will have a good idea of what these needs are.

Information can be acquired in numerous ways. Many newspapers have libraries that maintain clips and information on any company and/or person who has had an article written on them.

The local library may be a source as well. In the library, aside from annual reports, information on the industry can be found and some libraries even have clipping files on local companies. They may even have copies of house organs—internal newsletters that were published by the firm. Internal newsletters contain information about the firm's direction and philosophy that are not found in other publications. Frequently, these house organs are looked upon as puff sheets—and they are—but they get management's message and philosophy across. A newspaper article or advertisement may not.

Sales brochures are another source and give applicants an insight into what—and how—a company is promoting its products and services. The brochures also project an image of the company. For example, is the brochure on slick, glossy paper with color photographs, or is it on a mat finish with black-and-white photographs and duplicated at an instant print shop? One definitely says quality and spare no cost while the other says let's cut some corners and do it cheaply. It is an insight into how management is thinking.

There are other resources at the library that are of value. Moody's, for example, is a series of manuals that provides in-depth information on a company pertaining to its history, finances, products, services, subsidiaries, and executives. There are a number of different directories that cover companies in categories ranging from industrial to government.

Suppliers are another source. Companies that supply firms with stationery, janitorial, or even coffee supplies oftentimes have information. Will they give it? Not if they feel it is going to violate a confidence or endanger the relationship they have with the company. However, if the applicant makes it clear that he is researching the company because he is a possible employment candidate and he does not intend to reveal this information or the sources to anyone, he may find himself the recipient of little-known facts. If the applicant knows someone who, in turn, knows someone at the supplying firm, he may also obtain valuable insight.

Subsidiaries of the hiring company as well as brokers in the financial community are sources. So are bankers, accountants, and insurance agents. All of these usually have knowledge about local firms and what they are doing because they are either doing business with them or know someone who is.

An applicant may not know anyone at the firm or its subsidiaries, but there is an excellent chance he has contacts with a banker or accountant who does have information or access to it. Bankers, in particular, are an excellent source of information. They will not reveal confidential information about a client. However, if the applicant has a good banking relationship and rapport with an officer at the institution, he has one foot in the information door. Bankers talk to each other all the time and exchange information.

Another source that is often overlooked is the operator and/or receptionist who answers the telephone for the firm. They usually have a piece of information that is not readily available—how the employees feel about the firm. Annual reports list facts, figures, and a CEO's (or board chairman's) letter, but they do not go into the morale of the employees. Any applicant who is about to be interviewed should determine as much as possible about the internal environment.

Bledsoe spent several hours at the library, talked to the receptionist, and a local banker, and read and reread two annual reports, a 10k (financial report) supplied by a broker, and the firm's most recent sales literature. He had a good, working knowledge of the company and what some of its needs were.

A WINNING SCRIPT

When the vice president asked Bledsoe to tell him about himself, Bledsoe did not immediately jump in and give him a life history. Instead, Bledsoe did the smart thing. He turned to the executive and said "I would be delighted to tell you something about myself, but I could use your help. Could you tell me a little more about what this specific job involves and some of the requirements you feel are important?"

If a candidate poses a question in that (or similar) fashion and gets an answer, the answer tells the candidate exactly what the executive is trying to find. The executive is outlining his needs when he describes the requirements and the candidate can tailor his history to fit the requirements.

On the other hand, some executives will not say anything. "They will," says McDonald, "simply press the issue and say something like, 'Well, tell me something about yourself first.'"

If that happens, the candidate's preparation is critical. If he has studied the company, he can bring out his qualifications as he believes they relate to the company's (and position's) needs. If he has not studied the firm, he has to wing it. By not offering any insight into the company, the needs the applicant feels the company has, and how he might fill these needs, he becomes just another candidate.

The job interview is no different than a sales call and the salesperson who tries to make a sale without knowing what the customer wants has a difficult time closing a transaction. The same is true of the applicant.

THE THREE/SIX RULE

Even if the hiring manager fails to outline any of his company's (or the position's) needs, there are guidelines. McDonald maintains there are "at least three and no more than six" major responsibilities for a key position. Anyone applying for that position should certainly be aware of its responsibilities. For example, Bledsoe was applying for the position of Director of Communications. Based upon experience, he knew the three prime areas of responsibility were financial public relations, publicity in the marketplace where the company's customers (i.e., consumers or trade) were present, and internal communications via newsletters and other similar publications.

In examining the company, Bledsoe became aware of several weaknesses or areas that needed improvement. In the financial community, the firm's stock had dropped 6 percent during the past year. Although there were reasons for the drop, Bledsoe was certain the company's executives would be concerned because of potential shareholder unrest. Part of the reason for the drop in price was that the company had lost market share for one of its product lines. Bledsoe analyzed the product and saw several ways in which an effective communications program at the customer level might help.

When the vice president asked Bledsoe about himself, he immediately brought up several situations—similar to the ones with which this company was having trouble—that he helped solve for previous employers. He illustrated both with short anecdotes, none of which ran more than a minute each. The stories helped keep the interviewer's interest and the analogies were evidence that Bledsoe had the ability to solve similar problems.

Bledsoe could have worked out a solution to the problem his potential employer was having; however, that can be a dangerous approach. Even though an applicant has researched a company, he may not have all the facts and to propose a solution without them may indicate to the hiring manager that the applicant is impetuous and does not give sufficient thought to problems.

Another technique for determining needs is to take the three to six responsibilities (or criteria) of the position and pose questions to the hiring manager with them. For example, if the hiring manager had asked Bledsoe about himself without laying out any parameters of the position, Bledsoe could have come back with, "Well, Mr. Jones, in the position we are talking about, there are several critical areas of responsibility. One of the first is financial public relations. Has there been much done in this area and do you see any particular needs?"

The question shows the manager the applicant is aware. The manager may come back with a statement such as, "Yes, that has been a concern because . . ." Bledsoe, or any applicant, would then follow with examples of how he has handled the area. The manager might say something like, "Sure, that is a concern, but the area of most importance to us is . . ." This reply is a cue to concentrate on that area. If the manager does not focus on any one responsibility, the applicant continues to go down the list and cite questions along with examples.

Bledsoe went on to a second area of responsibility: publicity that concentrates on the firm's customers. He posed a similar question and, from the answer, determined how important the function was to the company. From there he went on to the third area: internal communications.

By working through each responsibility, the applicant was able to determine the hiring manager's concerns. Every applicant, regardless of the knowledge he has of the company, has the same ability. By being aware of a position's key responsibilities, it is possible to determine the exact needs of the firm. The applicant simply takes his cues from the manager's answers.

PLANNING THE CLOSE

The middle part of the interview is, once again, similar to the sales call. The client's needs are covered and his requirements are matched by the applicant's experience. As is the case with all sales calls, eventually there has to be a close.

This stage of the interview process takes sensitivity. The hiring manager has apparently run out of questions and the applicant has run out of examples. In moving towards the close, the applicant can ask, "Are there any questions you would like to ask me?" If the manager has a question about the applicant's abilities, it will surface here. He might ask something like, "Well, Mr. Bledsoe, I see how you have been quite active in financial public relations, but how about the consumer publicity?"

Although the candidate thinks he may have covered that area, he did not. The hiring manager still has a question—and doubt—as to the candidate's ability in that area. When questions of this type surface, the applicant should look upon them as an objection and they must be answered. This can be done through another story or illustration. The applicant must be sure, however, that there is no doubt left in the manager's mind.

A catch-22 question that many hiring managers pose is, "Tell me about your weaknesses." The applicant who says he does not have any is not believable. The applicant who says he does and goes on to describe them gives the manager a reason not to hire him. Some suggest naming a weakness and going on to explain how you have improved in the area. That still can be a minus in the eyes of the hiring manager.

TYING WEAK POINTS TO STRONG POINTS

There is a solution to this situation and that is to tie weak points to strong points. For example, someone who might be interviewing for a job that requires a great deal of writing might say, "I write fast and it appears as if I did not put any effort into it because I usually finish assignments quickly." That is a weak point tied to something strong but there is nothing negative about it.

Along the same lines, hiring managers will ask, "What was your greatest accomplishment?" A chance to brag, make points, or do both. Unfortunately, many applicants stammer and hesitate because they are not prepared. The accomplishment, like the weakness, should be determined before the interview begins and it should relate to something the hiring manager's company is doing. In Bledsoe's case, he was ready with an illustration of how he worked a consumer/product promotion for his previous company. It was so successful that it boosted sales 18 percent during one 30-day period. The hiring manager who has a similar product and problem can identify with this illustration.

Another question that has become popular recently is the hiring manager asking the applicant, "Why should we hire you?"

The unprepared candidate seldom answers correctly. The answer has nothing to do with "I can do the job" or "My qualifications are a perfect fit." It does, however, have a great deal to do with Dew's value-added selling. When the question is posed, the applicant has the opportunity to cite accomplishments in quantifiable numbers that relate to the open position.

Once again, in Bledsoe's case, it involved a promotional illustration in which he increased his previous employer's business by 18 percent. He also developed a financial relations program in which the CEO from the company made four speaking engagements in 45 days to various brokerage firms and, at the end of 60 days, the company's stock had increased 12 percent. In other words, Bledsoe is indicating he can do the same for this prospective new employer. He is stating what kind of bottom line results he might bring to the company. That is value-added selling—the additional value the candidate is going to bring to the company.

Accountants, engineers, systems analysts, and programmers can all do the same. The accountant could show where a new receivable system he designed sped up collections an average of 10 days per account and improved cash flow by a certain percentage as well. The engineer could show how an assembly line innovation eliminated three unnecessary steps and improved productivity by a certain percentage during the first month it was in place.

Once the hiring manager has posed all his questions and is convinced of the applicant's abilities, it is time for the applicant to pose his questions.

THE TOUGH QUESTIONS

The most difficult questions are those pertaining to past employment and why you were fired or laid off. Not all managers will ask—they will leave it to the human resource department to check—but some will.

"Why were you laid off?"

"It was an across the board 10 percent cut."

"Why were you fired?"

"There were some differences, but my firing had nothing to do with my performance and when you check my references you will find I did an excellent job. My former boss can give you some idea of the innovations and accomplishments I was responsible for during the time I was there."

Another frequently asked question is, "Where do you see yourself in five years?" The standard answer used to be, "In a job similar to yours." With paranoia rampant in industry and every hiring manager protective of his position, that answer is far from acceptable. The applicant should simply say something about contributing to a company like this one by doing this and that. In other words, bring up the value-added points.

"If someone does not ask questions during the process," says Ms. Senn, "to me that is a negative. It is a judgment I make. My assumption is that bright, interested people ask questions."

"It is a turn-on when you ask questions," says Adamo. "The interview is a two-way street and if the applicant has established rapport, he can ask pointed questions."

For example, "I notice the number of employees has fluctuated dramatically in the past three years, can you tell me why?" Or "Could you tell me about any weaknesses or areas in which you think the company should improve?"

McDonald suggests questions that may pertain to where the company is going, does it do strategic planning, and how does the position fit into the long-term goals of the firm.

A series of questions the applicant should definitely ask are those that pertain to the position itself. For example, applicants should ask about the areas in which they will have responsibility: What areas are they, what resources will the applicant have at his disposal, and, one of the most important questions, what do you, the boss/hiring manager, see as a priority?

"That is one of the key questions in any job," says Dew, "and it is one of the major causes of failure in a job. The person who takes the position sees the job being done one way and he has one set of priorities. His boss has another. Find the boss' pet project or interest. Just doing your job satisfactorily is not the thing, today. What the boss wants is. What is his priority or priorities."

THE CLOSE

Once the questions are disposed of, it is time for the close. This can be done with a statement like, "Well, Mr. Jones, you have seen my background and qualifications, how do you see me fitting into this position?"

Not every interviewer is going to reveal his or her feelings. Some may tell an applicant they like him while others hold back and refuse to give a clue.

Ms. Senn likes the direct approach. "If they want to know where they stand, they should ask. If I am definitely interested I will tell them. If they are borderline, I will be vague. I probably do not tell people where I stand more often than I do tell them."

The manager's answer could be, "Well, it is a little too early to say and we have two or three others to talk with." That means he has not made a decision and he wants to mull it over after he talks to the other candidates. He might say, "Mr. Bledsoe, I think you are perfect for the job." The response to that statement would be something like, "Where would you like to go from here?" Hopefully, it is an offer, as it was in Bledsoe's case.

There may be more than one interview the applicant goes through with the hiring manager. In today's environment where there are more resumes than ever for middle management positions, it is not uncommon for an applicant to be interviewed three or four times by the same manager before a decision is made.

Not every interview takes place in the office, either. Some managers invite applicants to lunch. The object of the luncheon may be more than a casual meal. It may be to see if the candidate smokes or drinks.

If an applicant can bypass the human resource department and go directly to the hiring manager, he has an advantage—he has avoided the screening where the object is to eliminate candidates, not find them.

In many cases, the human resource department will screen without interviewing. They will select the resumes they think are best and send them directly to the hiring manager. In other cases, they will interview and then send the best on to the hiring manager. An interview with the human resource department differs markedly from one with a hiring manager. The hiring manager's approach is loosely structured and subjective. He looks for best fit, that is, "Will this individual fit in with the rest of my group." He makes his judgment on instinct and the rapport he and the applicant have had.

The human resource department is going by a slate of objective requirements that have been given to them. The interview is structured and objective. In Bledsoe's case, the hiring manager wanted someone who had done consumer product publicity, worked in financial public relations, and put together internal newsletters. He did not particularly care about management skills or the person's ability to get along with others.

The human resource department will look for those three requirements in the cover letter and resume. For those applicants who survive the initial screening, the interview will concentrate on the same three areas. That means the applicant has to be well-versed in those responsibilities.

Applicants should not underestimate the importance of rapport with human resource interviewers. They are no different than anyone else and although the interview is structured and objective, it has an element of subjectivity to it. Their decision making, like that of the hiring manager, will be influenced by the rapport they have with the applicant.

Applicants should be prepared for questions from human resource interviews that they do not get from the hiring manager. For instance, is there a gap in the resume? If so, human resource interviewers will want to know why. Was the applicant fired or laid off? Why? Was there a personality conflict? If there was a conflict at one company, perhaps there will be one at this company.

They may also ask for references from previous places of employment. Human resource people want to talk to previous supervisors instead of the human resource department at the applicant's previous company. With the prevalence of wrongful termination lawsuits, human resource people have become extremely cautious when they give information out on a former employee. Thus, they will ask the applicant for the name of a previous supervisor.

What does someone do who has been fired? Fred Peters says, "you are in trouble. That is a definite strike and red flag for any employer. Human resource people may say it does not make a difference, but it does."

The answer is not to blame the firing on a personality conflict. If the applicant had a conflict at one firm, he could have it at another.

"There is," says McDonald, "a way around it. A supervisor can say something good about any employee, fired or not."

McDonald cites the case of an executive who was making a six-figure income and held down a CEO's position. He was hired by the chairman and, unfortunately, he had "terrible problems with authority figures." By not going by the rules, the CEO almost cost the chairman his job. Ultimately, the chairman fired him. The chairman was so enraged that he refused to even speak to anyone who mentioned the former CEO's name.

Eventually, the time came when the fired CEO was about to interview for another job, and his potential new employers wanted to call for a reference. The chairman, at first, refused and went into a rage. The human resource director reminded him about the possible legal problems the company could have and suggested there "must have been something good about the man. Is there one or two things you could say that he did well?" The human resource director went through a list of things he knew the CEO had accomplished. Begrudgingly, the chairman agreed and four things were written on a piece of paper and given to him. If called, he would give the CEO a positive reference on those four items.

Obviously, the case is extreme but the point is, there are positive things that can be said about any terminated employee. The applicant must make sure his previous supervisor is going to say them. That is one reason a fired employee should not become unpleasant and make accusations when he is fired. As difficult as it is to control one's emotions, one day the dismissed employee may have to come back to the supervisor and ask for a reference.

OVERCOMING A FIRING

Even a good reference will not always overcome the stigma of a firing. The human resource person is going to probe. Being fired does not necessarily mean you did a poor job, but they want to know why. The hiring manager is going to be curious, as well. Put yourself in the place of a hiring manager. Would you hire someone who has been fired? If so, what steps would you take to protect the company before bringing him in? Human resource people and hiring managers are going to think the same way.

Ms. Senn says if you have been fired, it is an "issue that is definitely worth exploring. That does not mean it is unforgivable, but I want to know why. And if you have been fired more than once, I get real curious."

The situation is not as dismal as it may appear. "It can be surmounted, but the key for the job seeker is to talk to the previous employer and make sure he is going to give a positive reference."

Aside from references, human resource people are also going to be looking for job tenure—how long did you spend in your last position?

"We have definite impressions as to how long a person should be on a job," explains Ben Greco, "For example, accountants and finance people should not be moving around as often as sales people. If we see an accountant come through who has changed firms every two or three years, a bell rings. Something may be wrong with this person. At the same time, if you see a salesman who has moved every 18 months, it may not bother the human resource department at all."

Job hopping does become a concern of interviewers when the position is high salaried and the company has paid a search or placement firm substantial fees for finding the candidate. They do not want someone who will only be around for a year or two.

Aside from firings and frequent job changes, there are two other things that companies take into consideration when interviewing—age and sex. Discrimination laws have eliminated any blatant overt actions, but there are guidelines that job seekers will encounter. The applicant may not run into problems until the interview because a power resume does not give any clue as to a person's age.

THE AGE FACTOR

Once the applicant is sitting across from the interviewer, age may become a factor. Certain unwritten rules apply. Assume there is a manager in his mid-fifties who applies for a position as a department head. In this particular company, department heads may be as young as 40 and as old as 53. In checking his previous history, the human resource person discovers the applicant is 55 years of age. Is he going to fit the organization? Why is he not a vice president? Is there something wrong with his skills? All those questions enter an interviewer's mind when age enters the picture.

A 60-year-old department head who has been laid off and is applying for a job will run into similar problems. The human resource person will wonder about his (or her) ability—why wasn't he in a more senior position. They will also wonder about how much longer this person will work—will he retire at 65? Age is a factor in this case.

The 60-year-old CEO may not have any problem. CEOs are expected to be older because of the experience required for the position. But there are still two questions remaining when someone 55 and over is interviewed—how long will they work and can they handle the job?

What is their energy level? Any executive who is 50 years of age or more should exhibit enthusiasm and energy at an interview because the human resource director (and hiring manager) is constantly evaluating these factors. Is this person too old to handle the pressure? Can he go 50 hours per week? The posture and energy that emanates from the applicant says a great deal about a person's physical ability.

"If a man walks in and he looks like he is 40 years of age and he is actually 55, that is a definite plus," says Adamo. "I think everyone looks for a healthy body. It influences them."

"If there is a guy 55 and one 43, and both are competing for the same job and have equal qualifications, I put my money on the younger candidate," says Fred Peters.

"Sure, every industry will hire a few older executives but age is going to hold them back; companies are definitely shooting for the younger executive if they have the qualifications."

THE GENDER FACTOR

Gender may be a problem, too. With approximately 50 percent of all employees female, the era of discrimination would appear to be gone, but it is not. Many women are still lower paid even though they occupy the same position that a man does. If a human resource director finds a qualified woman candidate for a middle management position, he (or she) is going to quietly weigh additional factors. Will this female fit in with the rest of the department? Has there been an unwritten policy insofar as the hiring of women as department heads?

If female job applicants examine a company, they may be able to determine the company's policies before they ever reach the interview stage. Does the firm have women in positions of responsibility? If not, why? Whereas most overt discrimination cases end in lawsuits, those behind the scenes never do and many female applicants wonder why they were not hired.

An excellent example of the subtle ways in which discrimination works is one involving a major corporation on the West Coast. A few years ago, the all-male board had a vacancy. The human resource director screened and interviewed dozens of candidates and found a female who would be a perfect addition to the group. He proposed the woman to the chairman who, without blinking an eye, turned her down. Why? It seems that every afternoon at 4:30, all worked stopped on the executive floor and the key managers gathered together for an hour or so of bridge in the chairman's office. This practice had gone on for years and the executives usually enjoyed a drink along with the game. The chairman's reasoning was that the language would be too raucous and the woman would not fit into the tight-knit group.

Despite this case, many human resource directors and search firms theorize that discrimination on the basis of sex may be disappearing in this country, but it is just beginning to appear in a different way. There are numerous foreign companies doing business in the United States. Some of those firms have set up subsidiaries and are hiring Americans. Recently, McDonald had an ideal candidate for one, a former human resource director whose qualifications matched the requirements of the hiring company. Enthusiastically, he called the firm and talked to the hiring manager. He immediately detected the low-key tone of the voice on the other end.

"Sorry, Bob, it will never work. This position has line authority over a similar one in the Far East. That position is occupied by a male and it is against the culture of the country to install a female as his supervisor."

It surprised McDonald but "I expect it is not an isolated instance and will increase as our dealings with foreign countries grow and they establish more subsidiaries in the United States."

THE VALUE-ADDED FOLLOW UP

Although each interview differs, there is one thing every applicant should keep in mind when the session is over—write a thank you note. Thank you notes can tip the scales primarily because not many applicants take the time to put one together. Ideal thank you notes should be handwritten and legible. Aside from saying thanks for the interviewer's time, the note should contain some additional information that the interviewer might find helpful. In Dew's words, it should contain "more value-added facts."

Value-added facts might pertain to something the applicant forgot to tell the interviewer. For example, if the position was for a departmental supervisor who was responsible for production or scheduling, the applicant might cite an instance in the note that he forgot to mention during the interview. It might relate to a creative scheduling mix that the applicant designed; one that enabled his former employer to save a certain percentage. The note might read something like the note in Figure 69.

Figure 69   Thank-You Note Containing Value-Added Fact

Dear Mr. Jones:

Just a short note to say how much I enjoyed our chat this afternoon.

Incidentally, I thought you might be interested in knowing that XYZ Trucking, the firm I worked for, had a production problem similar to your firm's. I solved it by revising the schedule and using the most productive drivers on the most difficult runs. Within 30 days after I put the program in operation, we were saving 12 percent in payroll costs and our shipments were arriving an average of three days earlier.

If there is any other information I can supply, please let me know.

Once again, I enjoyed the chat.

Sincerely,

If the applicant does not have any value-added tips to offer, the note should still be sent. In this case, the middle paragraph which outlines the applicant's accomplishment would be deleted. The key, however, is to remember to send the thank you note.

Thank you notes, along with other power resume tips, are discussed in Chapter 8.

8

POWER RESUME

TECHNIQUES

Never give your age. This gives a human resource director the opportunity to dispose of your resume if you are too "old." There are exceptions. If an executive is going after a CEO position, an age in the mid-fifties is perfectly acceptable. It shows maturity and experience. If he is going after a vice president position, an age in the early fifties is acceptable. But even if the position is for a CEO, as an applicant's age approaches 60, there is a good chance of discrimination.

Never give degree dates. This is a giveaway of age. Any human resource director or hiring manager will do some counting if the date of the degree is given, although in some cases, when a manager decides to pursue a degree later in life, these dates can be misleading.

Never give the number of children you have. If an applicant has five children, he may feel that by listing them he will give the impression to the human resource director that he is a "family man." That can be a detriment, however, especially if the position applied for requires travel. The human resource director (and hiring manager) will wonder if this executive can really travel without creating a hardship for his family. At the same time, some human resource directors may view the number of children as a sign that the executive is too family oriented—that he (or she) will not want to work late or on weekends.

Women should never give marital status. Corporate people look at these resumes and wonder when the person is going to have to take maternity leave. The female applicant may say, "Well, my kids are grown and out of the house." Fine, but if a resume lists two children, ages 27 and 25, the human resource director might wonder if, perhaps, this candidate isn't too old for the job.

Do not give salary. If you give a salary bracket you are searching for, you can be too high or too low. There is little chance you will be on the mark. If you are too high, the human resource department may surmise that you are overqualified for the job. If you are too low, they may wonder why you are willing to work for so little or they may wonder why you have never earned more.

Do not be negative. Never put anything negative in a cover letter or a resume. If you downgrade a former employer (or supervisor), the impression is that it would not be long before you downgrade this new company as well. If there was a problem with the former company, do not indicate it, either. Being positive and upbeat in cover letters and resumes is critical to opening doors.

Do not use present company letterhead. This is a dead giveaway that you are inconsiderate and not an employee who has high regard for employers. If you use a present company's letterhead, it implies that you are stealing two things: the letterhead and the time it took to write the letter. Companies do not want to hire disloyal workers.

Do not give previous salary history. Once again, this is an item that can be used against you. It shows what you made and where you fit, that is, if you are too high or low on the salary scale. Always leave salary for the face-to-face interview. Even if an ad requests salary history, do not include it.

Use chronological resumes. Power resumes are chronological. Functional resumes immediately raise questions in the minds of human resource people. What are you trying to hide? Why? They are also difficult to read insofar as finding companies and employment dates. When a human resource person (or hiring manager) is rushed and needs to get through as many resumes as possible, the functional resume slows him down and may be discarded because of it.

No typographical errors. In letters or resumes, this can be the kiss of death. If you do not take enough time to spell it right, the human resource screener may feel that you do not care that much about the position; if you are careless on paper, perhaps you are careless in the workplace. Companies are not interested in careless workers. The typo gives the screener an excuse to discard your resume.

No erasures. Computers erase, erasers on pencils or pens do not. They always leave tell-tale marks and are another giveaway to the hiring manager or human resource person that you do not care that much about the position. Keep it neat.

Professionally duplicated. Most important—applicants may take hours typing a resume or, perhaps, they prepare it on a word processor. Once the original is typed (or on computer), do not run copies through a duplicating machine that produces poor copies. The copies should be of quality equal to the original. An instant printer's offset press will duplicate this quality at an extremely low cost. Get it duplicated professionally.

Use letter quality printers. If a resume is put together on a computer, the printer should be letter quality. There is a temptation, especially among accountants, engineers, and computer applicants, to use the printers they have at work. Printers in these departments are not necessarily letter quality. They often produce poor copies and immediately say to the human resource department that this person is cranking out the same resume and cover letter to everyone. Computers are commonplace and most human resource screeners realize applicants utilize them. However, they cannot discern a computer resume from a non-computer resume when letter quality printers are utilized.

Summary or summary of experience a must. Every resume should have this at the top. It should be no more than one or two sentences and should give the screener a quick look at your experience and expertise. It immediately tells the screener if you can qualify. Typical summaries read like this:

Summary: Sales manager with 14 years of increasingly responsible positions including introduction of new products and management of sales teams ranging in size from 8 to 14.

This summary would be appropriate for an ad that asked for a sales manager who specialized in new product introductions and team management. The summary is always a direct answer to the ad or a match for the position's requirements.

Never say you were fired. Unfortunately, complete honesty does not pay off in the job market. Human resource people will say it does not matter if someone has been fired, but it does. If you could not get along with your former boss, perhaps you will not get along with the next one. Being fired is a major strike against an applicant. Some of the more liberal human resource people say they understand one firing, but never more than one. They would like to hear it explained. If it can be avoided, do not mention it. If you cannot avoid it, leave the entire explanation for the first face-to-face interview and make sure the firing can be tempered with a reference from your former supervisor. In most cases, fired employees can obtain a positive reference. There are always categories in which the employee did well and these are the areas that former employees should ask their managers to stress when called for a reference. Applicants should also remember never to denigrate former managers during interviews. The negative feelings reflect poorly on any applicant.

Hide the holes. If you have gaps in your employment record, human resource people are going to wonder. They will ask themselves what you were doing? Were you not able to get a job during that time period? If not, why? One way to avoid gaps is to remember that human resource departments will seldom check beyond your last two employments. If you have gaps prior to those two positions, there is no need to detail them in a resume. If you have three positions in your resume and they total seven to eight years, there is no need to put in gaps on the others.

Do not lie about nonjob experience. Some applicants may feel they can get an edge if they spell out something in their resume that is not quite accurate. For example, the person who only went to school three plus years and is only four units shy of graduating from college may be tempted to say he earned his BA or BS from X college. That is a definite mistake. Today, human resource directors are limited insofar as what they can get from previous employers. Many simply examine other parts of the resume and check them. A degree is something that can be checked and often is. If they find you have lied about a degree, that will eliminate you from consideration. The thinking is if you lied about one thing, you may have lied about others, and you may lie when you go to work for them.

Do not go over two pages. No one, not even a former president, need go beyond two pages in a resume. If you cannot say it in two pages, go through the resume once more and cut. Use bullets to highlight specific accomplishments. Human resource people get hundreds of resumes per job. They are in the business of eliminating resumes, not finding applicants. If a resume goes beyond two pages—unless it is exceptional and attracts the eye of the reader—it will kill the applicant. It is one more way of screening. Screeners are prejudiced against resumes that are beyond two pages. Their reasoning, while beneath the surface, is that they read all day long and they do not want to tire their eyes even more by going through a three-page resume. They may also feel that anyone who writes a three-page resume lacks the ability to be brief and succinct, and in many positions, missing that qualification can cost the job.

Stay away from narrative resumes. Too hard to read and they say too little. Highlight your accomplishments and do it briefly with bullets. Narratives also lead applicants into traps. They start using "I" and "we" too much.

Be specific in your resume. Use numbers and specific accomplishments wherever possible in the body of the resume. Avoid lines like, "While I was sales manager, I increased sales to their highest level." Concentrate on utilizing facts such as, "We reduced costs by 12 percent with the new accounting procedure I introduced" or "We increased sales by 22 percent in three years with the new telemarketing procedure I introduced. This was double our normal rate of sales increase." Hiring managers can sink their teeth into specifics, but can do little with generalizations.

Address the resume to someone. Find out the name of the person who is screening resumes. If it is in the human resource department, call and get the name of the director. Everyone attaches importance to their name. They will open a resume with their name on it first.

Use "Dear Sir/Madam." If it is impossible to find the name of the screener, hiring manager, or human resource director, address the cover letter to "Dear Sir/Madam." In many cases, this is the only alternative with blind ads.

Bypass the human resource department. If it is possible, do not send your resume to the human resource department; send it to the hiring manager. With ads that are not blind, this can be accomplished by analyzing the position and to whom you would report. Applicants should call companies and ask for the name of the sales manager, CFO, CEO, or whoever will be doing the hiring. If the resume goes to the hiring manager and he likes what he sees, he will "tune" in the human resource department to the resume.

Bypass contingency employment firms. Whenever possible, skirt the employment firm that is on a contingency. All this means is that the search firm gets paid only when they have an applicant who can fill the position. They send all resumes on to either the hiring manager or human resource department.

Do not bypass retainer firms. Retainer firms are exactly that. They are given a fee to locate the applicant. They search and screen for the hiring company. The company pays the firm and will usually rely upon them to screen all resumes and applicants. Retainer firms are utilized for several reasons and one is to save the time the hiring manager might have to spend screening. Thus, retainer firms are going to be involved in the selection process and it is not advisable to try and bypass them.

Target the resume. Every resume should be targeted to the position. Do not structure one resume for all jobs. Ads should be studied and requirements carefully thought out. The qualifications within the resume should match the requirements in the ad. Remember, when the human resource person (or anyone) screens resumes for a hiring manager, they are going to have two, three, or perhaps four parameters. If those qualifications do not immediately stick out, they may discard the resume.

Be qualified, not overqualified. Too much experience can be as harmful as too little. Firms look for people who fit, not those whose knowledge and experience goes beyond the job. They are afraid that people who are overqualified will leave the first chance they get . . . and they are usually correct. When you customize a resume and if you want the position, make sure the resume does not go far beyond what the ad is seeking.

Never put a photograph on a resume. Aside from it being passé, it gives screeners a chance to discriminate. They may not like people with dark hair, light hair, long hair, or so on.

Watch the job "space." Some occupations are perceived as having less longevity than others. For example, an accountant is usually thought of as someone who may spend three to four years on a job. On the other hand, a salesman may have two jobs to every one that an accountant holds. Salesmen hop more frequently. If the human resource director or the hiring manager perceives that your job history shows too many positions in too short a time, you can lose the position.

Extracurricular activities. Make sure your resume has room for your community involvement. In many positions (i.e., sales and marketing), involvement shows you are outgoing and are willing to put in time for important causes. Even in technical occupations, the extracurricular activities may come into play. Hiring managers relate these activities to your ability to relate to people within the workplace. That does not mean applicants have to load their resumes with community involvement. However, there should be two or three items on the resume to indicate the candidate has taken an interest in the community.

Do not offer references. In resumes, references are superfluous. When and if the hiring manager (or human resource department) wants one, they will ask. At the appropriate time, that is when the candidate has gone through the human resource department and one or two interviews with the hiring manager, he may offer to provide a reference. At this point, it may make sense. If the hiring manager has spoken to a candidate more than once, he is narrowing his options. Anything at this point that can focus him on the candidate is an asset. Thus, offering a reference at this point, when a few good words could make the difference, is tactically superior to offering references at the beginning of the game.

Last job first. Make sure your resume lists your last position first and all other positions, in chronological order, should follow.

Watch the three strikes. Do not put in layoffs, firings, or your age. Those three, when used together, are guaranteed to eliminate you from consideration for virtually any position.

Do not use colored paper. Print your resume on plain white paper with black ink. Colors may stand out but they are unorthodox and may reflect poorly on your ability to fit in the organization. Use at least 20-pound stock and, if possible, a white textured paper that gives the resume a clean, rich look.

Do not use all upper case letters. When you have a series of words or sentences, do not use all capital letters. Too many capitals—one right after another—make reading difficult. THIS TYPE OF AP-PROACH IS NOT NEARLY AS GOOD as this type of approach. Notice how much easier the latter portion of the sentence is to read. RESUME can be all capitals.

The importance of white space. Do not crowd everything together in a resume. Avoid narratives that gobble up white space on the paper. Use as much space as possible. Space aids the eye in reading. Use the bulleted approach for points you want to stand out.

Avoid acronyms. PR may stand for Public Relations, but most people outside the industry do not have any idea what it means. If you are in a particular profession and belong to any organizations or groups, make sure you spell out the name the first time you utilize it. After you spell it out, initials are permissible.

The three/six rule. There are seldom less than three nor more than six major responsibilities for any position. When answering an ad isolate those responsibilities and match your qualifications with as many as possible. When interviewed, make sure you are able to get the interviewer to name those three to six responsibilities so you can match your qualifications to them.

The extra resume. Always keep one handy, especially if you are about to go through an interview. Hiring managers have a habit of misplacing things, especially resumes, and if there is something you want to make sure he or she sees, carry an extra resume with you.

The magic words. Every resume should be tailored to fit each different position or different industry. There is no such thing as an effective generic resume. Resumes lose impact and can cost interviews if they are not slanted to fit the position and the industry.

Focus on accomplishments. Resumes should play down duties and responsibilities and focus on specific accomplishments. Those specifics should always be stated in measurable terms such as percentages saved, dollars earned, or production increased.

Do not send resumes en masse to search firms. They seldom keep them around. Search firms are usually only interested in the positions they currently have to fill. If you send in a resume without answering a specific ad, there is a good chance it will be discarded and never even read. If you are one of those individuals who is in a unique, hard-to-find profession, then the search firm may keep your resume. Remember, too, that search firms are usually only interested in recruiting employed executives. It is hard for them to sell a laid off or fired executive to management. That is why they always pursue those who already have a job. Hence the term *headhunter*.

How to tighten your resume. Hiring managers will seldom have any position checked beyond three previous employments. Many companies do not even maintain employment records beyond seven years. Consequently, resumes that run beyond two pages can easily be trimmed by eliminating older positions. If, however, a previous position is directly related to the opening the applicant is after, keep it in if at all possible.

Requirements vs. qualifications. Resumes are screened by human resource people who will match qualifications to requirements. If qualifications are not bulleted and do not stand out, the applicant could lose out. Human resource people do not spend time searching the resume for the qualifications. They must be obvious.

Objective. This term is fine when it comes to military targets, but is obsolete when it comes to resumes. Human resource directors and hiring managers recognize that objectives are put in for effect—and they seldom have any. There is also the danger that an applicant's objective may not meet the expectations of the hiring manager.

Eliminate adjectives. Do not waste space with flowery language. Hiring managers and human resource people are only interested in the facts.

The degree rule. If you list a degree on your resume, make sure you are accurate. With the limitations placed upon human resource people in checking previous employers, many look for other areas to check—and education is one of them. If you are inaccurate and it is turned up by the human resource person, you automatically lose the interview and chance for the position because the company may feel that your education inaccuracies are only one of many mistakes on the resume.

Education goes last. Education achievements and degrees always follow work experience on a resume with one exception—if the applicant is going for a position relating to instruction in a school. Degrees are highly prized in the education area and would precede work experience.

Avoid "complete responsibility." The temptation for many department heads, vice presidents, and CEOs is to use the "complete responsibility for." In the eyes of human resource people, hiring managers, and other employment specialists, no one has complete responsibility. To some it is even a turn-off. Avoid using "complete" because it says no one else deserves credit (or blame).

Resume turn off. Saying what the company (or department) did instead of what the applicant accomplished.

Resume turn on. Resumes following the 10 rules of power resumes.

1. Stay away from functional resumes.
2. Do not include objectives in the resume.
3. Leave out all clues and mention of age.
4. Use active words, not passive.
5. Tailor the resume to the job.
6. Use a summary at the beginning.
7. Limit the resume to two pages.
8. Leave out all reference to salary.
9. Include extracurricular activities when room permits.
10. Talk about specific accomplishments and do not waste more than a line on duties and responsibilities.

Resume and sales. Remember that a resume is a sales letter, not a chronological record of work experience. It must do much more than give a recap of employment history. It has to convince the prospective employer that you are the person for the job. Like any good sales vehicle, it must address the employer's needs.

Do not exaggerate. There is no telling what a human resource department will check on a resume. Exaggerations invite scrutiny and stretching the truth is one way to wind up without an interview.

Leave out short-term positions. Try to avoid listing short-term positions you may have had. If you had a job for six months or less, it is best not to list it. If, for instance, you were employed from June 1984 to July 1986 and then unemployed from July 1986 to December 1986, consolidate the listing. It would read from June 1984 to December 1986. Short gaps should be covered.

Do not hog the credit. If you were a member of a team that accomplished something specific, mention the word "team." If you claim the credit for yourself, there is always the chance the hiring manager may know differently (especially if he is in the same industry) or you may be tripped up later when a previous supervisor is called. If the team did something significant and you were part of it, that is substantial in itself.

Underlining. Underlining should be used in the resume but not overdone. Use it under titles such as *Work Experience, Education,* and anything similar. Underlining can also be effective when indicating the name of a previous employer and dates. Do not go overboard on the underlining, however. It is similar to using all capital letters: too much and the impact is lost.

Overcoming industry experience. If you are changing industries but staying in a position that is the same (i.e., data processing manager, communications manager, or CFO), be sure and stress accomplishments as they relate to the job and play down the industry.

Abbreviations. Like acronyms, they do not enhance a resume. They can be used for abbreviating months of the year in your work experience section, but not beyond that.

Cute is out. Whether it is the resume or cover letter, avoid trying to be funny, cute, or playing on words. You never know who will read the resume and it could be someone without a sense of humor.

Think like a hiring manager. When putting together a resume, think like the hiring manager. Put yourself in his position and ask what qualifications would you most like to see for this position?

Write slowly and edit. Letters and resumes take time to write and they should be read and reread—and edited. Read each one and put yourself in the place of the hiring manager. Try and imagine the reaction he or she will have when seeing the resume and/or cover letter. Does it leave gaps? Does it answer all the requirements?

Use active words. Use verbs that connote activity, movement, and excitement. Avoid adjectives and pronouns.

Never give a reason. Do not put reasons in your resume for leaving previous positions. Applicants run the risk of alienating human resource directors and hiring managers if the reason they put on their resume is a poor one such as, did not get along with the vice president.

Do not understate your accomplishments in the summary. Although the body copy in the resume may have clearly defined quantitative accomplishments, the summary should not be generalized or lack mentioning any outstanding accomplishments.

Watch for key words in advertisements. Certain key words in an advertisement will give you a clue as to whether you should slant your resume to and turn it into one with a great deal of experience or one with moderate experience. These key words usually ask for a candidate with more "general" skills, instead of specific.

Power Resumes concentrate on three things: (1) features, (2) benefits, and (3) accomplishments.

Public sector (and government) positions require more than a resume. Be sure to determine when answering a public/government sector ad that there are not a score of people already within the agency waiting to apply. These candidates usually receive preference over outsiders. To overcome this element it usually takes an inside contact or referral.

Remember the FAB format when stating positions and responsibilities in the resume. Follow the template in Figure 56 in order to determine exactly what your resume should say. Even experienced resume writers should utilize the FAB approach.

How many resumes should an applicant send to one job? Maximum would be two—one to human resources, the other to the hiring manager.

Index